KILMARNOCK

Champions of Scotland
1964-65

DESERT ISLAND FOOTBALL HISTORIES

Club Histories	ISBN
Aberdeen: A Centenary History 1903-2003	1-874287-57-0
Aberdeen: Champions of Scotland 1954-55	1-874287-65-1
Aberdeen: The European Era – A Complete Record	1-874287-11-2
Bristol City: The Modern Era – A Complete Record	1-874287-28-7
Bristol City: The Early Years 1894-1915	1-874287-74-0
Cambridge United: The League Era – A Complete Record	1-874287-32-5
Cambridge United: 101 Golden Greats	1-874287-58-9
The Story of the Celtic 1888-1938	1-874287-15-5
Chelsea: Champions of England 1954-55	1-874287-94-5
Colchester United: Graham to Whitton – A Complete Record	1-874287-27-9
Coventry City: The Elite Era – A Complete Record	1-874287-83-X
Coventry City: An Illustrated History	1-874287-59-7
Dundee: Champions of Scotland 1961-62	1-874287-86-4
Dundee United: Champions of Scotland 1982-83	1-874287-71-6
History of the Everton Football Club 1878-1928	1-874287-14-7
Halifax Town: From Ball to Lillis – A Complete Record	1-874287-26-0
Hereford United: The League Era – A Complete Record	1-874287-18-X
Hereford United: The Wilderness Years 1997-2004	1-874287-83-X
Huddersfield Town: Champions of England 1923-1926	1-874287-88-0
Ipswich Town: The Modern Era – A Complete Record	1-874287-43-0
Ipswich Town: Champions of England 1961-62	1-874287-63-5
Kilmarnock: Champions of Scotland 1964-65	1-874287-87-2
Luton Town: The Modern Era – A Complete Record	1-874287-90-2
Luton Town: An Illustrated History	1-874287-79-1
Manchester United's Golden Age 1903-1914: Dick Duckworth	1-874287-92-9
The Matt Busby Chronicles: Manchester United 1946-69	1-874287-96-1
Motherwell: Champions of Scotland 1931-32	1-874287-73-2
Norwich City: The Modern Era – A Complete Record	1-874287-67-8
Peterborough United: The Modern Era – A Complete Record	1-874287-33-3
Peterborough United: Who's Who?	1-874287-48-1
Plymouth Argyle: The Modern Era – A Complete Record	1-874287-54-6
Plymouth Argyle: 101 Golden Greats	1-874287-64-3
Plymouth Argyle: Snakes & Ladders – Promotions and Relegations	1-874287-82-1
Portsmouth: From Tindall to Ball – A Complete Record	1-874287-25-2
Portsmouth: Champions of England – 1948-49 & 1949-50	1-874287-50-3
The Story of the Rangers 1873-1923	1-874287-95-3
The Romance of the Wednesday 1867-1926	1-874287-17-1
Stoke City: The Modern Era – A Complete Record	1-874287-76-7
Stoke City: 101 Golden Greats	1-874287-55-4
Potters at War: Stoke City 1939-47	1-874287-78-3
Tottenham Hotspur: Champions of England 1950-51, 1960-61	1-874287-93-7
West Ham: From Greenwood to Redknapp	1-874287-19-8
West Ham: The Elite Era – A Complete Record	1-874287-31-7
Wimbledon: From Southern League to Premiership	1-874287-09-0
Wimbledon: From Wembley to Selhurst	1-874287-20-1
Wimbledon: The Premiership Years	1-874287-40-6
Wrexham: The European Era – A Complete Record	1-874287-52-X

World Cup Histories	
England's Quest for the World Cup – A Complete Record	1-874287-61-9
Scotland: The Quest for the World Cup – A Complete Record	1-897850-50-6
Ireland: The Quest for the World Cup – A Complete Record	1-897850-80-8

Miscellaneous	
Red Dragons in Europe – A Complete Record	1-874287-01-5
The Book of Football: A History to 1905-06	1-874287-13-9
Football's War & Peace: The Tumultuous Season of 1946-47	1-874287-70-8

KILMARNOCK

Champions of Scotland
1964-65

Series Editor: Clive Leatherdale

Rob Hadgraft

DESERT ISLAND BOOKS

First published in 2005
by
DESERT ISLAND BOOKS LIMITED
7 Clarence Road, Southend on Sea, Essex SS1 1AN
United Kingdom
www.desertislandbooks.com

© 2005 Rob Hadgraft

The right of Rob Hadgraft to be identified as author of this work has been asserted under The Copyright Designs and Patents Act 1988

British Library Cataloguing-in-Publication Data
A catalogue record for this book is available from the British Library

ISBN 1-874287-87-2

All rights reserved. No part of this book may be reproduced or utilised in any form or by any means, electronic or mechanical, including photocopying, recording or by any information storage and retrieval system, without prior permission in writing from the Publisher

Printed in Great Britain
by
Biddles Ltd

The photographs in this book were kindly provided by Allan Auld at killiefc.com, Kilmarnock FC, and private collections

Contents

	PAGE
Author's Note	6
Foreword by Davie Sneddon	7
INTRODUCTION: 'OH PLEASE, PLEASE, PLEASE GOD …'	8
1. FOUNDATIONS (1945-57)	17
2. RATTLIN', ROARIN', WILLIE (1957-64)	23
3. A CHANGE OF STYLE (August-September 1964)	33
4. THE NIGHT OF NIGHTS (September 1964)	43
5. WADDELL DROPS A BOMBSHELL (October-November 1964)	51
6. KILLIE GET THE JITTERS (December 1964 – January 1965)	97
7. UP FOR THE CUP (February 1965)	109
8. DOWN AND OUT IN GLASGOW (March 1965)	116
9. 'COME BACK WITH YOUR SHIELDS – OR ON THEM' (April-June 1965)	122
10. THE PAIN IN SPAIN (1965-66)	133
11. HOW THE MIGHTY FELL (1966 and beyond)	142
Guide to Seasonal Summaries	147
Seasonal Summaries	148
Subscribers	160

Author's Note

To win a major title is one thing. To win it by the narrowest margin ever, is quite another. As if the story of little Kilmarnock's one and only Scottish championship success was not thrilling enough in itself, the men from Rugby Park managed to capture the coveted flag in the most dramatic and heart-stopping manner possible – the last kick, in the last minute, of the last match proving decisive.

Had rookie goalkeeper Bobby Ferguson not flung himself across goal to finger-tip away a goalbound shot from Hearts' Alan Gordon in the season's dying seconds, the title would have gone to Hearts and not Kilmarnock. This truly remarkable save was quickly followed by the referee's final whistle, meaning Killie had won the title on goal-average – by 0.04 of a goal!

In the forty years since Killie's triumph, only two other clubs have interrupted the Celtic/Rangers title duopoly. And both of these (Dundee United and Aberdeen), come from far bigger populations than Kilmarnock. Given the way modern football has changed, it seems highly unlikely a club of Kilmarnock's size will ever triumph again.

In compiling the complete story of Kilmarnock's 1965 triumph, I was greatly assisted by club historian John Livingston. I also gratefully acknowledge the help of Davie Sneddon, David Ross (www.scottishleague.net), Allan Auld of the excellent website 'killiefc.com', Allan Wilson, Richard Cairns, Billy Lindsay, Alex Milligan, William Heron, Anne Marks, John C Wilson, Clair Fullarton, the staff of Kilmarnock FC, the Park Hotel, and the British Newspaper Library, the makers of the 'Killie Pie', and not forgetting my wife Katie, for encouragement and proof-reading skills.

My research sources included the following: 'We Were the Champions' by John Livingston (2000), *Every Game: The New Official History of KFC* by David Ross (2001), *KFC Images of Sport* by Gordon Allison (2002), *Charles Buchan's Soccer Gift Book* 1965-66, *Scottish League Players' Records 1946-75* by Beal/Emms (2004), *Jock Stein: The Celtic Years* by Campbell/Potter (1999), 'Killie: The Official History & Scottish Cup' (DVD), The *Kilmarnock Standard, Sunday Mail, Sunday Post, Scottish Daily Express* and *Scottish Football Historian* magazine (ed. John Litster).

No story concerning Kilmarnock would be complete without reference to Scotland's bard, Robert Burns, born nearby and forever associated with this town, where his work was first published. Each chapter of this book begins with a few lines of Burns' magical words, and I hope this enhances the sense of romance attached to Kilmarnock FC's remarkable struggle against the odds to become Champions of Scotland.

Rob Hadgraft

Foreword

I remember Kilmarnock's 1964-65 season starting so well, with fifteen games undefeated – eleven wins and four draws. That's a good basis if you are going to win the League.

We had a lean spell over January and February – just three points from seven games – but did well after that. Over the previous five seasons we'd been second four times and fifth once, so with that record we must have been a good side. At the back we didn't lose many goals and up front we had forwards who could win a game on their own. On the park we were hard on each other (crabbit), but off the field we mixed well socially and got on well together.

The week prior to the big decider at Hearts on 24 April 1965 (my 29th birthday) was similar to any other, for the boss and Walter McCrae made sure it was that way. On the Saturday morning the bus picked up the locally-based players at Rugby Park, the rest we met in Glasgow. We had something to eat at the BEA in St Enoch Square and then went on to Edinburgh to Tynecastle.

We all knew that in this game we had to stand up and be counted – there would be no hiding place. The dressing room was maybe a little quieter than usual. We'd talked among ourselves about Hearts' strengths and weaknesses, but in the end knew it would be about how *we* played.

The game itself is hard for me to describe, having been involved – I always tell people to read the description by John Livingston in his souvenir booklet 'We Were The Champions'. All I remember is scoring in the 26th minute and Brien McIlroy scoring three minutes later. Raold Jensen hit our bar and Alan Gordon brought a great save from Bobby Ferguson in the dying minutes. Then it was all over and we were the champs.

I will never forget the scenes that day. With the fans on the field, we struggled to get to the dressing room and I have never seen manager Willie Waddell in such a state. He was usually very calm, but not that day. He led us back on the field to thank the fans. On our return to Kilmarnock there were thousands in the streets. We had made their day and now they were making ours.

Davie Sneddon
January 2005

Davie Sneddon was Kilmarnock's record signing, arriving in 1961 from Preston. He made 113 League appearances and was a key member of Killie's title-winning side. He later returned to manage the club and led them to promotion into the Premier Division in 1979.

Introduction

'OH PLEASE, PLEASE, PLEASE GOD ...'

Now, auld Kilmarnock, cock thy tail,
An' toss thy horns fu' canty;
Nae mair thou'lt rowt out-owre the dale,
Because thy pasture's scanty
(Robert Burns 1786)

It is approaching 4.45 on Saturday, 24 April 1965 at the packed Tynecastle ground in Edinburgh, home of the mighty Heart of Midlothian FC. Squashed in among a screaming 38,000 crowd is schoolboy Allan Wilson, a devoted Kilmarnock supporter. He's only fourteen and, surrounded by jostling adults, can hardly see a thing on the pitch. Little Allan is a ball-boy at Killie's Rugby Park ground, so he knows the excitement of being close to the action. But never before has he experienced anything like this. Thrilled and frightened at the same time, these Tynecastle scenes will remain with him for ever:

'My heart is racing, time stands still and everything is going in slow motion. The Kilmarnock fans are in full voice, the air is full of smoke, people are praying out loud: "Oh please, please, please God" and the clock is ticking. Some guy shouts five minutes to go, then three minutes and I'm still trying to see what's happening. Then there is this great roar and surge forward and I get carried off my feet. "*Goal*," yell the Hearts fans around me. But suddenly the ground opens up and swallows the noise, for our goalkeeper Bobby Ferguson has found some incredible way of turning an Alan Gordon effort around the post.'

Meanwhile, up in the stand, white-faced and biting his nails, is Ayrshire's elderly and highly respected Police Judge Cairns, an ardent Kilmarnock fan. By the time four minutes of injury-time has passed, Cairns is up on his feet roaring at the referee to blow the final whistle to end the agony and tension. 'Sit down and shut up,' the home fans behind tell him. He screams back: 'I've been waiting seventy years for this day and you're no' keeping me quiet now.'

Suddenly that final whistle sounds – Hearts 0 Kilmarnock 2. The prayed-for miracle has occurred. Little Killie, the provincial underdogs have done it. Four times runners-up in the previous five seasons, they have finally won the Scottish League championship flag – against all odds.

Even a single-goal win by Killie could not have stopped Hearts taking the title – but the Ayrshire club had beaten them by two clear goals, on their own ground, and thus snatched the championship by the slimmest of goal-average margins – by just 0.04 of a goal. And, what's more, they'd done it by scoring a mere 62 goals and scraping just 50 points – the lowest ever tallies by any Scottish title-winning side in a season of 34 games.

Amid the mayhem of heaving humanity around him, 24-year-old Kilmarnock fan Billy Lindsay was stunned and hardly moving. Tears rolled down the cheeks of this carpet company mechanic. Clutching his arm, his wife Margaret was stunned to see her husband of five months crying unashamedly. 'Billy, why are you crying?' she yelled at him, her words almost drowned in the racket around them. Staring wide-eyed at the jubilation on the pitch in front of him, Lindsay struggled to find the right words: 'This is football history. I will never see this again with Killie.'

Lindsay wasn't the only Killie die-hard who could barely believe what had happened. The travelling fans looked on in amazement as the club's normally dour team manager Willie Waddell danced on the pitch like a complete idiot. This was truly surreal. The thing that really frightened Billy, however, was the thought that he'd very nearly missed all of this:

'On that final day I swithered if I should even go to Tynecastle as I really thought we couldn't do it – winning 2-0 was a huge hurdle when you are away. But my wife convinced me to go, saying if they did it and I wasn't there I would never forgive myself. So we both went and she was so right. I had only missed a handful of games all season, one being the home win against Hearts, which was the day we got married. I really didn't think we would do it, for we had been runners-up four times and seemed fated to [always] be just that.'

Eternal runners-up did indeed seem to be Kilmarnock's fate up until that day. In addition to all the near-misses in the League, Killie had been beaten in no fewer than six major Cup finals since 1932.

It wasn't just their supporters who struggled to comprehend what Kilmarnock achieved on 24 April 1965. The press were gobsmacked too. John Malkin of the *Kilmarnock Standard* wrote: 'There can never have been, and it is unlikely there ever will be again, a more dramatic moment in Scottish football than what was experienced at Tynecastle Park, Edinburgh. By the narrowest margin ever, one-25th of a goal, Kilmarnock had hoisted themselves above Hearts into first position … triumph at last after five years in which they have been so often on the fringe of top honours without ever winning one.'

Goals by Davie Sneddon and Brien McIlroy, within three minutes of each other midway through the first half, had put Kilmarnock in dreamland. The 2-0 scoreline they needed had been achieved after less than half an hour's play – and now the big problem was keeping it that way, with over an hour still to go. Had the 'goal-difference' system operated in 1965 instead of 'goal-average', 2-0 would not have been enough, and Hearts would have lifted the crown. It's a slim line between success and failure. Goal-average was a system that tended to favour sides with better defensive records and Killie had become renowned for their mean defence. Hearts were heavier scorers that year, but had a leakier defence, and it would be this difference between the sides that would be decisive.

It needed all the nerve and strength they could muster for Killie's players to survive that final hour at Tynecastle. Conceding just one goal would have lost the title. All eleven men were heroes. Rookie keeper Bobby Ferguson would capture the headlines for his injury-time save from Alan Gordon, but the rest of the defence merited equal praise.

For the thousands of Killie fans, this had been not so much a football game, more a life-changing experience. Allan Wilson says his memories of the day are 'all about being scared to death':

'The night before we travelled to Tynecastle I could not sleep. We went in a Kilmarnock Supporters Club bus and I remember it vividly as most of the buses were from Western SMT and were all black and white. My dad and I reported in at the KFC Supporters Club in the morning. The club at that time was above a fish and chip shop at the side of the river on a side street down to Howard Park. When we arrived at the ground in Edinburgh my dad paid to get me into the enclosure below the Main Stand and then he went off to join his friends on the main terracing. So I was fourteen and alone, in among a mixture of Hearts and Killie supporters who were all strangers to me.

'We were scared of the Hearts attack, and of course they were a bigger club, had more support, home field, and were two points ahead. It was an incredible atmosphere when the game kicked off. In those days most people smoked like chimneys and drank at the game, often having liquor in wee bottles in their jackets. We were squashed together and I was a wee fourteen-year-old – I'm only 5ft 9in standing on a brick today – so I stood no chance really. I just saw what I could of the game, stretching my neck as far as it would go while dodging the spit and trying not to get pissed on.

'Davie Sneddon scores – 0-1. All hell breaks loose. One guy yells: "I'll bet anyone ten shillings they don't score again". Did he say ten shillings? Shit, that's a fortune, I thought. Scuffles, some guy takes a swipe at another guy, fists fly, then it all calms down and the game is back under way. My God, I thought, we could actually win this. Brien McIlroy scores – 0-2. I get knocked flying and some guy picks me up.'

For supporter William Heron, it was not only the biggest day of his life so far, it was the day he became a teenager – his thirteenth birthday: 'I'll remember the scenes forever and how thrilled I was to have actually witnessed it all first hand. What a birthday present!'

David Ross, who would later write a definitive history of the club, was then a frustrated nine-year-old fan waiting anxiously at home for news of the big game: 'I wasn't allowed to go to Tynecastle. My memories of that day are of listening on the radio with my father and younger brother. Frustratingly, the commentary kept switching between Tynecastle and Hampden, where the Scottish Cup final was taking place. There was a fright when Hearts nearly scored towards the end and a false alarm when the commentator announced the end of the game, only for us to realise it was Hampden he was on about. There was a great cheer when the Killie match was finally over after about four minutes injury-time.'

Bill Costley, later to become chairman of the club, remembered carrying out his Saturday job delivering fish in Prestwick, listening for the score at Tynecastle on a radio taped to the handlebars of his bike. Frustratingly – perhaps typically – the radio station concentrated mainly on the Cup final, Celtic v Dunfermline, but Bill recalls they switched to Tynecastle to describe the tension-filled dying moments: 'On the final whistle I fell off my bike in excitement, only to see my sister running down Prestwick Main Street with her hands in the air in celebration.'

Everyone present at the game remembers clearly the drawn out tension of the last 61 minutes, during which Killie had to keep Hearts out. The agony was perhaps most acute for manager Willie Waddell, sitting hunched and helpless by the touchline. He barked orders that couldn't possibly have been heard in the din and chain-smoked nervously.

In almost eight years in charge, Waddell had turned Kilmarnock into a real force in the Scottish game, albeit one apparently destined to be eternal runners-up. For Waddell this was the 'last chance saloon'. He'd announced earlier that he would be quitting football and leaving Rugby Park at the end of 1964-65. The Hearts game would be his swansong, whatever the outcome. It really was a case of now or never.

A calm, articulate man who didn't suffer fools gladly, Waddell could normally be relied upon to show decorum and good sense in whatever situation he found himself. But this was not the case after the final whistle went at Tynecastle: he sprinted like a madman towards skipper Frank Beattie, hugging him and bouncing around wildly. After a brief departure down the tunnel, he was soon seen returning to the pitch, skipping along like an excited schoolgirl. 'I had never seen Waddell in such a state,' said goalscorer Sneddon. Later on, once the dust had settled, former Rangers and Scotland international Waddell would give an unusually fulsome and emotional interview:

'It was easily my greatest day in thirty years of football. The players thoroughly deserve this moment. No players have ever given more for the club and for me. They are eleven lads who played their hearts out [sic, no pun intended]. As far as I'm concerned, and looking at it from a personal angle, no club deserved it more. It was a well-earned triumph in the highly competitive field which football is nowadays.

'This club has been most progressive in their ideas and only the sheer hard work of everyone along the line has taken us to the pinnacle. No one man, no one player, has achieved this. It is the atmosphere and combined effort within these boundary walls that have brought success. I think it will bring the crowds back in greater numbers. It should. I am sure that everyone in Ayrshire is proud that Kilmarnock are champions and the players need support now more than ever to give them encouragement and the urge to reach further heights.

'I am leaving at the end of June and in many ways I am sorry. I have thoroughly enjoyed my stay with Kilmarnock and I could not have been with a better club anywhere. We have had most friendly relationships at all levels here, which is rather a strange thing in football these days. These relationships have operated from the bottom to the top – from the boot-boy to the chairman of the club – and it has been a great pleasure to me to work with them all. In all the thousands of words that have been written … one man has not received the praise he deserves … trainer Walter McCrae. He has done a wonderful job in getting and keeping the players superbly fit. He had proved himself to be Scotland's top trainer and that fact was deservedly recognised when he was chosen by the SFA to train the Scotland team that played England at Wembley.'

It had been a gruelling season for Kilmarnock and winning their first championship – and first major trophy of any kind in 36 years – sparked celebrations that resembled vapour escaping from a pressure cooker. The scenes in Kilmarnock town centre a few hours after the match were unprecedented. Crowds flocked into the central shopping area from early evening to welcome the team bus home. Behind the pavement railings around the Cross, they were packed in like sardines and whiled away the time by singing, including the familiar 'Killie, Killie' chant.

The squad had dined in Glasgow, en route to Ayrshire, from Edinburgh, and reached the outskirts of Kilmarnock shortly after 9pm. The single decker black and white Western SMT vehicle, registration plate XCS 903, crawled slowly into the town centre, preceded by a black Jaguar police car with its roof light flashing. Police struggled to hold the delirious crowds back as the bus stopped outside Grafton's store. Some club officials were in other vehicles and it was a long, slow procession that made its way eventually to Rugby Park.

Goalscoring hero Davie Sneddon somehow spotted his parents among the crowds and waved but wasn't able to speak to them. Worried about his wife, who was pregnant, he asked the bus driver to stop so that he could get off at Barbados Road, near his house. Pushing his way clear of all the fuss, he bolted towards his home, ran indoors and sprinted up the stairs. To his dismay he was told that his wife had decided to leave the house despite her condition, and had gone to the football ground so she wouldn't miss the fun. Sneddon then had to dash the half-mile to Rugby Park, push his way through the crowds and attempt to get in. At first he was turned away by an overworked policeman, but after a desperate 'do ye no ken me?' he was recognised and allowed to join his teammates inside.

Inside Rugby Park, players, officials, wives and girlfriends had started to party, and eventually thousands of supporters were allowed through the gates onto the terraces. Many of them gathered beside the Main Stand and called for Waddell and the players, who eventually emerged to huge acclaim. A few drams had clearly been imbibed, and the players enthusiastically hoisted their manager onto their shoulders. Eventually the celebrations continued inside for the players, and the crowds slowly departed.

The following at Tynecastle had comfortably been Killie's best turnout of the season, and a high proportion of them had hurried back from Edinburgh to be present at these scenes.

Club chairman Willie McIvor told reporters he was proud of the players who'd fulfilled his lifetime's ambition. A Wilson Strachan, chairman of Hearts, and Lord Provost Duncan Weatherstone of Edinburgh had been among the first to congratulate the new champions. Sir James Miller, Lord Mayor of London and a keen Hearts fan, acknowledged that Killie were worthy champs. Telegrams poured in, including one from Helenio Herrera, chief coach of Inter Milan. Kilmarnock's Provost D B Cunningham missed the fun as he was visiting Kilmarnock children boarded out in the north of Scotland. However, he made sure a message was relayed from Buckie in Banffshire to assure everyone that the Town Council would lay on a formal reception and celebration: 'It is the least we can do for Mr Waddell and the players.'

In parts of rural Ayrshire, news doesn't always travel fast and one local man didn't find out what had happened until he read a newspaper late on the Sunday afternoon. He'd bought the paper just before boarding a bus home from Troon. 'I wasn't the last [to find out],' he told the *Kilmarnock Standard*. 'My neighbour didn't even know about it until I told him on Monday morning.'

Fan Billy Lindsay recalls: 'That night the town was jumping and everybody, football supporter or not, was celebrating. Alex Milligan, who became a sports reporter on the local paper, says: 'The town centre was a mass of blue and white as the players' bus made its way down King Street.'

John Livingston, then twelve years old and later to become the club's historian, recalled the desperate effort to get back to Kilmarnock after the final whistle at Tynecastle: 'Some Killie fans invaded the pitch but I couldn't get on. I was so excited and wanted to get back to the town. I was with my friend and his cousin and we were itching to get back to Kilmarnock before the team bus. As a special treat we stopped on the way back in Strathaven for a fish supper, and there we met some Celtic fans who were celebrating winning the Cup. We made it back to Kilmarnock in time to chase after the team bus as it went down King Street. The streets were thronged with people. It was brilliant. We then ran home to watch the highlights on "Scotsport" later that night. It was a terrific day, like something out of a *Roy of the Rovers* story.'

According to Allan Wilson: 'I don't remember much about the bus ride home, other than singing, drinking, puking and stopping frequently to let the bus disgorge its contents on the side of the road for a piss and more puking. If we were not the first bus back at the Cross in Kilmarnock we were certainly one of the first. The bus came to a stop before the Cross as the crowds were too thick; the whole of the town was out. We all got out of the bus and joined the melee. Hugging, kissing, drinking, falling down, getting up, falling down again, waiting on the team bus to arrive. Then it came, us pressing forward banging on the side of the bus, the players inside waving. It inched its way down King Street and the falling over, getting up, drinking and falling over again continued well into the night.'

Anne Marks, a schoolteacher now exiled in the American city of Boise, Idaho, recalls: 'My Dad had decided earlier not to travel to the last game of the season if Killie needed to win – and he didn't change his mind when it came to pass. I did not get to go, but my sister did. We did go into the town to the Cross to welcome the team back home, however, and I got my picture in the *Evening Times*. That night Kilmarnock was the best place in the world to belong to – everywhere was blue and white. All the shops had the team picture in their windows and the air of euphoria filled the town. It came at a good time for Kilmarnock, which was reeling from closures.'

Having missed the game, young David Ross was determined not to miss out on everything that night: 'My father managed a pub at the time and he had to go to work straight after the game, so he handed me and my brother a ten shilling note each to celebrate. This was a tremendous amount. My weekly pocket money was five shillings at the time. My brother and I went to our village chippie and bought both evening papers [*Evening Citizen* and *Evening Times* late football editions]. The school janitor, a Rangers fan, was there and he grabbed the papers off us, made some comment about how lucky Killie were and then moaned about Celtic winning the Cup at Hampden. We called him something which nine-year-olds weren't supposed to know and ran off. He was also the school football coach and when we later reached Primary 7, neither I nor my brother made the team, even though there was a squad of fourteen and less than twenty boys in the class. I reckon he held it against us. My mother wouldn't take us into Kilmarnock that night because of the crowds expected. Two days later Killie met Ayr in the Ayrshire Cup and my brother, myself, my cousin the same age as me and older relatives – uncles, cousins, all males – went to see the League Championship trophy paraded around the pitch before the game.'

Older fans aired their views in letters to the local paper. William Wyllie of Greenford, Middlesex said any team which could defeat the league leaders 2-0 on their own ground in a deciding match were without doubt worthy champions. William Young of Fenwick, who was at Tynecastle, complained that the Killie supporters had urged their team on using songs borrowed from Ibrox and Parkhead: 'Now that we have won Scotland's premier award, it's time we had a song exclusive to Kilmarnock. Let's have a song for Europe.' A fan from Renfrewshire wrote to praise 'those teenagers who dominate the scene at every home game at the centre line'. He said these people had been at Tynecastle in great numbers, including many girls, three of whom had a big hug for the players, their shoes slipping off during their scampering on to the pitch. He claimed he had always been confident of the title and had placed a 9-1 ante-post bet of 90 shillings to 10 shillings last September. He had also correctly backed Liverpool to win the FA Cup at 18-1. He praised Waddell's 4-2-4 system which had been prematurely ridiculed in the press earlier in the season.

When the Scottish football writers announced their inaugural Player of the Year awards shortly after the Hearts game, there was disappointment that skipper Frank Beattie was runner-up behind Celtic's Billy McNeill. The players themselves were agreed that Beattie deserved the award, and also directed good-natured banter towards Davie Sneddon, normally a goal maker, who'd opened the scoring at Hearts with a rare header.

The title was a timely reward for the loyal service of men like Beattie, Bertie Black and Matt Watson, who'd all been at Rugby Park since the early 1950s. The new young faces, Ferguson and Tommy McLean, had also played major roles and it was proudly noted that the team at Hearts featured six Ayrshire lads in Ferguson, Andy King, Eric Murray, Jackie McInally, Black and Sneddon. Key men Ronnie Hamilton and Jim McFadzean were also local lads, but had missed the match.

Waddell announced the club would retain all 25 players on the books and he would be handing them over, hopefully all re-signed, to new manager Malky MacDonald in the summer. It was noted that the club had done well to win the title so soon after selling top performers like Andy Kerr, Sandy McLaughlan, Ian Davidson and Bobby Kennedy for a combined total of some £100,000. The only true import had been Sneddon.

The Scottish title had been won on goal-average for the first time since 1953, an occasion on which Waddell had also been involved – as a flying winger with the winners Rangers, who pipped Hibs by 0.23 of a goal.

Viewed with the hindsight of forty years, it cannot be denied that season 1964-65 was remarkable. It was the only time in the first 100 years of the championship that neither Celtic nor Rangers finished in the top four. Killie had become – and remain today – one of only three 'small-town' clubs to lift the title, Dumbarton in 1891 and 1892, and Motherwell in 1932 being the others. The remaining champions have all come from cities.

The wider world never expected Killie to become champions, but what about the fans? John Livingston admits: 'Not really. The team in 1964-65 was not as good as the ones who had been runners-up so often. Yet, even though the first half of the season had seen them do really great, most people felt they would stumble. Fortunately it was the other clubs for a change who stumbled. Only in the last few games did people think it could actually happen for us.'

Anne Marks reckons many fans had been ambivalent about the team's chances: 'Remember they had had their hearts broken before.' But David Ross recalls a degree of confidence: 'Kids of my age – unlike any previous generation – were growing up accustomed to Killie being one of the top teams. Between 1957 and 1964 they had reached two Scottish Cup finals, two League Cup finals and finished runners-up in the League four times. There was a feeling of "now or never" with the emphasis on the now.'

Killie captured the championship flag in defiance of the media pundits, who felt they'd never be more than runners-up. W G Gallagher, known to generations as 'Waverley' of the *Daily Record*, had scoffed at their chances of overhauling title-holders Rangers. Earlier that season, in *Charles Buchan's Football Monthly*, Gallagher had written about the Rangers team which had completed the domestic 'treble' in the spring of 1964 (winning the League by six points from Killie, the League Cup final 5-0 over Morton, and the Scottish FA Cup 3-1 over Dundee): 'The question is, do we have a club to stop Rangers again winning the lot? I find it difficult to see any side preventing the Light Blues from again winning the three major honours. Celtic have indicated a comeback but they have not yet the team to achieve greatness. Last season they met Rangers five times and were beaten in all. That is bound to have a psychological effect for some time.'

Gallagher was wide of the mark, for after lifting the League Cup in the autumn of 1964, Rangers faded. After the turn of the year they would take a back seat to neighbours Celtic, being revived by new boss Jock Stein, and to the likes of little Kilmarnock, the new champions.

So how did humble Killie manage to upset the traditional Old Firm domination in this way? This book examines the full story.

Chapter 1

Foundations
(1945-57)

Kilmarnock lang may grunt an' grane,
An' sigh, an' sab, an' greet her lane
(Robert Burns, 1786)

Sturdy provincials. Doughty cup fighters. A club lacking the class and resources to topple the Glasgow and Edinburgh giants in the Scottish League championship. That was the image firmly attached to Kilmarnock FC when football resumed after the 1939-45 War.

Traditionally, over the course of a gruelling season, Killie didn't have the wherewithal to go the distance. In the 49 seasons up to 1939, the title was won 43 times by Celtic or Rangers and three times by Edinburgh's Hibs or Hearts. The championship belonged to city slickers. Provincial clubs like Kilmarnock generally only shone in the cups. To prove the point, the boys from Rugby Park had made Ayrshire proud by reaching the final of the Scottish Cup in 1898, 1920, 1929, 1932 and 1938 (winning in 1920 and 1929) and had reached the semi and quarter-final stages on a regular basis. Not bad for an outfit who'd only finished in the top five once since Division One was enlarged to eighteen clubs in 1906.

The 1939-45 War hit Kilmarnock particularly hard. The Rugby Park ground was requisitioned by the authorities in 1940 as a fuel storage depot, forcing the club to close down for the duration. When Killie took control of their stadium again in April 1945 it was a complete wreck. Money wasn't so much tight as non-existent. Hardly the ideal situation to begin building a team to challenge the Glasgow giants. Kilmarnock FC would, effectively, be starting from scratch.

The immediate post-War years saw football in Britain enjoy its greatest ever boom period. It was a time when people longed to return to the normal lives they had led some six years before and the populace were desperate for entertainment. Despite great austerity, a climate existed in which the mass enjoyment of going to football could flourish once again.

Stadiums up and down Britain were packed every Saturday, often to dangerous levels, for little care went into spectator comfort or safety. In the period of post-War reconstruction it clearly seemed wasteful to use sparse resources to shore up decrepit football grounds. In many cases stands were held together by rusting girders and the terraces were crumbling in disrepair, but this did nothing to deter the huge crowds hungry for football.

Inevitably there was the odd tragedy, and in one 1946 game at Bolton, 33 spectators died after barriers collapsed.

Desperate to see the blue-and-white hoops back in action, almost 11,000 crammed into shabby Rugby Park for the first senior home game on the resumption of football in August 1945. It was too soon for the Scottish League to be resurrected, and 1945-46 would be tagged the 'Scottish Southern League'. Former Killie and Preston defender Tom Smith had taken over as manager and the first visitors were Aberdeen. But, although the home crowd raised the roof at being back in familiar surroundings, they had to endure a 1-4 defeat by the Dons, with even Killie's solitary success being a late own-goal.

As the realities of post-War austerity began to bite in Ayrshire, things got worse on the park too: the Aberdeen defeat was followed by a 1-6 hammering at Morton, then a 0-7 home mauling by Rangers in front of a bumper gate of 16,827. Results remained poor throughout 1945-46, the consolation being that attendances remained high. The average at Rugby Park was 11,267, the highest in the club's history. Prior to this, the league average had never exceeded 9,000. This upward trend continued. Over the following Scottish League campaign (1946-47), Killie's average gate rose to 13,622, even though the team again finished fifteenth, this time being relegated as a consequence. The drop had seemed inevitable, but was still a bitter pill to swallow. It represented the first time since 1899 that the club would not be playing at top level. Nevertheless the fans stayed loyal and gates remained at least as good as those of the immediate pre-War period, when Killie had been under the command of Jimmy McGrory – now managing Celtic.

The healthy crowds at Rugby Park reflected a nationwide trend. Rangers, for example, often played to an aggregate of over a million spectators in the late 1940s and early '50s. In 1952, 136,000 spectators crammed into Hampden Park to watch the Motherwell v Dundee Scottish Cup final. In England an all-time peak was achieved when 41 million fans watched the 1948-49 Football League programme.

Boom time it might have been, but for the men of Rugby Park times were tough. As a part-time outfit, the players mostly trained just two evenings a week and there was little continuity in terms of leadership. After Tom Smith left, the former Stoke and Newcastle boss Tom Mather took over but lasted less than a season. He gave way to Alex Hastings, a former Scottish international and Sunderland skipper. Success on the field was elusive and in their first three seasons in Division Two Killie languished in mid-table. There wasn't even a sniff of cup glory to provide excitement. Sometimes, emergency measures were necessary to patch up the side and on one occasion the physio-trainer Jock Brown was asked to play in goal.

Things reached a low ebb, and it took the appointment of Malcolm MacDonald as manager in April 1950 to usher in the dawn of a new era at Rugby Park. 'Malky' was no stranger to the area, for this celebrated ex-Celtic inside-forward had played for Killie for a short spell directly after the War, before a sojourn in English football.

MacDonald, 37, had been a Scottish schoolboy and junior international, joining Celtic in April 1932 from St Anthony. As the Parkhead giants possessed an abundance of inside-forwards, he served a long apprenticeship in the reserves. He won a championship medal in 1936 but was never sure of his first-team place until Willie Buchan was sold to Blackpool in 1937. MacDonald then established himself as a player who always seemed to have time to play the ball. He was a natural inside-forward but was versatile and played in many positions, including both full-back roles and at centre-half. He picked up a second championship medal in 1938.

MacDonald starred in Celtic's Empire Exhibition Trophy victory at Ibrox over Everton in 1938 and during the War played in three wartime internationals. He won a further winner's medal with Celtic – the VE Cup in 1945 – before signing for Kilmarnock in October 1945. But times were bleak at Rugby Park and it didn't take much to tempt him away. He accepted an offer from English First Division Brentford a year later. Reaching the veteran stage as a player, he became the London club's coach in June 1948 – by which time The Bees had slipped down to Division Two – working under managers Harry Curtis and Jackie Gibbons.

The chance to become a manager in his own right presented itself in the spring of 1950 and MacDonald returned to Kilmarnock, seeking to restore top-flight status at Rugby Park. Interviewed in later years, he recalled that expectations were low when he sat down behind the manager's desk for the first time. He remembered feeling lucky that the Killie directors and fans weren't expecting instant success and consequently there was little pressure on him. The club was struggling to find its place in football, let alone challenge for honours, but he was pleased to find some decent players had arrived at the club since his earlier departure.

Killie's lack of success was put into perspective in September 1950, when a local mining disaster made national headlines. Dozens of miners were trapped 700 feet underground at Knockshinnoch after a mine collapsed. Fourteen men lost their lives, one of them a rescuer.

MacDonald was having a tough but educational introduction to football management. On a couple of occasions he was even prompted to pull on the old boots himself, scoring once in a 3-4 home defeat by Queen's Park. In the course of 1951 austerity began to recede, Winston Churchill became Prime Minister and the patience of the Killie directors and long-suffering supporters slowly began to pay off. Before long MacDonald had been able to steer Killie into a position near the top of the table and in 1952-53 the club boldly made its way to the Scottish League Cup final. After finishing top of their section Killie posted a 7-2 aggregate victory over St Johnstone. This earned them a place at Hampden for a semi-final clash with Rangers. Memories of pre-War cup glory were revived for the Killie fans as Willie Jack's second-half goal toppled the Ibrox side in a tremendous display of giant-killing. The heroics couldn't be repeated in the final, however, and Dundee lifted the cup, thanks to late goals by Bobby Flavell, a man who would later sign for Kilmarnock.

Things were looking up as MacDonald slowly turned the club around. A year later the dream of a return to the top flight was realised. Killie were promoted after winning nineteen of their thirty league games in 1953-54 to finish Division Two runners-up, powering home 71 goals. Stenhousemuir, Morton, Dumbarton and Forfar were all on the receiving end of hammerings to the tune of six goals or more.

Promotion was clinched at Third Lanark, whose 1-1 draw with Dunfermline meant Thirds had failed to squeeze Killie out of second place behind champions Motherwell. According to the *Kilmarnock Standard*: 'After seven lean years in the financial purgatory of minor league football, the famous Ayrshire club was now fit to return to the arena of the giants.'

Many a wee dram and many a pint o' heavy was raised in Ayrshire pubs in honour of Malky MacDonald and the boys in blue and white hoops that Monday night. The misery of those lean post-War years was fast being forgotten. Among those with a celebratory smile was the club's mascot, a sheep known as Angus. Having a sheep in residence at Rugby Park was a Killie tradition that went back many years. Ruby and Wilma were among the earlier occupants of this important role. Angus, named after the farmer who donated him to the club, apparently loved to chomp on cigarettes, the supply of which increased when rationing was phased out and the good times returned in the mid-1950s.

The team made a poor start in the top division, only winning one of their opening twelve league games, but things slowly improved. One reason was MacDonald's signing of Willie Toner, a 25-year-old Glaswegian who'd been playing his football with Sheffield United. He would become Killie's skipper. Toner recalled that he'd been back in Scotland in 1954 to marry Annette, a local girl, when MacDonald collared him and urged him to sign. Toner recalled: 'They had just won promotion to the First Division and their aim was to stay there ... the playing staff were great to get along with. So were physio Walter McCrae, coach Ernie Nash and of course Malky MacDonald the manager.'

Toner was a clever player, originally a centre-forward, who converted into a centre-half and was more than just a crude stopper. Interviewed by the fanzine KTS ('Kissin' the Squirrels') not long before his death in 1999, MacDonald recalled: 'There were fixed ideas back then regarding styles of play. Because you were in a lower division you were expected to employ hard men to get you out. I bought a boy called Willie Toner. I had great faith in Willie. Instead of being a stopper centre-half, he was a fellow who could come forward with the ball and use it wisely. We would make allowances if he did come forward; someone would fill in behind. My goalkeeper of the time, Jimmy Brown, was another character and a right wag. He carried a lot of weight in the dressing room and he would sometimes manage the rest of the players.'

Another new face was that of Frank Beattie. Skilful, uncompromising in the tackle and strong in the air, Beattie made his debut in the No 8 shirt at home to Partick in October 1954 and would become a legend at Rugby Park, serving the club for eighteen years. Beattie's earliest footballing memories involved playing on the wing for his school at St Modan's in Stirling. This was followed by two years with Dunipace Thistle and Bonnybridge Juniors. MacDonald invited Beattie to Kilmarnock for a trial and the lad was asked to sign straight away. In his early years at Rugby Park, Beattie played part-time and continued with his day job as a miner. Twice a week he would leave home for work at 6am, do a stint on the coalface from 7 until 2.30, and then dash to his father's house for a meal. Then he would take the train from Larbert to St Enoch, and on to Kilmarnock for evening training. He would not arrive home until after midnight. This went on for five years until Frank was persuaded to become turn full-time in 1960. He was big but had bags of skill and for many years played at inside-forward. A change of position would come later in his Killie career.

The first two seasons back in Division One were helped by the scoring of Gerry Mays, who would ultimately total 111 goals for Killie in seven years (1952-59). That made him the club's fourth most prolific scorer of all time and he was still in the top ten more than forty years later.

During the early 1950s MacDonald demanded floodlights be installed at Rugby Park. The directors thought lights were an expensive luxury, but MacDonald dangled the carrot of a money-spinning visit from Manchester United. He promised the board that if they came up with the money, he would persuade Matt Busby to bring his all-stars to help pay for them. The proposal was accepted and the ground got its lights. They were unveiled for the visit of United in October 1953, a game United won 3-0.

The 1956-57 season turned into one of high excitement at Rugby Park, with a finishing place of third – behind Rangers and Hearts – and a glorious run to the final of the Scottish Cup. Ayr, East Fife, Airdrie and then – memorably – Celtic were shunted out of the competition as Killie roared to Hampden. There they faced lowly Falkirk. Mays in particular enjoyed the cup run, banging in six goals en route to the final, including a brace when Celtic were beaten 3-1 at Hampden in the semi-final replay.

Willie Toner recalled that Killie were hot favourites to lift the Cup as they were so much higher than Falkirk. But the final ended 1-1, meaning a replay the following Wednesday, also at Hampden. The game turned on one moment that would forever haunt Toner, who clashed with Bairns' forward George Merchant on 33 minutes. To Killie's horror, a penalty was given. Forty years later, Toner – who was never booked in his career – told the *Scottish Daily Record* that there was no way his challenge on Merchant merited a penalty: 'George was an awkward big player. I put my foot in to make a challenge as he came into the box and caught him at the same time as I pushed the ball away. It was a nothing foul – but the ref, Bobby Davidson, gave it. I found it hard to take but, unlike present day players, there was no question of me reacting. I was the Gary Lineker of my time. I was never booked in my twenty-year career. Anyway Falkirk scored and the game finished 1-1. The penalty changed everything though and I was the one who suffered.'

But Toner wasn't the worst affected when Killie's Cup dream died in the replay four days later, thanks to a 1-2 defeat in front of 79,960 and live TV cameras: 'Willie Harvey, our right winger, was totally inconsolable. He was crying his eyes out with his head between his knees. The poor lad just couldn't control his feelings. I was never one to show emotion, though I was obviously deeply disappointed. I was more concerned about the lads such as Willie who were finding it too hard to take. But, even after defeat, we went back to Kilmarnock on an open-topped bus and there were thousands of people to greet us.'

At the end of the season there was a shock when MacDonald – who'd always operated at Rugby Park without a contract – left to take up the post at Brentford, who he'd played for and coached, and who were now in England's Division Three (South). MacDonald's decision surprised many, but for him it represented a fresh challenge and a return to a club for whom he had a special fondness. For their part, Brentford saw the Scotsman as an ideal replacement for the respected Bill Dodgin.

Losing the man who'd played such a role in re-establishing Kilmarnock meant the summer of 1957 was crucial for the momentum of the club. Would MacDonald's replacement continue its advance, or would his departure signal another decline, a return to the bad old days of the late 1940s?

CHAPTER 2

RATTLIN', ROARIN' WILLIE
(1957-64)

Sittin at yon boord-en,
And amang gude companie;
Rattlin', roarin' Willie,
You're welcome hame to me!
(Robert Burns, 1787)

To maintain the momentum of finishing third in the League and runners-up in the Cup, Kilmarnock's directors knew their choice of new manager in the summer of 1957 was vital. Whoever replaced MacDonald would need to be a shrewd operator.

So would Killie seek to recruit an up-and-coming boss from one of Scotland's smaller clubs? Or a top player coming to the end of his playing days? Or maybe one of the many Anglo-Scots playing for big clubs south of the border? It would be none of these. Instead Killie appointed their man from the ranks of the pen-pushers at the *Glasgow Evening Citizen*.

Mind you, this was no ordinary soccer hack. This was Willie Waddell, the 36-year-old former Rangers and Scotland winger. Hailing from the Lanarkshire village of Forth, Waddell had forged a playing career as one of Scotland's finest flankers, starring on the Rangers wing for many years, scoring his fair share of goals and winning caps for Scotland. He'd hung up his boots in 1956 and moved into journalism, where he quickly gained a reputation for candid and acerbic football reporting on the *Citizen*.

Waddell was a perspicacious and articulate man; not for him the usual footballer's route of taking charge of a pub once his playing days ended. He'd played under the legendary Rangers manager Bill Struth, a single-minded disciplinarian whose influence certainly rubbed off. Waddell had gone to Lanark Grammar School and joined Rangers after impressing with junior side Forth Wanderers. His debut for the Ibrox club had come in a reserve game at the tender age of fifteen and his elevation to first team status came within another two years. He was a fast and powerful flanker, who could score and make goals.

In his one year out of the game, Waddell had been direct and uncompromising as a newspaper columnist, and he carried these qualities into his first football management role at Rugby Park. Struth was an interesting choice of role model. He'd become William Wilton's assistant at Ibrox in 1914 and when Wilton drowned in a boating accident in 1920, Struth took over as manager. The foundations for Rangers' dominance of Scottish football before the 1939-45 War were laid under Struth, who instilled in players a feeling of privilege to play in a Rangers jersey. They travelled first class but in return had to dress smartly and behave appropriately at all times. These values were admired by Waddell, whose wing play helped Struth accumulate eighteen League Championships, ten Scottish Cups and two League Cups. Struth became a director and then vice-chairman at Ibrox, dying aged 81 in 1956, the year Waddell retired as a player.

One of Waddell's first aspirations as Killie boss was to re-introduce full-time football at Rugby Park. His other changes included radical improvements to training methods and replacement of the traditional blue and white hooped jerseys with the vertical stripes that had been worn way back at the end of the nineteenth century.

On 10 August 1957 Waddell's first game in charge saw Killie beat Hearts 2-1 at Rugby Park in a League Cup-tie in front of a bumper crowd of 19,806. This would prove a rare defeat for the Edinburgh club, who romped to the championship that season, losing just one of their 34 league games. So victory on the opening day was a great afternoon's work by Killie, who set off on a run of eight unbeaten games. Waddell's honeymoon period would only come to an end at Ibrox, where Rangers inflicted his first defeat as a manager – 1-3. The result put Killie out of the League Cup at the quarter-final stage.

In that first season, Waddell worked with three players who would go on to star in the historic 1964-65 campaign. Frank Beattie was by now a regular at inside-forward, Bertie Black began to flourish in the No 10 shirt, and full-back Matt Watson came back into the side to claim a regular spot. Killie finished fifth in the table in 1957-58 but had a disappointing Scottish Cup exit at the hands of Queen of the South. Nevertheless, the new era looked full of promise. Waddell declared himself unimpressed by Killie's scouting system and worked hard to set up a more efficient network. It soon began paying dividends.

The autumn of 1958 saw construction of the Forth Road Bridge begin – and it was a time of rebuilding for Waddell at Rugby Park, too. His side slipped back to eighth in the league, but enjoyed another fine run in the League Cup, bowing out at the semi-final stage when reigning champions Hearts prevailed 3-0. By the time the 1959-60 season got under way, Waddell was beginning to impose a firm grip and was shaping the side as he wanted. He had now persuaded the directors to switch to full-time football, ending the many years where only a handful of players had been fully professional. Two other changes he made around this time would have far-reaching effects: Beattie was switched to wing-half and a raw Ayr-born forward named Jackie McInally was introduced to the side.

Recalling those heady days some thirty years later, McInally said: 'I signed for Kilmarnock in 1959 at a relatively late age [23]. I had just finished my National Service and had gone back to amateur football with Crosshill Thistle. Fortunately they reached the Scottish Amateur Cup final which was played at Hampden in front of senior club scouts.'

Kilmarnock talent spotter Norrie McNeill captured McInally's signature, just ahead of Queen's Park, and Waddell liked what he saw. McInally was made twelfth man for the opening game of the season with Hearts (a job that only involved sitting in the stands in those pre-substitute days). Killie were hammered 0-4 and Waddell threw McInally into the fray for the next game, at Stirling Albion. McInally's first goal in senior football came in his second outing, a 2-3 home defeat by Aberdeen, and he earned himself a regular place despite his lack of experience. Waddell was keen to keep the rookie's feet on the ground, however, and regularly gave McInally a hard time off the field.

The player recalled: 'Willie Waddell was very much his own man. Things had to be done his way. He was very sore on me as a player and I came in for a lot of criticism, but I think he was the type of man who knew how to deal with people and I probably needed a bit of goading, a bit of egging on, a kick up the backside every now and then. It worked with me because I would go in at half-time and if Waddell gave me a bit of stick I'd say to myself "I'll go out and show that bugger". The reaction he got from me was the right one. Others he dealt with differently. His attitude sometimes left a lot to be desired as far as I was concerned. He could have had a bit more give and take, but everything had to be his way.'

1959-60 turned into a successful campaign, with a shaky start being overcome after a no-holds-barred team meeting in which Waddell allowed experienced pros like Willie Toner and Jimmy Brown to have their say. This session seemed to work wonders, for Killie only lost four of their next thirty league games. This period featured a sensational mid-season run of fifteen straight league victories – stretching from mid-December to early April. On top of this, five Cup-ties were won and one drawn. Gates rose and in February 1960 almost 30,000 crammed into Rugby Park for a Cup-tie with Motherwell, a club record for any game not involving Celtic or Rangers. Killie ultimately ended second in the table, the club's best ever finish. The run of wins was not quite enough to close the gap on champions Hearts, who finished four points clear.

Being pipped in the League was matched by heartbreak in the Scottish Cup, for Killie marched to the final at Hampden, only to be beaten 0-2 by Rangers. They failed to capture their best form on the big stage, but finishing runners-up in the two main competitions was a wonderful achievement. The Cup final was a disappointing spectacle, and was put in the shade 25 days later, when, at the same stadium, Real Madrid beat Eintracht Frankfurt 7-3 to lift the European Cup.

In the summer of 1960, Kilmarnock's recent achievements saw them invited to represent Scotland in a new international tournament to be staged in New York. Six teams competed in each of two sections, with the two group winners to meet in the final. Killie were grouped with Glenavon from Northern Ireland, English champions Burnley, Bayern Munich and Nice. As no American Soccer League club was deemed strong enough to compete, a new club was hastily created, called New York Americans, to provide the local interest. The competition was the brainchild of William B Cox, a graduate of Yale who'd made a fortune in timber and mining, but had thus far enjoyed little success in various forays into sport. He'd invested in the hapless New York football Yankees of the early 1940s, Brooklyn's short-lived football Dodgers, and the inept Philadelphia Phillies baseball team. Notwithstanding his dubious track record, Cox was convinced that, if marketed properly, soccer could become as popular in the USA as in the rest of the world. Cox's tournament involved a hectic thirty-game schedule played in New York and Jersey City.

Kilmarnock were permitted to field St Mirren's Tommy Bryceland as a guest player to replace injured Bertie Black, and during the four-week trip did themselves proud, winning their group. Bayern were beaten 3-1, Glenavon 2-0, Burnley 2-0 and New York Americans 3-1. The game with Nice ended 1-1. The Burnley clash was rough and attracted the biggest group match crowd, 13,000. Bangu of Brazil won the other group ahead of Red Star Belgrade (Yugoslavia), Sampdoria (Italy), Sporting Lisbon (Portugal), Norrkoping (Sweden) and Rapid Vienna (Austria).

The final involved a return trip to New York. The contest at the New York Polo Grounds saw the Brazilians beat Killie 2-0 on a scorching day. Trainer Walter McCrae recalled temperatures and humidity levels were 'up in the nineties' and the players came off at half-time and headed into the showers in their kit in order to cool down. McCrae reckoned the trip was great for team spirit and saw Killie make many friends. Their public relations work included staging coaching clinics at various American colleges. The tournament lost money, but Cox was encouraged and continued staging it in subsequent years.

Although it took a hefty chunk out of their summer break, the Killie players enjoyed the experience. Frank Beattie said: 'A lot of harmony and team spirit was created by the trips made to the United States to play in the invitation tournaments, and by playing top continental teams.' After the idea was repeated in subsequent years, Jackie McInally wasn't so sure: 'I went to America four times with Killie, the first couple were enjoyable but the second two were a bit of a bind. The tournaments were far too long, the team changed and there were some guys each time that hadn't been before, but the novelty wore off for the older players. Four or five weeks is a long time out of the close season.'

Finishing runners-up in New York maintained Killie's record as 'the nearly men' of Scottish football, an image that would be maintained over subsequent seasons. The next episode of missing out would come just two months later, in October 1960, when the club reached the League Cup final again, but went down 0-2 to Rangers at Hampden. It was an identical outcome to the Scottish Cup final of six months earlier, but this time the Rugby Park side put up a better performance and came closer to upsetting the apple-cart.

League form was good throughout 1960-61 but once again Killie were bridesmaids. With chief rivals Rangers preoccupied with a run to the final of the first European Cup-Winners' Cup (they would lose 1-4 on aggregate to Fiorentina) Killie were in with a chance of the league title in the closing weeks – particularly after beating the Ibrox men 2-0 in front of nearly 30,000 at Rugby Park on April Fool's Day. However, although Killie won their final three league games, Rangers had games in hand and took the title by one point. There was some consolation when Killie centre-half Willie Toner was voted Scotland's Player of the Year.

The players had just three weeks to drown their disappointment before jetting out to New York again for the annual tournament. This time promoter Cox broadened his reach, inviting some up-and-coming young clubs to participate. Along with 1960 finalists Bangu and Kilmarnock, Cox persuaded Dukla Prague, Everton, Montreal Concordia, Karlsruhe, Dinamo Bucharest, Besiktas, New York Americans, Monaco, Red Star Belgrade, Espanyol, Rapid Vienna, Shamrock Rovers and Petah Tikva to participate. Killie could only manage to beat the two North American clubs, drawing with Dinamo and Besiktas and going down to Everton, Karlsruhe and Bangu. The final, played in early August over two legs, was anti-climactic, with Dukla Prague slaughtering Everton 9-2 on aggregate.

Back in Scotland, the sale to Manchester City of left-half Bobby Kennedy for the high fee of £45,000 (the British record at that time stood at £53,000) helped fund significant ground improvements at Rugby Park in the summer of 1961. It also meant the club could splash a record £17,000 on Preston schemer Davie Sneddon. A local lad from Kilwinning, 25-year-old Sneddon was a skilful and creative player who had joined Preston from Dundee two and a half years earlier. The fans were excited by the signing and their optimism was well placed, for Sneddon would become a major figure at Rugby Park for many years.

After the recent triple dose of runners-up syndrome, the new season of 1961-62 yielded less success (Killie finished fifth) despite the sensational goalscoring form of Andy Kerr. The thirty-year-old from the East Ayrshire village of Lugar was a former Manchester City striker who became a big crowd favourite at Rugby Park. He ran rampant after New Year's Day 1962, banging home 24 goals in nineteen games before the end of the campaign. Looking back, Jackie McInally reckoned Kerr was the best player he ever played alongside, an unpredictable and unique stylist.

Kerr continued his heroics at the start of the 1962-63 campaign, highlighted by his performance in the 8-0 hammering of Airdrie in September, in which he knocked in no fewer than five goals. By now, a promising centre-half called Jackie McGrory had established himself in the side, allowing Waddell to sell Willie Toner to Hibs.

Toner, a veteran of eight campaigns at Rugby Park, recalled: 'Walter Galbraith of Hibs asked me to sign for them as he wanted some experience to help them in their fight against relegation. I'm glad to say that his idea worked out as Hibs stayed in the First Division that year. I have good memories of all my time at Kilmarnock, especially the three Cup finals, but I'll never forget season 1957-58 when the supporters chose me as their first ever Player of the Year. I won two full caps and five League international caps while playing for Killie and was also the team captain. I consider that a major achievement. I do regret not getting a winner's medal from the three cup finals I played in though.'

Killie made a reasonable start to 1962-63 and enjoyed another good run of results in the early season League Cup competition. Their football was bright and entertaining. In addition to McGrory, another promising newcomer was winger Brien McIlroy. After overcoming Partick in the quarter-finals, Killie had a memorable night at Hampden, winning a 3-2 thriller against Rangers to reach the final once again. However, more heartbreak was just around the corner.

The final against Hearts is remembered to this day for one particular incident – a Killie 'goal' deep in injury-time that was harshly disallowed by referee 'Tiny' Wharton. It condemned unlucky Killie to being runners-up yet again. Once the dust had settled, even the Edinburgh lads felt sorry for Waddell and his men, for the 'goal' should clearly have been allowed to stand. Hearts' keeper that day was Gordon Marshall, who recounted the events to a reporter from the *Mirror*.

'Killie were playing with a strong wind behind them and had us pinned down in our own penalty area for the final 20 minutes. We were leading through a Norrie Davidson goal with seconds left when Killie's right-back Jim Richmond took a free-kick from the halfway line. He lofted it into the penalty area where Frank Beattie jumped to try to head the ball. As he went up, he also raised his arm. I tried to anticipate where the ball would go and committed myself early – but he missed it completely, as did everyone else.

To my horror, Richmond's free-kick ended up in the back of the net with neither defender or attacker getting a touch. But the referee was right up with play and immediately awarded us a free-kick for Beattie's intention to handle, though no contact was made. Even after all these years I still have to say it's the most brilliant piece of refereeing I've ever seen! He blew for full-time almost immediately. You can't say how things would have turned out, but Kilmarnock would have received a massive lift from rescuing the game at such a late stage.'

McInally confirmed Marshall's view when he spoke to the 'Killie Ken' fanzine: 'Beattie had a habit of jumping with his hands up, but I thought it was a good equaliser. Frank maintains to this day he never handled the ball, and he's not the type of guy who would lie. It was just one of those things. It was a most disappointing final for Killie because we were expected to win it after beating Rangers in the semi-final. It was particularly disappointing for me because I played very little part in it. I had just come back from breaking a bone in my foot and I got a nasty tackle early on which broke it again. I really played no part in the game after that – I finished up out on the wing, no subs then, and they were shouting at me to get the ball across and I couldn't even kick it properly! [1962-63] was a bad season for me. I broke my nose twice, had a fractured skull and broke the same bone in my foot three times.'

Plenty has been made over subsequent years over the constant heartbreak Killie had to suffer from being runners-up so frequently, but this League Cup final defeat in October 1962 was probably the hardest to swallow, simply because of the sheer injustice of it all. Once they'd got over the initial disbelief and misery accruing from Mr Wharton's error, the players converted their negative energy into determination against Motherwell four days later. Although fewer than 6,000 saw the game (51,280 had been at Hampden), Killie gave the Fir Park men the full backlash and smashed in seven goals – all scored by different players.

More emphatic wins followed in the League, including a 7-0 thrashing of Queen of the South and then, memorably, a 6-0 humbling of Jimmy McGrory's Celtic at Rugby Park. Rangers won the title that year by a nine-point margin, losing just twice all season, and no prizes for guessing who came second – yes, the men from Rugby Park. McInally recalled: 'Killie seemed to be eternal runners-up in various competitions and I know that was very frustrating for the fans, equally so for the players. We always seemed to fail at the last hurdle. Sometimes when that happens, the tensions and pressures get to you.'

So close and yet so far. Willie Waddell knew his team was only a whisker away from winning something, but what extra ingredient could he find to finally tip the balance?

In 1963 he visited Italy to study the methods of the great Helenio Herrera, chief coach of the highly successful Inter Milan. Accompanied by Killie trainer McCrae and the up-and-coming Jock Stein (then the forty-year-old boss of Dunfermline), Waddell was determined to find out what made Inter so formidable and what tricks he could learn. On their first morning at Inter's training ground, Waddell and Stein were puzzled to find themselves being kept waiting, while McCrae was being treated with much more deference and respect. It soon emerged that the Italians had noted that McCrae's title was 'trainer', which they confused with the Spanish term entrenador, which translates as manager or head coach.

After the pecking order was sorted, the Scots trio had their eyes opened by the attitudes and professionalism evident in top Italian soccer. McCrae later told *The Scotsman*: 'Stein liked the routines which Herrera had devised for training and their contrast with the deadly, unimaginative sessions which marked training at home. Where Stein [later] showed great originality was in adapting these techniques so that the end product was fluent, aggressive football – which he himself was to demonstrate against the master [Herrera himself] at Lisbon in 1967.'

Hererra was a striking example of an ordinary player who becomes an outstanding coach. By birth he was an Argentine, but was brought up in Morocco. The 1939-45 War seriously curtailed his playing career, which took him to French clubs Charleville, Stade Francais and Roubaix. He correctly anticipated the post-War explosion in footballing interest in Spain, and went there to coach Atletico Madrid, Valladolid, Seville, Corunna, Malaga and Barcelona. Real Madrid beat Herrera's Barcelona to qualify for the final of 1960 European Cup, where they beat Eintracht Frankfurt 7-3 at Hampden Park. This remains in many people's minds the finest single game of football ever seen in Scotland. It was a match that had a huge impact on the likes of 'local' managers Waddell and Stein, and made both eager to learn more from the Continentals.

Dismayed that his adventurous attacking style had been brushed aside by Real Madrid, Herrera relocated to Italy and apparently decided he would in future eschew adventurous football in favour of safety. In his eight years with Inter Milan he began to perfect a new system, encouraged by his club president, which yielded maximum return for minimum effort. He developed the theory of *catenaccio*, whereby a massed defence and a sweeper took care of all opposition attacks, while clever, speedy, breakaway raids would be relied on to produce the one goal that logic said would be sufficient. Easy to understand on paper, but how could a dour Scotsman like Willie Waddell bring such a system to bear back home?

The type of game Herrera espoused was intellectually admirable but emotionally sterile. 'Mobile chess' was one of the kinder descriptions of it.

Nothing could be further removed from the robust, hell-for-leather, old fashioned Scottish game. This didn't overly concern Waddell, though, for he was fed up with continually coming second with Killie and knew that tough challenges demand tough decisions. He vowed to try and introduce the Inter method in the near future at Kilmarnock. More of that later.

Poker-faced Waddell, known to some as 'the old growler', already believed in a disciplined regime, so he was gratified to find in Italy that Herrera ran a hard school where players were subjected to what was, even by the stricter Italian standards, a severe regime. One of the most intelligent British footballers to play abroad, Gerry Hitchens of Aston Villa, described parting from Inter Milan and Herrera in 1962 as 'like coming out of the Army all over again'.

Back in Ayrshire, the locals wondered how on earth Waddell's trip to Italy would help their team. Did he really propose to bring a touch of Milanese sophistication to austere Rugby Park?

Waddell and McCrae returned to Scotland with much food for thought. By now Killie had become a consistent side, and had remained near the top of the Division One table since Waddell's arrival in 1957. The pre-War dominance by the Old Firm had been loosened, even though the Glasgow giants continued to pull in by far the biggest crowds wherever they went. Before the War there were only six seasons out of 49 when neither Celtic nor Rangers claimed the championship. But in the seventeen seasons since 1945, the balance of power had shifted a little and four 'outsiders' were able to finish top of the pile. When in 1963-64, Waddell's seventh season in charge, his men finished runners-up to Rangers yet again (this time six points adrift), he began to think about his future. Although he had new ideas up his sleeve and his resolve to win something remained firm, he knew he couldn't battle against the odds like this for much longer.

His team by now had a strong, compact look about it, with goalkeeper Campbell Forsyth, right-back Andy King and wing-half Eric Murray having been introduced to become regulars in seamless fashion alongside a core of McGrory, Beattie, Brown, Watson, McIlroy and Sneddon. King and McGrory were called up to represent Scotland at Under-23 level around this time.

By the end of his first full season in the keeper's jersey at Kilmarnock, the ex-St Mirren man Forsyth had made his debut for the senior Scotland side, playing in front of 133,245 screaming fans at Hampden in the 1-0 victory over England in April 1964. It was a well-deserved honour, but because Forsyth played for a provincial club, his call-up didn't go down well in some quarters – particularly among Rangers fans. They felt their own Billy Ritchie was a better bet for the England game and they let their feelings be known during the game. Before the kick-off against England, they were heard singing 'Campbell Forsyth, we wish you were Ritchie ...' to the tune of 'Campbeltown Loch'.

Big Forsyth did well, however, doing Killie proud as he kept a clean sheet against Bobby Charlton, Roger Hunt *et al*. His elevation to the full Scotland side came shortly after a superb display in Kilmarnock's 4-0 humbling of Celtic in March 1964. Two particularly courageous saves stood out in the first half of that game: He dived bravely at the feet of the inrushing Steve Chalmers and then John Hughes to prevent certain goals, injuring himself in the process. He outdid even these saves later on, pushing a fierce ten-yarder from Chalmers around a post. His bravery and agility inspired his teammates, particularly Eric Murray, who had been restored to the attack and had his best game for the club to date. It was a great day for Killie and a shame the appalling weather restricted the Rugby Park crowd to fewer than 12,000.

Beating Celtic comprehensively at Rugby Park was becoming a welcome habit and Jackie McInally recalled: 'Celtic were in a bit of a transitional period in the early sixties, and Killie seemed to make a habit of thrashing them at Rugby Park. They had players like [John] Hughes and [Jimmy] Johnstone, who were just breaking through. Possibly their style suited the way we played; they would be pushing forward and we would give them the midfield and hit them on the break.'

By the end of 1963-64 the first-team squad at Rugby Park looked in better shape than ever, and although in recent years Killie had become established as one of the top two or three sides in Scotland – they now looked to have every chance of taking that extra step and actually winning something.

Inspirational skipper Beattie reflected on the side's development under Waddell: 'Willie's arrival had signalled great changes at Rugby Park and I felt that he and I [developed] a good rapport. We had a great bunch of guys then, too. Willie put a very good team together and we came so close to major honours on numerous occasions. Unfortunately [up to 1964-65], we always seemed to come out second best. We were definitely the most consistent team in the country in the early 1960s and if you keep knocking at the door, eventually you will get in.'

CHAPTER 3

A CHANGE OF STYLE

(August-September 1964)

Ye sons of old Killie, assembled by Willie,
To follow the noble vocation;
Your thrifty old mother has scarce such another
To sit in that honoured station.
(Robert Burns, 1786)

Viewed forty years on, the summer of 1964 appears a time of great optimism and change. Bob Dylan was singing *The Times They Are a Changin'*; London magistrates were punishing young women who went out in 'topless' dresses. And in Kilmarnock, the local football team were at last deemed suitable to take part in the glamorous and mysterious world of European competition.

Having finished Scottish League runners-up four times in five seasons, this first taste of European soccer seemed long overdue for Kilmarnock. Up to now the Scottish FA had always 'shunted them off' to the international tournament in the USA as a reward for finishing second, apparently preferring to nominate bigger, but lower-placed, clubs like Hibs for the limited places available in the Inter-Cities Fairs Cup. Some Killie fans felt hard done by over this, but even they had to admit the competition had been designed for city clubs. Thankfully, times and attitudes change, and by 1964 Killie were no longer provincial 'outsiders'.

The 1964-65 season would, however, begin under a black cloud. Fans across the nation were shocked by the death of one of Scotland's greatest players, then at his peak. Brilliant international midfielder John White, 27, was killed by a bolt of lightning while playing golf. The tragedy occurred in North London, but reverberated powerfully in White's home country. He'd been hugely popular among the tartan hordes. A memorial match would later be played in White's honour, with a Scottish Select side beating Spurs 6-2, although a fixture clash ruled out Kilmarnock's players.

Meanwhile, the draws were made for the opening rounds of European competitions. Kilmarnock were handed the mouth-watering prospect of facing Eintracht Frankfurt, who had outclassed Rangers 12-4 on aggregate in the 1960 European Cup semi-final, and then taken part in a classic final with Real Madrid at Hampden. Killie boss Willie Waddell thought long and hard about the challenge posed by the West Germans and decided the time was right to introduce a new tactical formation. It would be based largely on what he'd learned on his recent trip to study Inter Milan, but it would not prove popular with the supporters.

Pre-season training was as strenuous as ever at Rugby Park for the eighteen full-timers and seven part-timers then on the books. Killie players may have begged to differ, but trainer Walter McCrae's methods were acclaimed in the sporting press, the bouquet coming from former assistant trainer Ernie Nash, who had recently joined St Mirren. Nash told a reporter that McCrae's uncompromising regime was not bettered anywhere in Scotland, even by Rangers and Celtic. As the Killie players nursed aches and pains from the gruelling pre-season workouts, the last thing they needed was public praise for McCrae's methods.

One victim of the McCrae regime was forward Jackie McInally, or 'Jake the Rake' as many fans called him, who said: 'I wouldn't criticise [Walter] as a physio, nor as an organiser of the dressing room. That side of it was first class. As a trainer – and Walter knows this because I probably argued with him every day I was there – he was far too much the hard taskmaster. I think you should enjoy training, up to a point. You have to work hard in training to get fit, but there should be a spell sometimes when you can enjoy it. Humour was never Walter's strong point.'

For his part, McCrae knew full well that some of his methods weren't popular. Interviewed for a club publication many years later, he pointed out that the antics of some of the players meant 'I had my work cut out'. He recalled the sessions which involved players running laps of Rugby Park. Some would sprint past him as if working hard, but, on reaching the darkened corner areas of the ground, they would hide away for a quick smoke, having hidden cigarettes and matches in their tracksuits. Skipper Frank Beattie admitted he was among those who used to call McCrae 'all sorts of names', but did acknowledge that the trainer's methods ultimately resulted in a high standard of fitness.

Although the swinging 1960s were well under way by now, there wasn't much of the colour and vibrancy of London's Carnaby Street in chilly Killie. At the town's Co-op department store you could rent a TV for ten shillings and sixpence a week, get a new Hoover washing machine for £62 (as long as you part-exchanged your old wash-board and scrubbing board), and buy a tin of Scotch broth for tenpence-ha'penny. Housing had become a major social problem in the area and sanitary inspector James Baird reported that only 52 new homes had been built in the past year. Mind you, if things got too depressing, there was always the pub – and Mr Baird was pleased to announce that Kilmarnock's hostelries had improved beyond recognition recently.

Although much of the post-War austerity had abated across the UK, there were still signs that tough economic times could lie ahead. Problems

A Change of Style (August-September 1964)

were beginning to beset the Kilmarnock area, with a general decline in heavy industry and rising unemployment. The town had established itself as a regional capital of industry, with Johnnie Walker whisky, BMK Carpets and Saxone shoes among the better-known names established there, and although the new Forth Road Bridge was about to open, times were generally tough and provincial High Streets were showing the strain. Sporting bodies struggled for cash, and the public was urged to support a £5,000 appeal to enable Scottish athletes to travel to the upcoming Olympic Games in Tokyo.

The stop-go economic policy of the Government was having a marked effect on life in Scotland. In 1961 there had been a 'stop' budget which saw taxes increase, but in 1963 – with a General Election looming – the Tories attempted to boost the economy by reducing unemployment and encouraging consumer spending under policies that became known as the 'dash for growth'. However, in the autumn of 1964 Prime Minister Douglas-Home was toppled by Labour in the General Election. In such a climate it was no real surprise when football clubs like Kilmarnock announced an increase in admission prices for the 1964-65 season. Killie's went up to four shillings for adults (extra for seats), with kids up from one shilling and sixpence to two 'bob' (two shillings = 10p).

The 1964-65 action at Rugby Park began with the visit of Hearts for a League Cup-tie in which the major excitement was a freak thunderstorm which hit the ground just before 4pm, forcing the second half to be delayed for nine minutes. In contrast to the weather, the football was a lifeless affair and many fans were dismayed and confused by a new tactical formation on show. It had a distinctly negative look. Players didn't seem to be playing in a position that corresponded to their shirt number. Could this be the result of Waddell's visit to Milan last year?

Murray, wearing an unfamiliar No 7 shirt, was playing in a withdrawn position in midfield, McInally (8) was out wide on the right, Beattie (6) had moved inside to play alongside centre-half McGrory. It was all baffling for the Rugby Park faithful and, even worse, it seemed to be stifling the home side's attacking instincts. The press concluded that Waddell was experimenting with a new-fangled 4-2-4 system, and – like the fans – they didn't like what they saw. It was unworkable in Scottish football, they said. Poet Robert Burns once famously said that even the best schemes 'gang aft a-gley' and the *Sunday Mail* warned this might be the case for Waddell's plans. The paper described his formation as a concept involving 'the double centre-back, with a three-man attack and a floating inside-forward'. The match wasn't much of a spectacle and ended one goal apiece, with Brien McIlroy's fine hooked shot putting Killie ahead, only for Tommy Traynor's cross to set up a Billy Higgins equaliser.

As if to emphasise that this was a formation based on Milan's *catenaccio*, Killie ground out a goalless draw in their next League Cup-tie, at Partick, four days later. The defence looked more at home with the new formation and Davie Sneddon was lively in the middle, but the only time Killie went close was when a twenty-yarder by full-back Andy King flew wide. Waddell seemed determined to place a priority on solidifying his defensive unit. If Killie were to win anything, he felt, they needed to frustrate the opposition and base their game on being difficult to break down. Some observers agreed with this outlook, but others feared Killie would become an unattractive side to watch. Waddell's hardening attitude would be summed up by his later comment: 'We like the big, strong, powerful fellows ... with a bit of strength and solidity in the tackle rather than the frivolous, quick moving stylists like Jimmy Johnstone [Celtic winger], small tiptoe-through-the-tulips type of players who excite the people.'

On Saturday, 15 August the controversial new system had to be abandoned mid-match at Parkhead when Kilmarnock left-back Matt Watson was crocked and had to hobble out to play on the wing. By this time opponents Celtic were already a goal ahead and although the limping Watson somehow managed to snatch an equaliser, the disrupted Killie eventually capitulated to the tune of 1-4.

At Rugby Park on the same afternoon, Killie's reserves were beating Celtic's 3-1 in a stormy game that saw talented youngster John Hughes sent off in his comeback match following a ban. Hughes later appeared before a disciplinary panel for his repeated indiscretions, as did Celtic trainer Neil Mochan, charged with 'inappropriate conduct'.

The League kicked off on the evening of Wednesday, 19 August with Third Lanark visiting Rugby Park. Being a midweek game, issues of cost and logistics led to Killie not bothering to issue a match programme. It would be the first of five games this season (four at home) where there would be no programme – all of them midweek games. Third Lanark, who had struggled over the past three campaigns, upset the applecart by taking the lead after half-time through Billy Todd's drive from an acute angle. Killie were stung into action. After McInally hit the Thirds' crossbar, full-back Watson rifled in from 35 yards. Seven minutes later Pat O'Connor netted a free-kick from twenty yards and Ronnie Hamilton rounded off the win with a close-range flick.

Manager Waddell assured sceptical journalists that his 4-2-4 formation would eventually work well, once the players got familiar with it, and his words began to ring true on Saturday, 22 August when Killie subdued Hearts at Tynecastle to win 1-0 in the League Cup. With Sneddon and McIlroy constantly swapping wings, the home side looked confused. The game was won after the interval when McInally crashed home part-timer

Hamilton's pass in off the bar. Four days later Partick were thrashed 4-0 at Rugby Park, but by half-time the news had filtered through that Celtic were 3-0 up against Hearts, meaning Killie's chances of progressing to the knockout stages were effectively over.

So with the League Cup group already decided, Celtic came to Rugby Park for a meaningless final game on Saturday, 29 August. Nevertheless, based on events at the corresponding reserve match a fortnight earlier, many suspected a stormy affair was on the cards – and they weren't wrong. There were free-kicks galore, missiles were hurled and there was a menacing pitch invasion. Celtic stars Billy McNeill and Bobby Murdoch were both hurt in clashes with Hamilton and had to be taken by car to Glasgow's Victoria Infirmary. Clearly fired up, Hamilton was also warned twice by referee McKenzie for kicking the ball out of the hands of keeper John Fallon. Things heated up further when Mr McKenzie consulted a linesman about missiles thrown from the crowd, only to be hit by a beer can for his trouble. After McNeill was 'removed to the pavilion' in agony, the referee called the two captains together in an attempt to cool things down. He was wasting his time. Hamilton thrashed home a penalty after McInally was upended, and McIlroy sealed victory with a late screamer. O'Connor was booked for an off-the-ball flare-up and later picked up a nasty ankle injury. Sadly this would keep him out of the trip to Frankfurt, an occasion he'd been looking forward to as he'd served there while serving in the Army. Celtic fans gave their verdict on Killie's 2-0 win by invading the pitch. The terracing and turf was left blanketed by thousands of beer cans. 'One could hardly have taken a step without standing on some souvenir from a public house,' reported one paper.

With the Celtic hullabaloo out of the way, Killie prepared to go into battle in West Germany, their first competitive game in Europe, just four days later. O'Connor was out of the reckoning and another absentee would be part-timer Hamilton, who had to stay behind to take his first-year accountancy exams. Bertie Black and the previously injured Jim McFadzean were drafted into a fourteen-man squad. Waddell had flown to West Germany in advance to spy on Eintracht in a domestic fixture. When the Killie squad arrived, they politely declined an invitation from the Frankfurters to enjoy a pleasure trip down the Rhine before the game, preferring to use the time for training. The hosts then offered to take them on the trip after the match, but again Killie declined as they needed to fly back quickly to prepare for their next fixture.

Killie travelled in confident mood, having won four domestic games in a row. They faced an outfit which still regularly fielded five survivors from the European Cup final of 1960. Behind the scenes, a deal was struck for Killie to receive £12,000 for keeper Sandy McLaughlan from Sunderland.

It raised cash and also allowed the promising Bobby Ferguson to become outright deputy to Campbell Forsyth. McLaughlan had been in the party of fourteen in West Germany, but flew straight back alone to sign for the Rokerites.

McFadzean and Black would now make their first appearances of the season. Killie understandably took a while to settle in the vast Waldstadion. Their defence looked in good shape, however, and they made it to the interval without conceding. Stinka, despite his name, had a superb game and was reminiscent of 'Slim Jim' Baxter with his silky skills. The contest was played out in a good spirit, the only untoward incident being when Beattie, apparently accidentally, kicked Stein in the face. It was, in fact, against the run of play when the home side made the breakthrough. Stein seized on Hubert's miskick to crash the ball past Forsyth. After this the Germans dominated and a second goal came when Trimbold scored at the second attempt. Killie twice went close to pulling one back before Stinka lashed in a loose ball to give Eintracht an emphatic advantage to take into the second leg. The crowd, said by some to have been 35,000, but much smaller by others, sportingly applauded the Scotsmen off the field at the end. The next day's press condemned Waddell's negative tactics – but the manager dismissed this and said he believed the tie was not yet over. Even Killie's most ardent fans raised an eyebrow at such optimism.

The trip to St Mirren on Saturday, 5 September was Killie's ninth senior game of the season but only their second league contest. Having little time to recover from the thrashing in West Germany, Waddell decided to make changes, pushing the versatile McFadzean into midfield, and abandoning his controversial 4-2-4 formation. This seemed to pay dividends, for the home side lacked punch and made little headway. Killie looked the superior side from the moment McInally miskicked when presented with an open goal in the opening minutes. The breakthrough arrived after the turnaround when Hamilton let fly from outside the area, the ball crashing against the bar and rebounding to Brien McIlroy, who tucked it neatly past Pat Liney. Twelve minutes later McFadzean forced a corner and, from Sneddon's kick, Hamilton sent a header goalwards. The ball was blocked by John Wilson, but rebounded to Hamilton who made no mistake. Although Killie had an indifferent start to the campaign, with Waddell tinkering with the formation, this result made it two wins out of two in the League. Killie topped the table.

Whatever the merits or otherwise of Waddell's new-look formation, it was becoming clear that it certainly frustrated domestic opposition and made Killie look impregnable at the back. Discounting the Eintracht game, the defence would keep seven successive clean sheets over this period, which spoke for itself.

A Change of Style (August-September 1964)

The fifth of those clean sheets came at home to Airdrie on Saturday, 12 September when the lack-lustre visitors rarely threatened. A slick move on the right flank provided Killie's opening goal, with Sneddon supplying McInally who skipped past two defenders before cutting the ball back for Hamilton. To the fans' frustration, it took nearly an hour for the second goal to come. Sneddon was again the architect, his speculative lob eluding the defence and giving McInally an easy task.

Sneddon's midfield prompting and deft touch had by now earned him at least two nicknames – he was sometimes known as 'Chippy' and sometimes as 'The General'. He was in great form at that time and teammate McInally remembered how influential he was: 'Wee Davie ... wasn't a pacy player but he had a great head for the game and could calm things down when they got hectic.'

A week after beating Airdrie, Killie travelled to Perth to be tested more severely by St Johnstone. The new formation came into its own as the defence was put under heavy pressure, which was soaked up. McInally then notched the visitors' winner with a fine piece of opportunism against the run of play. It came after Sneddon and McIlroy combined well, before a lucky bounce saw the ball spin across goal to McInally. It seemed a lucky goal from The Saints' point of view, especially as they'd had a strike cruelly disallowed. As their frustration grew, Willie Renton began kicking lumps out of McInally and was booked.

This had proved to be a business-like single-goal victory – the type of result so essential for a team with genuine title ambitions. There was an element of luck about it, but when the chips were down Killie had rolled their sleeves up, worked hard and kept their nerve.

While Killie were getting used to their lofty position, news came from an old friend now playing in South Africa. This was Vernon Wentzel, born in Bulawayo. Wentzel was a lively forward who'd had four years at Rugby Park. He had endured a lean patch in his local league in South Africa and was ready to try just about anything in order to get the goals flowing again. So, before kick-off in a match between his side Addington of Durban and Arcadia of Pretoria, a witch doctor was invited into the home dressing room to work his magic with Wentzel's boots. The voodoo man picked up the boots, performed his ritual and handed them back. The result? Wentzel scored six times in an 8-0 victory. The flabbergasted player said afterwards: 'I am not superstitious – but this worked.'

Campbell Forsyth kept his seventh successive clean sheet in domestic games as the end of September approached. This fine run helped persuade the Scottish international selectors to stick with Forsyth for the upcoming British Championship game with Wales in Cardiff. It would be his second full cap, but his selection was once again not welcomed throughout

Scotland. In the Sunday papers, Forsyth's clubmates jumped to his defence, and claimed that big city clubs and their supporters were thumbing their noses at provincials like Kilmarnock. Willie Waddell joined in the row and told one paper: 'After all his clean sheets, he's playing exceptionally well and deserves the call-up.' Forsyth himself said: 'Maybe it's because of [Killie's] 4-2-4 system, but I don't get so much to do these days. But this kind of criticism gets me down because it's not correct.'

Born in the Stirlingshire village of Plean, Forsyth could be described as a late developer. Although his date of birth has been recorded differently in the various record books, Forsyth's senior debut for St Mirren is generally thought to have been as a 21-year-old. He was transferred to Kilmarnock at the age of 27 and made his international debut just a few days before his thirtieth birthday. Stepping out at Hampden against England in front of 133,000 sounds likes a daunting experience for anybody, let alone someone making a 'controversial' debut. But Forsyth took it in his stride. He told *Charles Buchan's Football Monthly*: 'I was confident everything would go right on the day from the moment I learned of my selection, and I wasn't nervous as kick-off time drew nearer. I felt I had been picked on merit and I knew I was not playing for myself, but also for a lot of people connected with my club Kilmarnock.'

Forsyth said Waddell, and the Killie trainers McCrae, Ernie Nash and Gerry Mays had all spent time helping improve his game in special afternoon sessions at Rugby Park and his call-up was partly a reward for them, too. As he looked around at the vast crowd at Hampden he remembered wondering if Jerry Dawson and Bobby Brown were there, for those ex-Scotland keepers were his idols and he'd studied them as a youngster.

Forsyth grew up in the same mining village (Plean) as Killie skipper Frank Beattie, but while his pal moved straight to Kilmarnock from junior football, Forsyth made slower progress into the football limelight: 'While playing for my Army unit, the Herford club [in West Germany] wanted me on the pay-roll. But my CO [commanding officer] would have none of it and I struggled along on a soldier's pay. When I went back to Scotland I had a trial for Falkirk. They sent me to juniors Kirkintilloch Rob Roy, and they weren't very impressed. Rob Roy didn't object when rival club Shettleston signed me and then I was really on my way.'

Within nine months of signing for Shettleston, Forsyth joined St Mirren and in 1957 was called up by Scotland Under-23s. Disappointment followed. The Love Street club reached the 1959 Scottish Cup final, but an injury in an earlier round put Forsyth out and The Buddies stuck with his replacement Davy Walker for the final. In 1961 a swap deal was set up with Kilmarnock and Forsyth arrived at Rugby Park, with Jimmy Brown and a £2,000 cheque going the other way.

A Change of Style (August-September 1964)

'Willie Waddell made it clear the moment he signed me I was to go into Kilmarnock's second team and fight for my place. But I was still a part-timer – I had a good job as a General Post Office technician – and I found the travelling took the edge off my training so decided to switch full time to soccer. The benefit was soon obvious. Finally, in March 1963 at the end of the long freeze-up I got my chance [to stake a regular claim].'

Forsyth's first full cap would have been followed by another in Hanover against West Germany, but injury put him out and Hearts' Jim Cruickshank got the call. This proved a blessing in disguise, for it meant Forsyth could stay at home for the birth of his daughter Kirsty. Now, in late September 1964, that belated second cap was on the way.

Forsyth provided the best possible response to his critics by turning in a fine performance for Kilmarnock at home to Dunfermline on Saturday, 26 September. He made what the *Sunday Mail* described as 'a save in a million' to keep out Tommy Callaghan late in the game, denying the visitors a point-saving goal. The big goalkeeper wasn't the only star, for Killie handed a league debut to seventeen-year-old winger Tommy McLean, a brilliant prospect. The local press praised the new boy's footwork and distribution skills, and reckoned his only fault was a tendency to hang onto the ball too long. The winner against Dunfermline came after a corner, which led to a fierce drive by McInally being prodded past keeper Jim Herriot by the alert Hamilton. The local paper noted a 'new enthusiasm' among home fans at this game, and pointed out that it was the first time in ages that 'ricketties' (wooden rattles) had been seen at Rugby Park. One fan was spotted twirling a giant-sized model, painted in blue and white.

The Pars were a lively outfit and the Killie back line had to keep a close eye on Alex Ferguson (the future Manchester United manager), who wore their No 8 shirt. A week earlier Fergie had bagged a hat-trick against Clyde, but on this day had left his shooting boots at home, for in the early stages he made the miss of the game, blasting high over the bar after a rare slip by Forsyth presented a gaping goal.

Killie's new formation was bedding in nicely and the defence generally looked tight. The idea of twin centre-halves, as opposed to one stopper with half-backs either side, was looking especially effective. Jackie McGrory was in great form at No 5 and Beattie, more of a ball-player, highly influential alongside him. They were becoming an awesome barrier for the opposition, with the motto 'they shall not pass' metaphorically written all over them.

For John Livingston, these were exciting times: 'The ground was neat and tidy in those days, although not spectacular to look at. It was as good as most grounds then, with possibly only Ibrox and Tynecastle having better looking terracing and stands in the First Division. The atmosphere with a big crowd was tremendous and Killie had a good home record, so the opposition was always up against it when they visited us. It was always looked upon as a shock result if Killie lost at home to anyone.

'I always walked to the home games and if my dad was going I got a lift-over at the turnstiles and got in for free. If my dad wasn't there, then I still got a lift-over from some kind man who saw me standing at the turnstiles. The toilets were outside and *al fresco* affairs and very primitive indeed. Getting in free meant I could afford a pie *and* Bovril, and also get the bus home after the game. My aunt, who lived en route to the game, always gave me threepence for a programme. I usually went to the away games with my dad on the bus, or with my friend's uncle, who would take us in his car.

'The place to be at Rugby Park for the sing-song supporters was in the area known as The Middle. This was in the covered terracing enclosure, about midway up to the back of the terracing, directly in line with the halfway line on the pitch. As a youngster it was great to get in there beside the older or bigger boys and to sing along with them. Of course, I was not allowed to stand beside them if my dad was with me. However, if he was not at the game, I always managed to get near enough to soak up the atmosphere and feel a part of the Killie choir. At the age of twelve it was a great feeling. I can remember finding a set of false teeth one day and a man said they were his and he gave me sixpence for finding them. Seemingly he had shouted for a penalty and the top set of his teeth had flown out of his mouth to land near me. It was one of many memorable incidents, but one that proved bizarre and profitable for me.

'Fans of other clubs treated Killie with the greatest of respect as we were then a team to be feared because we had good players and a good manager. If luck had been with Killie in the early sixties then they could have been champions and Cup winners on a few occasions, and other supporters acknowledged this. When their respective teams beat Killie they knew they'd beaten a good team. Some of our fans didn't like Rangers or Celtic because of the religious bigotry which both sets of supporters inflicted on one's ears. Partick Thistle were a bit of a bogey team to Killie and games against them were often boring, tedious affairs.

'Occasionally you would see the players in the town, particularly local ones like Andy King, Ronnie Hamilton, and Davie Sneddon who lived near my aunt, plus Jim McFadzean who was a schoolteacher during the week. They were just like ordinary people and not big-headed or overpaid like the wealthy stars of today. As a twelve-year-old it was a major event if you even walked past a player. I can still recall the excited feelings if and when it happened. Later on, Jim McFadzean was my PE teacher for a year, but as I was then older it didn't have the same effect on me.'

CHAPTER 4

THE NIGHT OF NIGHTS
(September 1964)

We'll ne'er permit a Foreign Foe
On British ground to rally!
(Robert Burns, 1795)

There was great excitement surrounding Kilmarnock's first campaign in European football. Enthusiasm remained high even after the team lost 0-3 in their Inter-Cities Fairs Cup first round, first leg tie in Frankfurt. It was felt Eintracht were flattered by the scoreline and the Rugby Park lads would do much better in the return. Perversely, being well beaten in the first game lifted pressure from Killie shoulders, meaning the players could now go out and 'enjoy' the second leg.

The visiting West German party – pride of the recently formed Bundesliga – made their base at the Marine Hotel, Troon. Set on the beautiful Ayrshire coast and looking out to the Isle of Arran, it was the same HQ they'd used four years earlier for their European Cup final with Real Madrid at Hampden. Their schedule now involved staying at this coastal hideaway for five days, and then flying direct to Berlin for a league game. Waddell would have noted with interest that shortly before their arrival Eintracht were hammered 0-7 by Karlsruhe in a friendly, although several first-team regulars were out injured that day, one of whom was centre-half Landerer, a broken leg victim.

To enhance the atmosphere of this first European game in Kilmarnock, a special souvenir match programme was prepared and crack Army bands were laid on to entertain the crowd. The military and pipe bands of the 6th/7th Cameronians (Scottish Rifles) would perform before kick-off and at half-time. Terrace prices were raised for the game, from four to five shillings for adults, but prices for youngsters were pegged.

On the morning of the game on Tuesday, 22 September, the Queen Mother was in Ayrshire to perform two ceremonies – firstly the opening of a £2 million terminal at the expanded Prestwick Airport, and then the commissioning of the world's most powerful nuclear generating station at Hunterston. Her Majesty couldn't be tempted to round off her day by popping into Rugby Park for the football, it seems. Perhaps she was put off by the torrential rain that soaked the area that day. It turned into a really ugly night weather-wise, and, combined with the fact that Killie started out three goals down, helped keep the attendance below the 15,000 mark.

Those who chose not to turn out in the miserable conditions must have regretted their decision ever since.

An injury to full-back Matt Watson meant Waddell had to ponder long and hard over team selection. Switching versatile Jim McFadzean to fill the No 3 shirt surprised nobody, but the decision to play raw seventeen-year-old Tommy McLean on the right wing in such a big match certainly raised eyebrows. The wee lad's previous first-team experience was restricted to two Summer Cup games, so this was a true baptism of fire. To accommodate the youngster, experienced Davie Sneddon was shifted to inside-left to replace McFadzean. It was a bold move by Waddell.

McLean, who'd taken his father's advice to sign for Kilmarnock despite strong representations from Glasgow Rangers, was astonished to be picked and was only given an hour to prepare himself for the match. Many years later, McLean recalled: 'Maybe [Waddell] was only thinking about giving me a bit of first-team experience. I was just a raw kid. There was a note on the notice-board instructing *all* players to report for the big game. Then at 6.20 – just over an hour from kick-off – the manager read out the team, which included the name "McLean". There was a stunned silence among the players in the dressing room, but no one was more surprised or astonished than me. Waddell had never taken me aside to hint that I had a chance or anything like that, so it was a staggering decision.'

With a mountain to climb, Killie's main priority was to pull a goal back in the early stages. To the horror of the 14,930 crowd, it was the West Germans who got that early goal, bulging Campbell Forsyth's net with only ninety seconds gone. A stunned silence blanketed Rugby Park after left-winger Schamer gathered a loose ball and slipped it inside to Huberts. The No 10 strode forward with Killie men backing off, and then cracked the ball high into the top left corner. Now Killie were four down on aggregate and the mountain had just got considerably higher.

It was the very last thing they needed, but luckily the players had no intention of caving in. After twelve minutes, Forsyth sent a big drop-kick upfield and Sneddon fed the ball to McInally in the inside-left position. The big man clipped the ball into the box, clearly hitting an Eintracht arm en route, but it ballooned into the path of Ronnie Hamilton. With several players screaming for a penalty, Hamilton drove a smart half-volley high into the net from close range. Although they were still a long way from saving the tie, the whole atmosphere changed at this point. The crowd ratcheted the noise levels up even further. Game on.

Just three minutes later, skipper Frank Beattie collected a throw-in and supplied Andy King, who skipped down the right, the Killie fans roaring him forward. The ball was shipped inside to McInally who returned it wide where young McLean was waiting out on the touchline. McLean's low cross

The Night of Nights (September 1964)

reached the near post and eluded full-back Blusch, who made a hash of things and lost his footing. The ball fell to McIlroy, who turned and shot in one smooth movement from five yards. His low drive rippled the back of the net and Killie were now ahead on the night.

Rookie McLean was involved in many of the Killie attacks as the home side bossed the first half, and certainly wasn't overawed by the occasion. The youth international tormented full-back Herbert with his speed and skill as the driving rain continued to lash down. Despite some heart-stopping moments there was no further scoring by the interval, meaning Killie would have to score three times without reply afterwards to get through. The odds were stacked against them.

Playing to a backdrop of bedlam, Killie threw everything forward in a splendid do-or-die effort. Seven minutes into the second period a free-kick just inside the Eintracht half was taken by centre-half Jackie McGrory, who lofted the ball towards the towering figures of McInally and McFadzean. The latter jumped to head a simple goal. Now Killie were just a single goal adrift and there were 38 minutes left.

Killie poured forward with the crowd making an almighty racket. Beattie showed deft footwork as he moved into Eintracht territory at a swift lick before unleashing a shot from 25 yards. The ball soared towards the top corner, but goalkeeper Loy flung himself into a wonderful diving save to touch it round for a corner. McIlroy then had a goal disallowed. It was heady stuff, but the real excitement was yet to come.

With ten minutes to go, it looked like Killie had left it too late. But then McFadzean went on a jinking run before passing to McIlroy, who crossed from the left flank. McInally got there first and headed in from close range. The sides were now level at 4-4 on aggregate. The goal sparked unprecedented scenes, hundreds of youngsters invading the pitch. If there were no further goals a third game 'replay' would be needed, for away goals – fortunately for Killie – didn't count double then. But Killie weren't thinking in terms of a replay, they had the scent of victory in their nostrils.

Once the field had been cleared, a free-kick in the Eintracht half was taken by King and cleared desperately by the weary West German defence. However, the big punt went straight to Forsyth, who belted it straight back again. There was clearly going to be absolutely no respite for the visitors. Forsyth's huge kick took one bounce to reach the opposite penalty area. Hamilton flicked the ball wide to McLean, and the teenager shot from the corner of the box, the ball slamming against a post with the keeper beaten. McFadzean was first to the rebound and returned the ball into the danger area, where King slid it back out to the right flank. McLean sent in a deep cross which caused yet more chaos, but the ball was somehow scrambled away. The scenes beggared belief as Killie drove relentlessly forward and threw everything at Eintracht in search of the winner. For the West Germans it was all hands on deck to repel the blue and white hordes in the driving rain, the fans screaming them on. Surely a fifth, and winning, goal was now only a matter of time?

Skipper Beattie recalls asking the Belfast referee Jack Adair at this point how long there was to go. He clearly recalled the reply: 'Never you mind what's the time, there's still plenty of time for you to get another.' Even the official seemed to sense what was coming.

With two minutes left, unsung hero Eric Murray sent the ball forward for the umpteenth time. McInally lashed at it but miskicked. The ball fell for Sneddon, who was felled on the edge of the penalty area. Sneddon's forward momentum meant he actually fell inside the box and the possibility of a penalty reared its head. The referee, however, indicated that the infringement had taken place outside. Sneddon hobbled up to stand over the ball alongside King. It looked like King was shaping to try a shot around the five-man wall in front of him, but crafty Sneddon fooled everyone and suddenly poked the ball sideways.

It rolled into the path of Hamilton, who cracked a low left-foot drive goalwards. The ball took at least one deflection as it evaded the wall and ended up in the net, poor Loy diving to his left, the ball flying down the middle. Cue another mass pitch invasion, this time far more bodies than previously. The ecstatic TV commentator, struggling to take everything in from his lofty vantage point, clearly didn't know who had hit the decisive shot, but screamed wildly all the same. 'All the boys in Ayrshire are swarming onto Rugby Park,' he cried. The impossible had happened and a 4-0 deficit had been overturned.

'Killie, Killie,' chanted the crowd at deafening volume as the dying seconds ticked away. Then, as the ball went out of play near the halfway line, referee Adair raised both arms and sounded his whistle for the last time. It was over. A game that will never be forgotten by all who saw it. On came the crowd again, one or two players escaping the melee by quickly diving for the tunnel, but most were engulfed by the invaders, including the weary and bewildered West Germans.

Amidst the mayhem, John Livingston recalls that even the supposedly neutral pressmen, who had lambasted Waddell in recent weeks for his tactics, were standing on their seats high in the stand, applauding as enthusiastically as anyone. Waddell and his boys had outmanoeuvred and outgunned one of the top sides in Europe. 'Waddell had won a lot more than a game that night – he had won respect from the critics,' said Livingston, adding: 'It was one of the greatest atmospheres ever at a Killie game that night. It was astounding. It was the greatest game and feeling I have ever experienced – you had to be there to understand it.'

The Night of Nights (September 1964)

Years later, match-winner Ronnie Hamilton said when people debated which had been the club's greatest ever game, people usually plumped for this one. There were no more than 16,000 in the ground, he said, but it genuinely felt like 160,000. He reckoned the fans had sensed that something special was about to happen, even after the huge blow of going a goal down early on. 'It was simply one of those one-off occasions,' he said. 'We would have beaten anybody on that night.'

This was the first time in the competition's history that a 0-3 first leg deficit had been overturned – let alone a 0-4 one. 'That was some performance,' said Everton manager Harry Catterick, watching the game to run the rule over his team's opposition in the next round.

The crowd demanded their heroes make a reappearance. The players emerged from the dressing room wearing big smiles and little else. Mostly barefooted, they took a bow and young McLean was hoisted on the shoulders of Sneddon, McIlroy and McInally. Rugby Park had never witnessed scenes like this, said the *Kilmarnock Standard* later that week, announcing emphatically that this had been the club's 'night of nights'. Chairman Willie McIvor marvelled at how the heavy rain had failed to dampen Kilmarnock spirits and neither had the blow of that early goal. He admitted that the early setback saw 'my heart sink into my boots'. Waddell admitted: 'I have never been so proud of any team. I have never witnessed scenes like this in my life.' Eintracht's injured skipper Herman Hoefer sportingly praised Killie's indefatigable spirit and the enthusiasm shown by the fans.

Jackie McInally says this game was the pinnacle of his sixteen years in football: 'We thought we were in for a hammering. But it seemed the whole of Ayrshire was crammed into the ground that night, not just Killie fans, and they gave us incredible backing. The excitement was unbelievable, the whole ground was in a frenzy as we began to break them down.'

Even though Tommy McLean would enjoy a fine career as player and manager, packed with big-occasion matches, he also regards the Eintracht game as the greatest of them all. He recalled: 'When we lost a goal in two minutes we just threw caution to the wind and with the rain belting down the goals just kept coming. From a personal point of view everything I touched seemed to turn to gold. It was incredible. Away goals didn't count double in those days and I have to admit when it went to 4-4 I was delighted because I thought I was going to get a trip to a neutral venue abroad. Then, amazingly we scored again to make it 5-4 and that was how it stayed. It was one of the greatest European comebacks of all time. I set up a few of the goals and I even hit the post, I remember. It was some way to make a debut. I felt like Roy of the Rovers.'

The excitement took its toll on the McLean digestive system, and on his way home the youngster threw up: 'My brother, Willie, was at the game and on the drive home I had to get him to stop the car so I could be sick. It all just caught up on me – the whole thing of playing when I thought I would be just watching, doing so well and the result. But the experienced lads in the side then – guys like Frank Beattie and Jackie McInally – were brilliant with me and I've always remembered that.'

Young David Ross, later to become a journalist, recalled: 'The next day Scotland awoke to find Killie's deeds plastered all over the front pages. Britain was in the middle of a general election campaign, as was the USA. China was on the brink of exploding an atom bomb and a coup was in the offing in the Kremlin. But none of this was allowed to intrude on the story of the day – Kilmarnock's magnificent fightback. Perhaps even more significant in the world of Scottish football than knocking Harold Wilson and Lyndon Johnson off the front pages, Killie even managed to knock the Old Firm off the back ones'

The next morning the shell-shocked Eintracht players and officials were guests at a civic reception in the Ossington Hotel, Kilmarnock. Provost David Cunningham spoke, hoping 'you lads from Germany' were not too disappointed. Killie had been known for years as eternal runners-up – but fortune had favoured them this time and this was their first real success for some time. He apologised to the West Germans for the pitch invasions, explaining 'their enthusiasm ran away with them'. Eintracht centre-half Richard Weber – a university student and one of several part-timers in their team – translated the official reply from the visiting officials, which included glowing references to the beauty of the local landscape. Afterwards the 21-strong party toured Johnnie Walker's distillery nearby and were given souvenir samples to take away with them. They flew home on the Friday from Renfrew and were seen off by Willie Waddell.

Killie officials knew the pitch invasions would displease UEFA and could prove embarrassing, having happened at the club's very first staging of a European tie. To reassure the authorities, and the public at large, the club hurriedly issued an announcement that strict measures would be put in place in future to prevent any recurrence.

This remarkable episode in Kilmarnock's history is, not surprisingly, etched deep into the memories of those who witnessed it. For example, Anne Marks, a young girl at the time, but now teaching in the USA, says unequivocally: 'That was definitely the greatest night in Rugby Park history. I still have the blue and white scarf from then, rather well worn now. The pies were the best, by the way, and my grandfather had the first hot pie stand at Rugby Park. Perhaps my strangest memory from back then, though, is watching the club's sheep mascot keeping the grass trim.'

Another fan, Allan Wilson, saw things from a different perspective. He was lucky enough to be a KFC ball-boy and was therefore closer to the

The Night of Nights (September 1964)

action than most. Originally from Bonnyton, Kilmarnock, Allan is these days Chief Executive Officer of a software company in Austin, Texas, USA, but his days as a Killie ball-boy are still vividly recalled:

'I'd begun my ball-boy career around 1960 and continued through the glory years, including the Eintracht game. As you can imagine, being fourteen years old and being a ball-boy I had the type of access to the players that the regular supporters did not, and they seemed larger than life to me. Heroes, gods, rock stars all rolled into one. In those days, for a wee boy growing up in Scotland, especially working class Kilmarnock, fitba' was everything. Killie was larger than life to me, bigger than the Beatles. The crowds of course were larger then and they were jammed in like sardines for every home game, especially when Rangers and Celtic came to town. Leading them out of the tunnel – the ball-boys always ran out ahead of the teams – was incredible. It was like I was part of the team and the roar was for me. I will never forget that feeling as long as I live.

'My dad first took me to Rugby Park when I was about seven or eight. He commentated on the games with three other guys from a little wooden enclosure stuck up in the back corner of the old West Stand at the Dundonald Road end. This service was for the Ayrshire hospitals and while he was doing that my mother was working in the little Pie-and-Bovril huts that were around the ground. Dad was treasurer and secretary of the KFC Supporters Club for many years, so it was not surprising when he managed to swing it for me to become a ball-boy.

'When I started, the old West Stand was still there and we entered through the players' and officials' entrance, which was on the Rugby Road end, and had just one little single door with a doorman who sat in a little booth. It was just like getting into the pictures. I was paid half-a-crown (12½ pence) and I thought that I was the bee's knees. The old stand was a rabbit warren of little corridors and cramped dressing rooms – I'm sure that down in the lower divisions in Scotland there are still stands like that in existence today. The ball boys were given really good kit. I remember getting a bag and tracksuit, boots and rain-gear. When I arrived on a matchday and had to push through the crowds waiting on getting players autographs, and then enter the players' entrance, it was, as I mentioned earlier, like being part of the team. What a feeling.'

Wilson remembers being fascinated by the players: 'The players were each very different characters, as they are today, some very serious and focused and others always joking and winding each other up. One of the larger than life characters I remember was goalkeeper Jimmy Brown. He was a riot. At the end of some games when it had been freezing out on the park and the rain had been lashing down – as we all know it can in Ayrshire – he would come into the ball-boys' dressing room and take us all into the big bath with the team. In those days it was one big communal bath in the home dressing room – can you imagine the uproar that would cause today?

'A big favourite was Jackie McInally. The chant was "McInally, McInally – Jake, Jake, Jake!" To see big Jackie in full flow, running at the defence after a flick on from wee Bertie Black was something to behold and then the finish, which was invariably a crashing fifteen or twenty-yard drive into the top corner – magic! Another, of course, was the late Brien McIlroy, a prolific goalscorer. I was at Rugby Park recently and asked Davie Sneddon about the best Killie player he had played with. He mentioned Tommy McLean, but as far as a natural goalscoring talent goes, he did not hesitate to name McIlroy. I also asked Davie who was the fastest player. His answer stunned me – goalkeeper Ferguson. He said that Big Jake and Bobby used to race each other after training and it was always Bobby who won.

'When fringe players tried to break through, perhaps due to injury, they were sometimes given a hard time. Big Jim McFadzean was one. Jim was typically played at left-back when Mattha Watson was out and he was a different player from Mattha. Jim was tall, athletic and strong so his attacking skills were better, but he was a little slow on the turn and would get caught in no-man's-land and let players get behind him. Mattha on the other hand did not get forward as much but was a better defender and anyone who tried to get behind him would end up on the cinder track – ask Willie Henderson of Rangers about that. Away from the field of play there was a major difference as compared to today's players. Yes, they would have a drink and party with the best of them, but my memories are that they were more committed to the game then. The Old Firm players had more money of course and did get caught doing some stupid things – and of course the *Daily Record* was there to report it all – but all in all the game came first.

'Frank Beattie was a great player, given the life-style and training methods of the day. Frank's style was not unlike Steve Bruce when he played for Manchester United, or even Patrick Vieira at Arsenal. The training and conditioning available today result in the game being played at a far greater pace and as such the Frank Beatties could not have survived in today's environment. However, if Frank had been born later and grown up with all of this training and conditioning he would have coped well for he had all the skill and leadership and tenacity exemplified in Roy Keane today.'

Not all Wilson's memories of the mid-1960s are so kind: 'I can remember seeing bottles thrown and exploding on people's heads back in those days, when they allowed alcohol in the ground. I've also seen darts thrown and spit running down the back of heads.'

CHAPTER 5

WADDELL DROPS A BOMBSHELL
(October-November 1964)

We've lost a birkie weel worth gowd;
Willie's awa!
(Robert Burns, 1787)

Barbara Windsor and the 'Carry On' team were starring at Kilmarnock's ABC cinema at the beginning of October 1964, and for Killie it was a case of 'Carry On Winning' as far as their Scottish Division One campaign was concerned.

They'd maintained a 100 per cent record after five league games, and the new-look defence had conceded just once, with that minor aberration coming on the opening day back in August. Throw in the extraordinary events against Eintracht Frankfurt and it all added up to a highly satisfactory start to the season. The loyal band of Killie fans who headed to Edinburgh for the tussle with Hibs on Saturday, 3 October were in good heart.

That afternoon's league fixtures clashed with the British International Championship programme, meaning Killie would have to do without goalkeeper Campbell Forsyth. He had been rewarded for his seven successive clean sheets in domestic games by being called up by Scotland to face Wales at Ninian Park for his second full cap.

As ever, the goalkeeping position was giving the Scottish selectors cause for concern in the early 1960s. Since the humiliating day when Celtic's Frank 'Happy' Haffey conceded nine at Wembley in 1961, Scotland had called upon Lawrie Leslie (Airdrie), Bill Brown (Spurs), Eddie Connachan (Dunfermline), Adam Blacklaw (Burnley) and Tommy Lawrence (Liverpool) before giving Forsyth the nod in 1964. The selectors kept returning to the experienced Brown, but by now he'd reached the age of 33 and was perhaps past his best. The situation was crying out for a youngster to come through and make the jersey his own, but nobody seemed ready to claim it. As it happened, there was a bright young prospect on Killie's books – Bobby Ferguson, a nineteen-year-old who hailed from nearby Kilwinning – who had shown bags of promise in the reserves recently.

Forsyth's absence meant Ferguson would be making his League debut for Killie in the game at Easter Road, and in front of a big crowd in the capital it was a great chance for the youngster to show his worth. He grabbed the opportunity with both hands, so to speak, and had a wonderful game, thwarting the home side time and again and leaving their new manager Jock Stein grim-faced in the dug-out. Few chances came Killie's way and they relied on breakaways, one of which saw Ronnie Hamilton open the scoring just before the interval. He headed home after keeper Willie Wilson had only parried an outswinging cross from Brien McIlroy. The second half was a matter of hanging on grimly, but there was glee among the Killie ranks when a second goal came against the run of play, Hamilton nodding his second from a McInally cross. Ferguson's goal came under heavy pressure in the closing stages, and Killie's long run of clean sheets against Scottish opposition ended when a Pat Stanton lob was glanced in by the head of Neil Martin. It set up a grandstand finish, during which Jim Scott hit the bar and Ferguson was kept on his toes.

The 100 per cent league record was thus maintained and for Ferguson in particular it was a day to remember. However, down in South Wales, Campbell Forsyth had an unhappy afternoon as Scotland – apparently cruising to a 2-1 win – were beaten by two goals in the final three minutes by Ken Leek of Birmingham City.

The lead at the top of table was reduced to just one point a week later, when Killie's run of wins came to an end in their seventh league encounter of the season. Partick Thistle were the visitors on Saturday, 10 October and their feisty defensive display won a point in a goalless draw that left the home fans frustrated – but grudgingly praising visiting keeper George Niven, who had one of those afternoons when everything went right for him. Waddell had recalled young McLean, with McFadzean dropping back to fill in for the injured Andy King, but not even the teenager's deft footwork and darting runs could break the Jags down.

Supporter David Ross recalls the visit of Partick that day as one of the rare occasions when a spot of bother occurred at a game not involving the Old Firm. Said David: 'After the game two Thistle fans, aged about thirteen or fourteen, grabbed hold of me and my cousin, who were just eight, and threatened us with a right kicking unless we kissed their scarves. They weren't joking either. We pretended to oblige, but actually left a few globules of spit instead and then shouted for help, the arrival of which sent the Jags pair scurrying off.'

A goalless draw at home to Partick Thistle on a chilly afternoon is not the ideal route to a Killie supporter's heart, but most were not complaining – after all their heroes were still top of the league and there was the tasty prospect next month of a visit from the so-called 'School of Science' club, Everton, in the second round of the Inter-Cities Fairs Cup. Not only were Kilmarnock folk satisfied with their football team, they were also happy with their man at Westminster – for that same week they returned Labour

MP William Ross with an increased majority of nearly 15,000. Moreover, Labour supporters across the land had cause to celebrate because, led by 48-year-old Huddersfield Town supporter Harold Wilson, the party gained a slim majority and ousted the Conservatives for the first time in thirteen years.

On Polling Day, Willie Waddell – presumably having registered his vote first – headed down to Goodison Park to watch Everton finish the job against Valerengens of Oslo and confirm their meeting in the next round with Kilmarnock. Harry Catterick's side won this second leg game 4-2 to qualify by 9-4 on aggregate. After what they did to Eintracht, Waddell must have thought his team would be a match for anyone, but he was nevertheless impressed by what he saw at Goodison – particularly the silky skills in the middle of the park of Scot Alex Young, widely known as The Golden Vision. Everton were at that point third in the English League and a formidable side, although they were without the services of highly rated wing-half Tony Kay, suspended pending a police investigation into match-fixing allegations. In fact, the day Everton beat Valerengens to set up the tie with Kilmarnock, Kay was facing magistrates alongside several former teammates. The whole sorry episode would lead to Kay being jailed.

Waddell followed up his Goodison visit with a second trip to spy on Everton, seeing them lose 2-3 to Blackburn, after which he met up with Catterick to get down to the business of agreeing dates for the Fairs Cup meeting. The first leg was fixed for 11 November. This clashed with the John White memorial game in which a Scotland side was to face Tottenham. Waddell therefore put in a formal request to the SFA for Campbell Forsyth and Jackie McGrory to be released from the White game. To Killie's relief, the request was granted, which meant Scotland's tightest defence would be at full strength when it faced England's brightest attack.

Thoughts of the Everton clash had to be put aside as unbeaten league leaders Killie headed for Dundee on Saturday, 17 October. They were shocked by an early goal, Steve Murray winning a race with Forsyth to scramble the ball goalwards where it rolled gently in off a post to send Dens Park into raptures. The Dundee lead lasted almost forty minutes, Eric Murray equalising after a corner and then Sneddon firing home after a King free-kick was only partly cleared two minutes later. This double blow meant the home side were out for the count and Killie rubbed their noses in it by grabbing a third, McInally heading home after a dreadful defensive mix-up. Kilmarnock's defence had again been impressive and by now their record was just three goals conceded in the season's opening eight league games. They looked on course to achieve the best defensive record in Division One since the 1939-45 War.

As a happy Killie party returned home from Tayside, more good news filtered through from Japan that Britain's Olympians were at last getting among the medals. Anne Packer in the 400 metres, Mary Rand (pentathlon), Maurice Herriott (steeplechase) and Louis Martin (weightlifting) had all won silver in the Tokyo Games earlier that same day.

Kilmarnock reserves also made the news that day, thanks to the fact that transfer rebel Alan Gilzean turned out at Rugby Park for Dundee's second string. The highly-rated forward had been embroiled in a dispute known as 'the Gilzean affair' which started with a rebuffed transfer request and saw him refusing to play for five months. Effectively he was on strike. But after twenty weeks of kicking his heels, Gilzean had by now agreed to sign a short-term contract and the reserve game at Kilmarnock was his much-heralded 'comeback'. The press descended on Rugby Park in droves to see Gilzean put himself in the shop window. Killie defender Pat O'Connor had to mark him and told the journalists afterwards that considering he'd been out so long, Gilzean had been very mobile. The man at the centre of the row, who celebrated his 26th birthday that week, announced that he was glad to be back and was not fussy which club he joined next, as long as the terms were right. The saga would ultimately drag on for another seven weeks until Tottenham came in with a £72,500 cheque, Gilzean moving south to form a lethal partnership at White Hart Lane with Jimmy Greaves.

There was cause for celebration in the Killie camp shortly after the Dundee win when 22-year-old centre-half Jackie McGrory was called up to win his first full Scotland cap. The selectors were without Celtic's Billy McNeill, Arsenal's Ian Ure and Liverpool's Ron Yeats – all injured. McGrory wore the dark blue No 5 shirt against Finland at Hampden in a World Cup qualifier, and played his part in a 3-1 win. McGrory was helped that night by his Killie teammate Forsyth, who was winning his third full cap. Supporter David Ross believes the call-up was well deserved and reckons McGrory was the finest centre-half he has seen play for Kilmarnock in more than forty years: 'McGrory was as important a player for Kilmarnock as his sadly pre-deceased contemporaries Jim Baxter and Bobby Murdoch were for the Old Firm.'

McGrory started out playing wing-half or inside-forward for Kilmarnock Amateurs and Dreghorn Juniors before joining Killie in 1960 and was converted to centre-half by manager Waddell. Frank Beattie was moved from the right to the left-hand side of midfield and McGrory made his debut, ten days before his nineteenth birthday, in the heart of defence. It looked a makeshift arrangement at the time, but the McGrory-Beattie partnership would go on to achieve legendary status in subsequent years. McGrory became a regular after an injury to Willie Toner in August 1962 and went on an unbroken run of 114 competitive first-team matches until December 1964. Looking at his career as a whole, it is clear McGrory was consistent and rarely injured, for during ten seasons he would only miss thirteen league matches – five of those due to contractual disputes. In October 1964 it was regarded as a tremendous achievement for a player from Kilmarnock to force his way into the international reckoning and line up alongside the star names from Celtic, Rangers, Liverpool and Manchester United.

Meanwhile, Killie's scheduled opposition on Saturday, 24 October was Celtic, but the Parkhead club had qualified for the League Cup final that day, against Rangers at Hampden, which meant Rugby Park was without a game. The clash with The Bhoys was therefore rearranged for the following Wednesday night. Local householders drew a collective breath and the town of Kilmarnock battened down the hatches and prepared itself for the usual mass invasion.

Often the main talking point surrounding a Celtic visit would be the havoc created by their fans, but this occasion was different. Shortly before the game an important statement was issued by Kilmarnock chairman Willie McIvor. His words stunned fans, players and officials alike – Willie Waddell, after seven years managing Killie, was planning to quit.

The shock statement read as follows: 'At his request, Mr Waddell is being released from his duties on the expiry of his contract on July 31, 1965. Mr Waddell feels that for personal reasons his future lies outwith the area of football management. The directors are very proud of the performance of Kilmarnock during the period since Mr Waddell was appointed manager. Unfortunately, as yet, we have not won any national competitions but we think we can claim without fear of contradiction that for a provincial club our record over the past few years is second to none. Most of the credit for this sustained performance is due to Mr Waddell, for whom the directors have the highest regard. The phrase "personal reasons" is often used as a euphemism to hide some measure of disagreement, but in this case it happens to be the truth and the whole truth. The directors deeply regret Mr Waddell's decision to leave football management, but they respect it and in agreeing to his request they would like to take the opportunity of placing on record their deep appreciation of his services and their best wishes for his success in whatever future career he may choose.'

McIvor added that Waddell had agreed to accept a place on the Kilmarnock board of directors after his departure as manager, as long as it didn't conflict with his new career. A stunned Scottish football world was left guessing what Waddell intended to do next – and the man himself was offering no clues. He explained that he'd made his decision known now, so as to give the club time to look for a successor. The *Sunday Mail* praised him for building a team that had done everything except win major honours, and had made Rugby Park the best organised producers of provincial talent in recent years.

The rumour mill was in full flow and it was widely thought Waddell intended to make a clean break from football. In the gap between the end of his playing days and the start of his stint at Kilmarnock, Waddell had worked as a football journalist, and it was suggested he would return to a media job. He was only 43 and still had plenty of time to forge a new career, after all.

The press pointed out that he certainly wasn't the first Scottish club manager to make a clean break from football. David Halliday of Aberdeen had a spell as a hotelier and George Young quit Third Lanark to concentrate on various business ventures. One of Waddell's predecessors at Killie, Alex Hastings, had become disillusioned with football and became a shopkeeper and hotelier, while St Johnstone's Jimmy Crapnell went into engineering. Other names could be recalled who expressed delight and relief at quitting the pressures of football management, including Bobby Flavell of St Mirren and Willie Fotheringham of Airdrie, both of whom jumped ship of their own volition. 'Let's hope it's not the Kilmarnock people who have chased Waddell away by their very indifference to his fine team,' said one report, referring to Killie's relatively small home gates.

News of Waddell's decision had spread far and wide by the time the home game with Celtic kicked off, and judging by the way the Killie players tore into the opposition, the announcement had not prevented them focusing on the job in hand. King fed Hamilton, who sprinted down the left, roared on by the home fans, and crossed for McInally to slide the ball past the advancing figure of keeper John Fallon. Before the half-hour mark, Killie were two ahead, Hamilton outjumping Tommy Gemmell and Fallon to nod home a free-kick from King.

Despite the backing of their huge following on the terraces, Celtic had little answer to the onslaught, and seven minutes before the break Killie made it 3-0, McInally hammering in a corner-kick by Sneddon. The big lead didn't flatter the home side, who could have had many more – and there was no let-up after the restart. Big Jim McFadzean headed home twice in two minutes early in the half, both from Sneddon assists, to give Killie a 5-0 lead they fully deserved. The home fans were ecstatic and loving every second. It had turned into one of those glorious, atmospheric nights that live long in the memory. Inevitably the pace slackened a little after an hour and Celtic took advantage to pull a couple of goals back, via good shots from Gemmell and Charlie Gallagher – the latter a former Kilmarnock Amateurs player. But even this couldn't take the gloss off a wonderful night for the home fans.

John Livingston recalled: 'When Celtic came to Kilmarnock there was often trouble – probably because Killie in the early to mid-sixties always used to thump them at Rugby Park, and their fans didn't like it one bit. I remember seeing one game where we beat them 6-0 and I was hit over the head with a large fishing rod by a Celtic supporter in his twenties. There was no segregation in those days and regularly Celtic would bring 10-15,000 supporters, with Rangers bringing well over 20,000.'

Having crushed the mighty Celtic, Killie found, three days later, that they wouldn't get things all their own way at Tannadice, home of lowly Dundee United. In the first half United did most of the attacking but failed to find the target, and just before the break referee 'Tiny' Wharton missed a blatant handball in his own area by Matt Watson – to the fury of the home fans. Another close thing was a cannonball shot by Stewart Fraser being blocked by the head of Frank Beattie, laying out the Killie man in the process. It took a single goal, deep into the second half, to see off the home side. And what a goal it was. Hamilton gained the ball inside his own half and pushed a through ball in the direction of McInally. Only moments earlier the pair had responded to trainer Walter McCrae's instruction to swap positions. McInally gathered the pass and set off at speed and beat four defenders en route to goal, ending the run by skipping past keeper Don Mackay and curling home a marvellous shot. It was a sensational strike and McInally recalled it years later as the best of his career: '[I went on] a mazy run from the midfield, beating four or five players. I probably beat some of them twice, and then rounded the goalkeeper to stick it into the net.'

McInally was a colourful performer who often polarised opinion among Killie fans. Some loved his powerful, mazy runs and worshipped him, but others barracked him and were constantly critical of his style. John Livingston recalls: 'Jackie could dribble from his own penalty area into the opposition's, round the keeper, but then put it past the post or fall over the ball. He was such a deceptive player – tall, slim with a long awkward stride, but he could be a match-winner at times. I think he was a better player than his son Alan, who went on to play for Aston Villa, Celtic, Bayern Munich and Scotland.'

McInally himself accepted that his inconsistency caused opinions to be divided. He said anyone who took players on, as he did, would look like a world beater when it came off, but would look bad when it didn't: 'I got on well with the majority of the Killie fans. But everyone who plays football has a section of the support who don't like them. It doesn't matter where you go, or what you do on the park, you'll never please them.'

McInally's solo effort in that hard-earned victory at Tannadice on the last day of October maintained Killie's two-point cushion at the top of the table, a lead that would have been even more substantial had the two Edinburgh clubs not embarked on impressive unbeaten runs of their own. The top of the table on 1 November looked like this:

	P	W	D	L	F	A	Pts
KILMARNOCK	10	9	1	0	20	5	19
Hearts	10	7	3	0	33	12	17
Hibs	10	8	2	0	24	14	16
Dunfermline	10	6	2	2	24	10	14
Celtic	10	6	2	2	22	16	14

November 1964 kicked off at Rugby Park with the spoils being shared with Motherwell, a rather disappointing outcome in these heady days of topping the table. It was a fair result in view of the fact that Killie looked below their best and by the end were hanging on for a point. Eric Murray was injured and off the field for ten minutes, which may have disrupted things, but they missed several good chances in the first half before McGrory set up Hamilton to net a fine goal. Former Killie favourite Joe McBride, and George Lindsay, looked dangerous on the break for the visitors and it was no surprise when the latter equalised soon after the restart. His firm shot was pushed against a post by Forsyth but rolled over the line with McGrory stretching desperately and unsuccessfully to stop it. The crowd numbered 9,698, which was disappointing in view of the club's league position, and was described as 'a disgrace' by the national pressmen at the game, who were used to the bigger city clubs leading the table.

Perhaps Motherwell had benefited from Killie having their minds on the Everton Fairs Cup-tie, scheduled for the following Wednesday, 11 November. Ever since the amazing night against Eintracht, this game had been the subject of huge interest. In the last couple of weeks, Everton had dropped from third to eighth in the English table, suffering three successive defeats. And their manager Harry Catterick certainly wouldn't be under-estimating Killie, for he'd watched their 5-2 win over Celtic. On the Scottish TV show 'Scotsport' he described Kilmarnock as 'the best-drilled Scottish team for five or six years'.

Everton's last game before their trip to Kilmarnock was a stormy affair which became known as the 'Battle of Goodison' against Don Revie's unpopular Leeds side. Everton's Grangemouth-born defender Sandy Brown was sent off in the early minutes and, before long, overworked referee Ken Stokes of Newark ordered the remaining 21 players off the field, too, instructing them to 'cool off for ten minutes' before returning. According to the *Sunday Mail* it was the first time in the history of English football that a game had been suspended in this way. Amid the mayhem, some players apparently misunderstood what was going on and thought the match had been abandoned altogether. They were preparing to jump into an early bath before it was made clear. Missiles were thrown by irate Goodison fans and there were loudspeaker announcements appealing for order. Leeds ended up winning 1-0 and Everton were left with at least six men injured, including winger Derek Temple, who'd departed on a stretcher. A furious Catterick revealed that Sandy Brown had six stud marks on his stomach after the clash with Johnny Giles which provoked the dismissal. Police had to intervene at the end when angry Everton fans gathered outside the dressing room area. The mob was ushered away and the Leeds players escorted to their bus.

News of their opposition's injury list was obviously encouraging for Kilmarnock, whose cheaply assembled side faced the prospect of coming up against an Everton line-up that cost around £250,000. Everton had recently earned themselves bragging rights as unofficial 'champions of Great Britain', having beaten Rangers over two games in a contest designed to find the best side in the UK.

Having been physically battered by Leeds, Everton took the field at Rugby Park missing Scottish internationals Alex Scott and Alex Parker, while Killie brought in Bertie Black to replace McInally, who'd failed a late fitness test. The tie was watched by a bumper crowd of 23,561, which was way above Killie's average, although it didn't reach the level of some of the Old Firm games, which involved huge away followings. The Everton game turned into a real anti-climax as far as Killie was concerned. The visitors won 2-0 after scoring twice in a five-minute spell early in the second half, both goals coming as a result of errors by the unfortunate Campbell Forsyth. The first came after a long-range shot by Dennis Stevens was deflected off Beattie to the edge of the Kilmarnock penalty area and seemingly out of danger. As Forsyth hesitated, Derek Temple set off in pursuit of it. Temple got there first and chipped the ball goalwards, Forsyth getting a touch on it, only to see the ball roll agonisingly slowly over the unguarded goalline. It was an embarrassing goal to concede for the current Scotland first-choice keeper, but worse was to follow. Johnny Morrissey fired in a shot which Forsyth attempted to punch clear, only to see it fly off his fist into the net. It was a mortal blow to Kilmarnock's hopes, but, to his credit, Forsyth pulled off a magnificent save from Jimmy Gabriel soon afterwards.

There was no time to wallow in misery, for reigning champions Rangers were in town three days later. This contest was regarded by many as the most important league game thus far. Victory for Killie would surely leave mid-table Rangers with too much ground to make up to retain their title. Rangers had recently won a European Cup preliminary round play-off tie with Red Star Belgrade at the neutral venue of Highbury, but knew they'd have a big battle on their hands at humble Kilmarnock, who had now gone fourteen domestic games without defeat, despite the Everton debacle.

A huge crowd of more than 32,000 squeezed into Rugby Park, well over half of these being visiting fans, and the contest was a thriller. Killie gave as good as they got from the reigning champions and Forsyth bounced back brilliantly from his Everton woes. Killie were lucky to survive early penalty appeals when Willie Johnston was tripped. Meanwhile, the maestro 'Slim Jim' Baxter had a masterful game in the middle of the park and it was his low, firm drive which opened the scoring just after the hour mark.

The *Kilmarnock Standard* noted how Baxter was spoken to in stern terms by the referee on two occasions, but had not been booked: 'Few other players seem to get this lenient treatment,' wrote their irritated correspondent. He had a point. Even after being warned about his behaviour, late in the game Baxter blatantly shoved McFadzean on to the track surrounding the pitch as the Killie man went to retrieve the ball for a throw. The ref consulted a linesman, but still kept his book in his pocket. The *Standard* man reckoned it was 'tragic that such a skilful player chooses to misbehave and mar his performance, but also bad that officials don't clamp down on such disrespect for their authority.'

Fortunately Frank Beattie took the spotlight away from the talented but petulant Baxter by steaming in towards the rebound after Hamilton's 25-yarder was parried, and bulleting a header into the Rangers net on 74 minutes. It was a magnificent goal, which saved a deserved point for Killie and prompted what the *Sunday Mail* called 'one of the biggest roars ever heard at Rugby Park'.

Unlike his opposite number Baxter, skipper Beattie was praised for his exemplary conduct during the height of the battle at Rugby Park. And another man who came in for praise was Rangers' Jimmy Millar, who claimed that he'd sportingly got himself injured in a bid to prevent hurting Killie's Davie Sneddon! Millar explained to reporters that as he and Sneddon hurtled into a challenge, he'd realised the Killie man was about to be injured and therefore stopped suddenly to avoid this. But, as a result of this generous manoeuvre, Millar ended up injuring himself.

Shortly after this stormy game, Jim Baxter's run of good form would come to a nightmarish end. In a European Cup-tie in Vienna his leg was broken, putting him out of action for months. This injury was perhaps the final blow to Rangers' realistic hopes of successfully defending their League title in 1964-65.

The season was now well into its stride and moving along at a cracking pace, with important matches coming one after the other for Kilmarnock. Waddell knew it was important his players should relax properly between games, and 48 hours after they had held Rangers he sent some of them to wind down at the beautiful Crow Wood Golf Club, on the Garnkirk Estate, north of Glasgow. Players Sneddon, Beattie, Murray, Forsyth and Watson were given the task of defending the *Daily Record* Soccer-Golfers championship they'd won previously. Despite the fierce gales overhead the Killie group beat Motherwell to retain their title. Manager Waddell showed his players how it was done, completing his round in an excellent 67, some nine shots better than any of his players.

After the gales of Crow Wood, the next weather hazard confronting the Kilmarnock players was the thick fog which rolled off the sea and enveloped Aberdeen's Pittodrie stadium when Killie visited on Saturday, 21 November. The Dons ripped into the league leaders in the opening half and Tommy Morrison put them ahead. With winger Charlie Cooke and former Killie favourite Andy Kerr wreaking havoc, Killie were fortunate to get to the break just one goal down. The fog descended in the second half and with it Killie took a grip on the contest. By the end the battling visitors were coming out of the shroud toward John 'Tubby' Ogston's goal in relentless fashion, but it wasn't until the last minute that they levelled, a grounded McInally deflecting a wayward Hamilton shot in off the goalpost. Due to the conditions, only a fraction of the crowd would have seen this valuable point-saving effort. It represented Kilmarnock's first away point to be dropped this season, but in the circumstances it was a draw well earned.

John Livingston, shivering alongside his dad among the away supporters that afternoon, recalls: 'Not many people could have seen McInally's equaliser because of the heavy sea haar. I certainly didn't. It was quite frightening trying to find our way back to the bus. I think it was well after midnight before my dad and I got home because the bus took ages to get out of Aberdeen and down the road back to Ayrshire.'

Back in Kilmarnock that same afternoon, Killie's reserves were tackling Aberdeen's second string in a game that featured a bizarre controversy over a penalty. The kick was apparently clouted home by Killie's Frank Malone, but the goal was then disputed in animated fashion by the Aberdeen goalkeeper. The small crowd couldn't understand what he was complaining about, until it emerged that he'd retrieved the ball from outside the goal and was therefore trying to convince the referee that it had never entered the net at all. After inspecting the netting, the official stuck to his original instinct that the ball had gone in, and must have gone through the net. From then on, Frank Malone could call himself a true 'net-buster'.

During the week Kilmarnock and other clubs were circulated by the SFA about the Summer Cup, which had been introduced the previous close season and was seen as reasonably successful, despite the non-participation of the Old Firm clubs. Most clubs voted for a repeat event in 1965, but ultimately the absence of enthusiasm from the bigger clubs would prove decisive and the competition died a death.

With international football on the calendar for Wednesday, 25 November, Everton and Kilmarnock scheduled the second leg of their Fairs Cup-tie for the preceding Monday, meaning the Killie players had to spend their Sunday travelling to Merseyside by rail. The club's followers were invited by their Everton counterparts to join them at their official clubhouse, a converted cinema situated a short walk from Goodison in the City Road. They were staging a cabaret evening with dancing and bingo, with Chinese food brought in from a nearby restaurant. A number of Killie fans took advantage of this cordial invitation.

The start of the Goodison tie was briefly delayed, after Killie players were ordered back to their dressing rooms to change their jerseys. The West German referee reckoned their blue and white stripes clashed with Everton's blue shirts. With no suitable gear to change into, it was left to the home side to step in and offer to wear white tops. Frank Beattie had failed a fitness test and Pat O'Connor was given a rare opportunity in this game. Killie were determined to peg back the Toffees in the early stages and McIlroy reduced the deficit after just six minutes with a brilliant opportunist goal from McFadzean's pass. They continued to press forward and with just eleven minutes on the clock had forced five corners to the home side's none. Everton's inexperienced young stand-in keeper Andy Rankin was put under heavy pressure.

The brave Killie challenge effectively ended after 24 minutes' play, however, when Colin Harvey shot Everton level. Within minutes Fred Pickering embarked on a long run and smashed in a second. By the time man-of-the-match Alex Young made it three, the tie was well beyond Killie's reach and it was no surprise when Pickering added a fourth, direct from a free-kick. The 6-1 aggregate loss seemed a little harsh on Killie, and Everton boss Harry Catterick agreed that the pivotal point had clearly been Killie's narrow failure to grab a second goal in the first twenty minutes when they had been so dominant. Everton went on to lose in the third round to Manchester United, who in turn were beaten by eventual trophy winners Ferencvaros.

Killie's Forsyth and McGrory had no time to dwell on the Fairs Cup defeat, for 48 hours later they were in action at Hampden, helping Scotland beat Northern Ireland 3-2 in a British Championship fixture.

On Saturday, 28 November newly promoted Clyde were beaten by Killie 2-1, thanks to two first-half goals, headers by McFadzean and McInally. Clyde came close to snatching a point in a hectic second half. Centre-forward Kenny Knox was making his debut and capped a sparkling game by netting a 63rd minute header. It needed some gritty defending and some great saves by Forsyth to keep the lead intact.

Despite winning, Kilmarnock lost their leadership of the table, for Hearts' 3-0 win at St Johnstone saw them inch ahead, thanks to a marginally better goal-average. It was the first time all season Killie had been off the top, and the margin was by a mere fifteen-hundredths of a goal. In view of what was to happen later on, it was ironic that Hearts should be the team sitting precariously on top in this manner. If Killie fans felt sore over this situation as November ended, they only needed to wait a few months for sweet and final revenge. The table at the end of November 1964 read:

	P	W	D	L	F	A	Pts
Hearts	14	10	4	0	44	15	24
KILMARNOCK	14	10	4	0	25	9	24
Hibs	14	9	2	3	32	20	20
Dunfermline	14	8	2	4	30	16	18
Celtic	14	8	2	4	28	21	18

The new leaders' crucial win at St Johnstone represented the first fixture played under new floodlights at the Muirton ground – and this now meant that every First Division ground in Scotland was equipped with floodlights, allowing all winter Saturday games to kick off at 3pm instead of earlier.

The month ended with some sad news. Kilmarnock officials were informed that popular former Killie and Scotland full-back Joe Nibloe's son John had been killed in a car accident near his Sheffield home. John had followed his dad into professional football and had played for Sheffield United, Stoke, Doncaster and Stockport.

Meanwhile, just a few miles down the A77, Killie's neighbours Ayr United found themselves facing a bleak Christmas. The Somerset Park club announced that it was in serious financial difficulties and issued a bleak warning that unless gates improved soon, they could go out of business. Sadly the warning didn't have much effect on Saturday, 28 November, for only 667 turned out to see their game with East Fife. The 3-3 draw left Ayr rock bottom of Division Two with just ten points from seventeen games.

Killie fan Billy Lindsay, then in his early twenties, has vivid memories of this period and recalled the thrilling emergence of talented young winger Tommy McLean over the weeks leading up to Christmas 1964: 'He was a delight to watch and in an age when wingers were abundant he was one of the best. Bertie Black I also particularly admired, for he was a very skilful player and scored his share of goals. And Frank Beattie was a great captain who led by example and was a stalwart defender.

'I lived in the town, so in those days I walked to the ground via the Loudon Bar, had a couple of pints with a crowd of mates and then headed over to Rugby Park. I started off on the terracing across from the Main Stand and was there for a number of years, then moved to the Enclosure in front of the Main Stand. I then became a season ticket holder in the Main Stand and am still there to this day [2004]. Scarves were in those days the main supporters' wear, the food on offer was quite basic – a pie and Bovril – and toilets were primitive to say the least. The crowd behaviour was pretty good, although supporters got into matches having consumed more drink than is the case today.

'It was great really, always a good atmosphere and we would mix with opposing fans to a degree, with plenty of banter going on, but few fights. We could learn from that era! At games against the Old Firm the atmosphere was a bit hostile and there was always the odd bit of trouble, but considering the size of the crowds, I suppose it was minimal.'

Kilmarnock: Champions of Scotland 1964-65 65

Between 1958 and 1964, Killie were the nearly men of Scottish football. They finished runners-up in the League four times and lost four cup finals and three semi-finals. This 1961 team group came agonisingly close to a League and League Cup 'double'

The match programme for the League Cup semi-final with Rangers at Hampden in 1962, which ended in a thrilling 3-2 win for Killie in front of 76,000. They would lose the subsequent final to Hearts

66   *Kilmarnock: Champions of Scotland 1964-65*

The final whistle has blown at Tynecastle in April 1965, and Kilmarnock have won the Scottish Championship against all odds

Jackie McGrory (1941-2004), kingpin of the title-winning side's defence. Between 1961 and 1972 he missed only a handful of games

KILMARNOCK STANDARD
AND AYRSHIRE WEEKLY NEWS

NOW... THEY'RE THE CHAMPIONS

Football history was made at Tynecastle, Edinburgh, last Saturday, when Kilmarnock defeated Hearts to win the Scottish League Championship by a hair's breadth after a succession of near misses in season after season. On this, and other pages, the "Standard" tells the story of the triumph in words and pictures and pays its own tribute to the heroes of Rugby Park.

Willie Waddell Talks To The 'Standard'

WHEN the excitement had died down a bit I visited Rugby Park this week to have a talk with Kilmarnock's "Man of the Year," Manager Willie Waddell, in the peace of his office, writes the "Standard" sports editor. There I found Willie "back down to earth" and very much a man of business getting on with his office work and other duties.

To my opening question on the great title win he said: "As far as I am concerned, and looking at it from the personal angle, no club deserved it more. It was a well-earned triumph in the highly competitive field which football is nowadays. This club have been most progressive in their ideas and only the sheer hard work of everyone along the line has taken us to the pinnacle. No one man, no one player has achieved this. It is the atmosphere and combined effort within these boundary walls that have brought success."

A VALUABLE ASSET

I asked him if he thought this breakthrough to a big soccer prize could lead to better support than the team have received in recent seasons. He answered: "I think it will bring the crowds back in greater numbers. It should. I am sure everyone in Ayrshire is proud that Kilmarnock are champions and the players need

(Continued on page sixteen).

It's all over at last. The long, long wait has ended. Kilmarnock are the champions now, and here we have a back view of Manager Willie Waddell as he throws decorum to the wind and leaps into the arms of Frank Beattie. Andy King raises his arms in victory salute, and Bertie Black hugs Bobby Ferguson in appreciation of that last-second save from Gordon. A smile from Wallace shows he understands the mood of the occasion.

The Championship Hung in the Balance During Four Tense Minutes of Injury Time---Then...

The Final Whistle---And Triumph For Killie At Last

UNFORGETTABLE MOMENT AT TYNECASTLE

On Other Pages

The *Kilmarnock Standard* tells its readers how it was done

68   *Kilmarnock: Champions of Scotland 1964-65*

Joe Mason (right) scrambles home Killie's goal in a vital 1-1 draw at Ibrox against reigning champions Rangers (March 1965)

Killie lost 0-2 to Bangu of Brazil in the final of the 1960 New York International Tournament

Forty years after the title win, Rugby Park is almost unrecognisable
with its modern facilities and smart appearance

Loyal club servant Frank Beattie was granted a testimonial match in May 1971. Visitors Celtic won 7-2, with their new discovery Kenny Dalglish scoring six times

70   *Kilmarnock: Champions of Scotland 1964-65*

FRANK BEATTIE

AN APPRECIATION—BY THE CHAIRMAN

In over 20 years of football administration, at S.F.A., League Management and Club level, there is one player I lift my hat to—our own Frank Beattie.

Frank joined us over 17 years ago and no more self-effacing and kindly being has ever been a member of our club. His humility, his sense of responsibility and his dedication to his chosen profession made him an ever popular and ideal member of a team and the type of player that managers respect and make their task lighter.

In the years he has been with us and now approaching the evening of his career, Frank Beattie has been an example of everything that is good in football and a model of what is best in the game without dressing room or field of play 'histrionics'.

I welcome this opportunity of saying on behalf of everyone who has come in contact with Frank; not only my colleagues on the Board of Directors, the Manager and his staff or all our players, but everyone in Scottish football and all our football public.

Well done, Frank, and thanks for those memorable years.

WM. MCIVOR,
Chairman, Kilmarnock F.C.

FRANK BEATTIE
is acclaimed for his

Performance
and
Reliability

... So also is the
CHRYSLER

Chairman Willie McIvor spoke for all Killie fans when he penned this tribute to Frank Beattie in the player's testimonial match programme (May 1971)

Killie full-back Andy King was a consistent one-club man who really came of age during the championship-winning season

The title-winners with their trophy.
Back: King, Watson, Ferguson, McInally, McGrory, Murray.
Front: McLean, Black, Beattie, Sneddon, McIlroy

72 *Kilmarnock: Champions of Scotland 1964-65*

Rugby Park was requisitioned in 1940 for use as a wartime fuel storage depot

Bobby Ferguson and Andy King celebrate the championship win after the final whistle at Tynecastle in April 1965

Kilmarnock: Champions of Scotland 1964-65

The champagne begins to flow – mostly over Jackie McGrory's head – after the Hearts game at Tynecastle (April 1965)

Frank Beattie, skipper during the title-winning season and a highly influential figure for many years

74 *Kilmarnock: Champions of Scotland 1964-65*

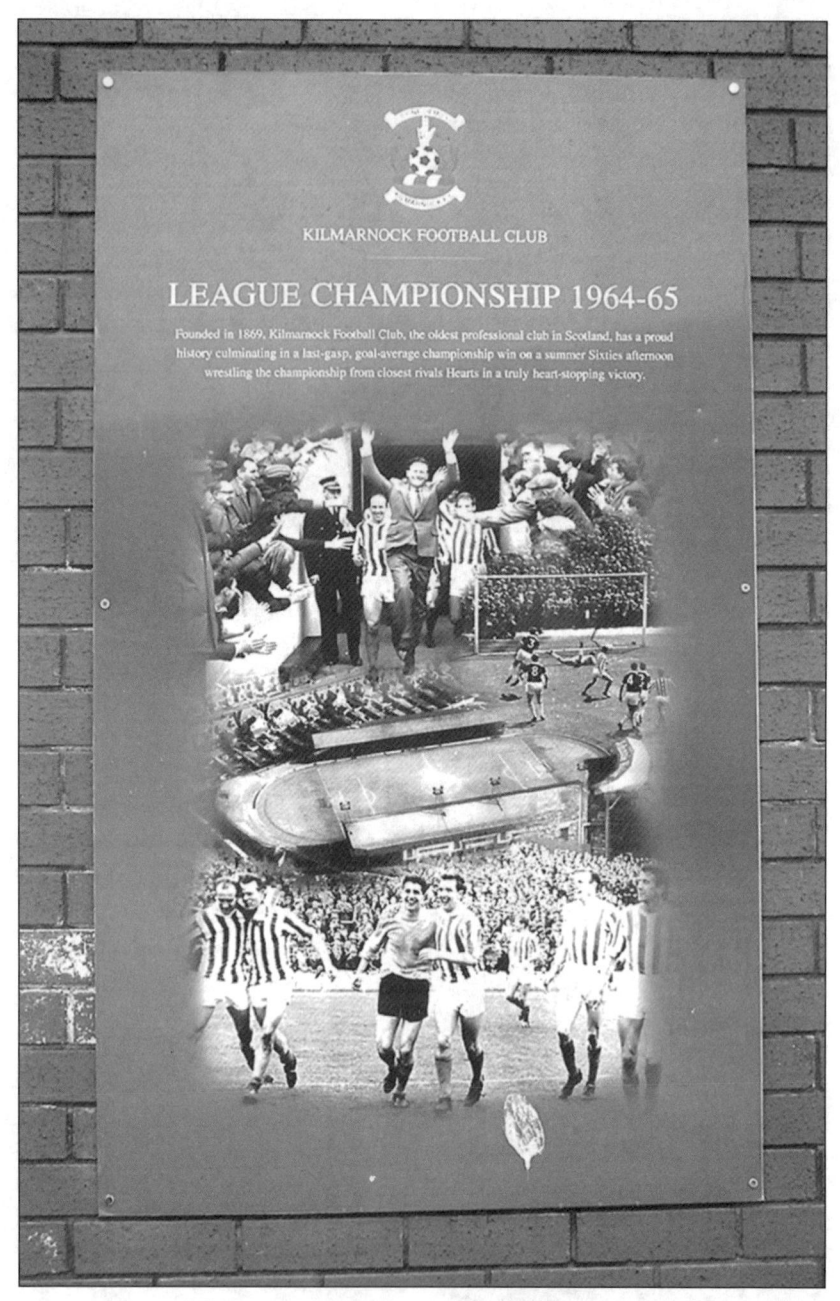

New generations of Killie fans are reminded of the 1964-65 title win by this illustration on a wall at Rugby Park

Kilmarnock: Champions of Scotland 1964-65

Hearts players are stunned, and one is on his knees, as Killie celebrate the final whistle at Tynecastle (April 1965)

Midfield general Davie Sneddon with the championship trophy at a players' reunion in 2004

76 *Kilmarnock: Champions of Scotland 1964-65*

Bobby Ferguson has just saved an injury-time shot by Alan Gordon (out of picture) to preserve Killie's 2-0 title-winning lead at Hearts (April 1965)

Killie's 'holy grail' – the Scottish League Championship trophy

Kilmarnock: Champions of Scotland 1964-65 77

The great comeback begins: Ronnie Hamilton scores Killie's first goal to reduce the deficit against Eintracht Frankfurt to 1-4 (September 1964)

78   *Kilmarnock: Champions of Scotland 1964-65*

Davie Sneddon, who cost £17,000, was the only true 'import' in the title-winning side – yet even he was born locally

The full Kilmarnock FC squad pictured shortly after winning the 1964-65 title

Kilmarnock: Champions of Scotland 1964-65

Soviet leader Alexei Kosygin meets Killie players before their 1-2 defeat by Rangers in 1967. On a week-long visit to Britain, Kosygin visited Hunterston Nuclear Power Station and had lunch at Troon before arriving at Rugby Park

Malky MacDonald, pictured after his retirement from football. He had two stints as manager of Kilmarnock, the second when he succeeded Willie Waddell a few weeks after the championship was won in 1965

80   *Kilmarnock: Champions of Scotland 1964-65*

Jubilant youngsters invade the Rugby Park pitch after Kilmarnock level the aggregate scores at 4-4 against Eintracht Frankfurt (September 1964)

An unprecedented show of delight by manager Willie Waddell, as he leads his players back on to the Tynecastle pitch after the title win (April 1965)

Manager Willie Waddell (left) and trainer Walter McCrae relieve the Tynecastle tension with a cigarette (April 1965)

82 *Kilmarnock: Champions of Scotland 1964-65*

Over the years it became traditional to have a sheep as a club mascot at Rugby Park. Angus (pictured) followed in the footsteps of Ruby and Wilma

Jim MacFadzean (left) and Campbell Forsyth – key players during the championship season – seen reminiscing at a players' re-union (April 2004)

Kilmarnock: Champions of Scotland 1964-65   83

Brien McIlroy steers home the title-winning second goal at Hearts, past the despairing dive of Jim Cruickshank (April 1965)

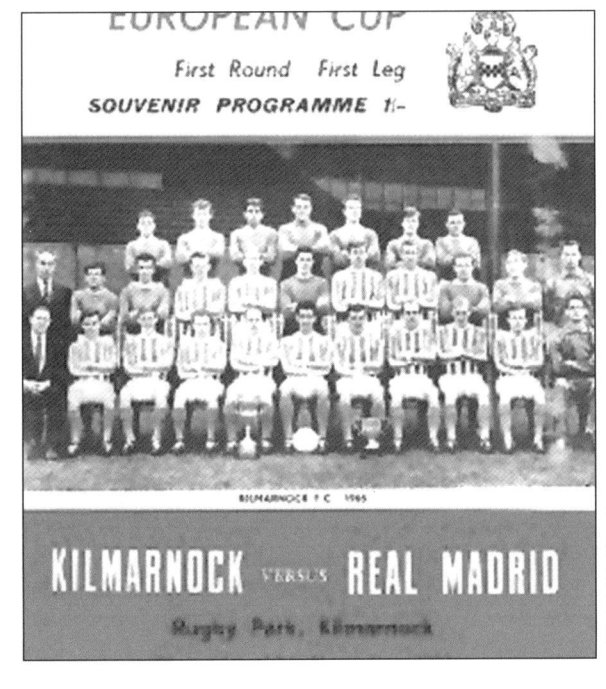

The match programme for the European Cup home tie against Real Madrid, which finished 2-2 (November 1965)

84 *Kilmarnock: Champions of Scotland 1964-65*

Trainer Walter McCrae, famous for his tough approach, made Kilmarnock one of the fittest sides in Scotland during the early and mid-1960s

Kilmarnock: Champions of Scotland 1964-65   85

This *Sunday Mail* cutting shows Rangers' Ralph Brand scoring a disputed penalty in the stormy 1-1 draw with Kilmarnock at Ibrox (March 1965)

The match programme for Killie's Fairs Cup-tie at Eintracht, which they lost 0-3 (September 1964)

86   *Kilmarnock: Champions of Scotland 1964-65*

Campbell Forsyth, pictured at a players re-union in 2004, played 75 League games for Killie before losing his place to Bobby Ferguson in the title-winning season. Forsyth won four full caps for Scotland

Lanky but elegant skipper Frank Beattie, who spent a remarkable 19 years on the Killie playing staff

Kilmarnock: Champions of Scotland 1964-65

Friday, May 12, 1995

ENTERPRISE AYRSHIRE

Kilmarnock Memories

When Killie won the league

In Kilmarnock's long history there must have been many great moments in sport, at local, national and international level. But from that wide selection, most sports enthusiasts would say that the greatest of them all was the Saturday in 1965 when Kilmarnock Football Club took the Scottish league championship in 1964-65. That the honour was won by a whisker didn't matter. What did matter was that Kilmarnock had the best football team in Scotland and all the members of the team were local heroes. The winning players and managers above are: Back: T. McClean, R. Black, R. Ferguson, D. Sneddon, B McIlroy. Middle: W. Waddell (manager), E. Murray, J. McGrory, J. McInally, F. Beattie, M. Watson, A. King, W. McCrae (trainer). Front: T Lauchlan (director), R. B. Thyne (director), W. McIvor (chairman), D. R. McCulloch (director), T. Kerr (director).

Thirty years after the event, this was one of several articles published to mark the anniversary of Kilmarnock's historic title win

88   *Kilmarnock: Champions of Scotland 1964-65*

The moment the title was won. With Killie 2-0 up, Bobby Ferguson dives to save Alan Gordon's shot in the dying seconds. Had Ferguson missed it, Hearts would have been champions (April 1965)

Thanks Bobby! Andy King congratulates his goalkeeper when the final whistle sounded, just moments after the save pictured above

Skipper Frank Beattie recalls fondly those title-winning days

Hearts and Scotland goalkeeper Jim Cruickshank gets down to block an effort by Kilmarnock's teenage winger Tommy McLean (April 1965)

Bobby Ferguson tips a high cross over the bar to foil another Hearts attack at Tynecastle
(April 1965)

Ronnie Hamilton, a member of the title-winning team,
who later had a spell as club chairman

Photographers and club officials pour onto the pitch as the final whistle blows at
Tynecastle (April 1965)

Teenager Tommy McLean, making his senior debut, is chaired off the pitch after the remarkable win over Eintracht Frankfurt (September 1964)

The coveted Championship flag, raised over Rugby Park during the summer of 1965

Jackie McGrory played 52 games, including cup-ties, in the title-winning season and won full Scotland honours

Davie Sneddon heads a rare goal past the diving Jim Cruickshank, and the League title is on its way to Kilmarnock (April 1965)

Davie Sneddon was a key figure in the No 10 shirt in the 1964-65 campaign. Fourteen years later he managed the club to promotion to the Premier Division

The Kilmarnock party head off to board their plane to West Germany for the Fairs Cup-tie with Eintracht Frankfurt (September 1964)

96 *Kilmarnock: Champions of Scotland 1964-65*

Willie Waddell – a legendary figure at Rugby Park. His League record as manager of Kilmarnock was: fifth, eighth, second, second, fifth, second, second, and first.

Huge crowds gathered in Kilmarnock town centre to greet the return of the team from Edinburgh after the title was won (April 1965)

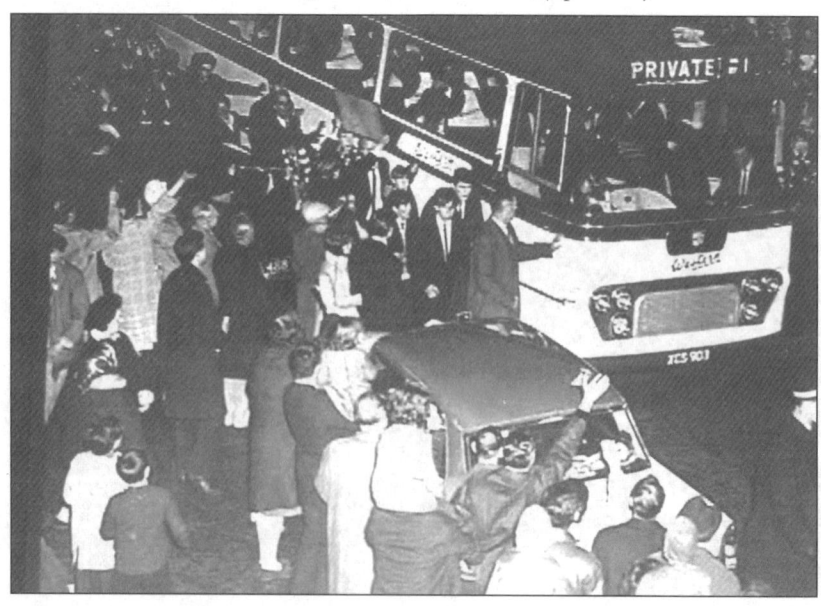

Chapter 6

Killie get the Jitters

(December 1964 – January 1965)

*Though fickle Fortune has deceived me,
She promis'd fair and perform'd but ill*
(Robert Burns, 1782)

As 1964 drew towards a close, the United Kingdom was being swept by Beatle-mania. On the same December day that drummer Ringo Starr had his tonsils removed, *I Feel Fine* shot straight to No 1, alongside *Beatles For Sale*, which already topped the album charts. And that very evening, youth was also having its fling at Rugby Park, Kilmarnock, as the old stadium was hosting an Under-23 international between Scotland and Wales.

Killie officials smartened up the ground for the occasion and put everyone on their best behaviour. There was much local pride in the fact that a trio of players – Jackie McGrory, Andy King and Ronnie Hamilton – were that night wearing the dark blue of Scotland. All three had picked up knocks in Killie's victory at Clyde a few days earlier, but were passed fit. The Welsh party had made their base on the coast at Troon, while the Scots assembled at Kilmacolm under the control of Killie trainer Walter McCrae. A crowd of 6,211 turned out to see Scotland win 3-0, with a King effort deflected in by Ollie Burton for one of the goals. Man-of-the-match was Leeds' tigerish young wing-half Billy Bremner. Another outstanding starlet was winger Charlie Cooke of Aberdeen.

Meanwhile, Kilmarnock began December with a routine win over lowly Falkirk on a day of appalling weather. In the second half Killie failed to build on a 2-0 interval lead and the punters, their mood not helped by the weather, vented their frustration at what looked like a lackadaisical display by their heroes. No doubt they remembered events of the previous season when Falkirk were taken apart 9-2. In view of the barracking, it was ironic, then, that the two points gained returned Killie to the top of the league, on goal-average from Hearts. The Jambos had won 3-1, but by conceding that single goal, their goal-average became inferior to Killie's. With things so close, it was all the more galling that Killie hadn't taken the opportunity to boost their goal figures against an injury-hit Falkirk. Davie Sneddon played a crucial part in the goals that did come, crossing for McInally to head the first, and six minutes later netting a powerful 25-yarder.

On an otherwise forgettable day, a feature of the game was the excellent display at centre-half by Jim McFadzean, who shone as deputy for the injured McGrory. Were there no limits to this man's versatility? According to the *Sunday Mail* this was the eighth different position that McFadzean had filled this season alone. Big Jim was a local lad who had played for Troon Juniors before joining Hearts in 1956. After a spell at St Mirren, he was signed by his home town club on a free transfer from Raith. Waddell had always liked the look of him and took him to the USA international tournament in 1963 and he'd been a key part of the squad ever since. He was a true utility player, willing and able to play in virtually every position. 'Jim's a real Kilmarnock man now,' said Waddell. 'When I saw him with Hearts I knew he had ability all right, and when he was freed by Raith Rovers I knew I could make him into something.'

Off the field, all was not well at Rugby Park, with bickering behind the scenes over whether Willie Waddell should be invited onto the board once he'd vacated the manager's job in the summer. There were differences aired among shareholders at their annual meeting at Dunlop Street Cooperative Hall on Monday, 7 December. It was eventually agreed by the narrow majority of 29 votes to 25 that the Articles of Association be amended to allow the board to expand to six members instead of the current five – thus leaving the way clear to make Waddell a director. The resolution was moved by chairman McIvor, but was opposed by an amendment which insisted things be left alone. The latter was supported by local schoolmaster James Henderson, a former chairman of Killie, who said it would be a retrograde step to change the size of the board. In 1937 it had been reduced from nine to five directors, citing economic difficulties and other circumstances, and increasing it again would be wrong, he felt. He conceded that creating a seat for Waddell was a 'high motive', but having six directors could lead to stalemates when there was divided opinion. He felt a better way to repay Waddell's fine service to Kilmarnock would be a golden handshake or a testimonial. It wouldn't be right for Waddell to become a director and sit in judgment on his successor as manager.

Henderson asked why Waddell could not become an adviser rather than a director, and maybe a paid one? And if he was so clearly worthy of a place on the board, why didn't one of the others graciously stand down to allow this, and thus keep the five-man status? Waddell, who was not entirely convinced he wanted to become a director anyway, seemed embarrassed by all this fuss. He addressed the meeting and said when the idea of a directorship had first been mooted he'd been honoured and surprised and willing to accept. Now he was somewhat less chuffed:

'I only know now that I regret I had to be here tonight to listen to what has gone on. I have had good relations with Kilmarnock FC everywhere along the line but I have been most disappointed that I have been forced to sit here and listen to this tonight. I regret that very much indeed. If I can

Killie get the Jitters (December 1964 – January 1965)

be of any service I will be only too delighted to help, whether as a director or not. Anything I have put into football has been for the love of the game and it will never change no matter what was offered.'

Ultimately, Waddell would turn down the chance to become a director and would leave football for a spell, for a job on the *Scottish Daily Express* – but more of that later.

As this would be his last annual meeting, Waddell's speech amounted to a valedictory address. He added that he had been in football as a player, pressman and manager for 28 years and his seven at Rugby Park had been as happy as any. He felt he was leaving at a time when the club could afford to be without him: 'When a club is healthy, that is a time when it is easier to get a replacement. I am sure Kilmarnock will prosper whoever comes after me. He will get the right guidance.'

Waddell paid tribute to the club's trainer Walter McCrae, backroom man Norrie McNeill and others who made the club what it was today. 'There are players there who could get more money elsewhere, but with these lads I have had little or no trouble from that angle, and that takes a bit of doing these days.' He said he did not kid himself that the club would win the League this season, and he would only believe that fact if and when it was accomplished – but given the rub of the green they were in a better position to achieve it than ever before: 'If a club gets through December and into the second week in January with a successful run, they are well on their way [to the title].'

Talk of finally winning the League, after all those near misses of the past, began to look premature after the events of Saturday, 12 December. The first league defeat of the season had to come some time, and today, at Morton, proved to be that day. Moreover, not only were Killie beaten, they were hammered. Morton's No 10 Allan McGraw scored four goals as the home side romped to a 5-1 victory. It was a shock to the system for Killie, but nobody could dispute the result. According to Rex of the *Sunday Mail*, the ineffective Kilmarnock forwards spent the game 'poking at the ball like it was about to squirt grapefruit juice in their eyes'.

It had been a weekend of torrential rain – roads and homes were flooded in the Glasgow area – but nothing could dampen the spirit of McGraw on this day. Killie were left ruing the absence of injured defensive kingpin McGrory. John Caven had put The Ton ahead early on, but when McGraw first found the net just before the break the game was as good as over. McGraw was a folk hero in Greenock, having scored a club record 62 goals the season before (51 in the league), a total he unsurprisingly never came close to matching again. After the final whistle, Morton fans chanted for McGraw to return to do a lap of honour, but the modest hero had been first off the park and there was little chance of him returning.

Even after conceding five and relinquishing the leadership again, the league table showed Killie still had the best defensive record in the country. Waddell said there was no need to panic: he only got depressed when his team lost a game they should have won. That was clearly not the case here. He was not worried by the heavy scoreline, for his players had always kept their heads up and had continued to graft regardless. Interestingly, he signed off his post-match remarks with the following: 'I am convinced the title will be won by points and not goals alone.'

It emerged that Morton had been fired up for this particular game, having been warned by their director-manager Hal Stewart that it was a 'make-or-break' contest. The team had recently suffered a bad patch and Stewart was determined to halt the slide. To fire his players up, he brought out a cine film that he had stashed away of Morton's fine opening day win over Dundee. He took his team through the film in detail, replaying certain parts repeatedly. It certainly had the desired effect.

A worry for Kilmarnock at this time was the continuing low gates at Rugby Park for any side other than the Glasgow or Edinburgh giants. Some games pulled in fewer than 6,000, even though Killie were at or near the top of the table. This bugged Chairman McIvor. He launched an attack on the stay-aways: 'It's distressing that our gate drawings for the past season reveal an income of 50 per cent greater for away games than home games – representing approximately 60,000 more spectators who were keen to see us play away from home. Why is it that we are poorly supported? Do we suffer from an affluent society with their motor cars and televisions and all their orders that football does not occupy the priority of choice on a Saturday afternoon that it used to hold?'

Although he was unhappy over their numbers, McIvor had no complaints about the enthusiasm of the die-hards who did come regularly. He noted that his appeal of twelve months earlier for more vocal support had yielded positive results – and he thanked 'all the boys and girls and everyone else' and urged them to 'shout not just when we're one up but even louder when a goal down.'

The humiliation at Cappielow meant the long-awaited clash with Hearts at Rugby Park on Saturday, 19 December could no longer be treated as a clash of the two unbeaten titans. Nevertheless it was still a crunch game, with the Edinburgh side currently two points ahead of Killie at the top. Hearts hadn't won any of their last eight league matches at Rugby Park, not even during their title-winning year of 1958.

Although Jackie McInally was out with a virus, McGrory and Tommy McLean returned and a crowd of approaching 19,000 came to see the fun, resisting the pressures of Christmas shopping. Alan Gordon was first to find the net, his overhead kick raising the noise levels yet further among the travelling Hearts support. Killie hit back immediately. McIlroy, who gave Chris Shevlane the run-around all afternoon, drove home an equaliser two minutes later and the game went from strength to strength. Memories of Cappielow were erased as Sneddon converted an awful back pass by the beleaguered Shevlane. Beattie got away with a blatant handball in the area, but Killie capped a fine display with a third goal when Hamilton guided a McIlroy cross into the net off a post.

While Killie were ending Hearts' long unbeaten run, their neighbours Hibs were involved in some bizarre goings-on in their Easter Road game with Partick Thistle. The fun started when referee Elliott of Barrhead was knocked unconscious for four minutes when struck by the ball. The crowd had been baiting him over a number of disputed decisions, but their anger turned to mirth when he ordered a free-kick to be re-taken, turned his back and was then hit by the ball. He had to be carried off for treatment. The incident must have left the ref confused, for after returning he blew for full-time three minutes early. Partick skipper John Harvey and a linesman spotted this error and were quick to inform him. Mr Elliott admitted his watch had malfunctioned, meaning he was unsure what the correct time was – a state of mind presumably exacerbated by his accident. Most of the Partick players were still on the pitch, and were told to stay there while red-faced Mr Elliott chased into the changing rooms to fetch the Hibs players back. The match re-started and ended 2-1 to Hibs. It was a pre-Christmas pantomime, with many of the laughs due to the *schadenfreude* surrounding poor Mr Elliott. Football spectators can be very cruel.

A more benevolent Christmas spirit was in evidence in the town of Kilmarnock, however. After a few years of looking rather austere over the holiday period, this time the town centre was illuminated in attractive fashion. Happy with the effect, the local council announced it would buy £1,200 worth of second-hand Sauchiehall Street lights from Glasgow to improve the display even further for next year. Campbell's department store in King Street got into the spirit by stocking up on all the latest popular toys, including Play-doh, Lego, Meccano and Sindy and Tressy. It was also the best place to buy the current chart-toppers – The Beatles, Rolling Stones and Georgie Fame.

To get into the spirit of things, local shoppers snapped up bottles of the finest South African sherry for eleven shillings and many a football fan got a 17s 6d Kilmarnock FC scarf in their Christmas stockings, purchased from McMurrays clothing store in Portland Street. Up the road at All-Sports in Titchfield Street, wide-eyed boys pressed their noses against the window to stare longingly at the special football kits on offer for Christmas – bearing the names of Kilmarnock, Rangers, Celtic and 'Denis Law' and priced at 25s 6d each. Families who could afford to dine out booked up a

Christmas Day dinner-dance and cabaret at the Marine and Curlinghall Hotel at nearby Largs for 35s per ticket. More affordable for the working class folk was the six-course Christmas lunch at the Broomhill Hotel for 12s 6d. Live entertainment on offer in the area included international TV and recording stars The Applejacks (*Tell Me When*) and locally-based acts like The Anteleeks and Tommy Truesdale and The Sundowners (the latter still going strong forty years later!).

Killie players had to take it easy on the turkey and trimmings, for on Boxing Day they had a game scheduled with crisis club Third Lanark at Cathkin. The Thirds were having their worst season in memory and their problems were compounded by a mounting financial crisis. They would end this season with thirty defeats from their 34 league games and suffer inevitable relegation. Shortly before Christmas, sheriff's officers walked into Cathkin and seized a £1,750 cheque which had just arrived from Rangers as the club's share of the Ibrox gate money the previous weekend. Before kick-off on the day of the Killie game, one of Third Lanark's creditors warned: 'Every time Third Lanark get a big game we will claim the gate money till the debt is cleared.' Unfortunately for him, the Cathkin attendance against Kilmarnock was a paltry 2,549.

Third Lanark had debts totalling £9,000, despite selling players valued at £90,000 over the past two years. Relegation looked a certainty even at this stage of the season, and within another two years the club nicknamed The Hi-Hi would go out of business altogether. Exactly how things got so bad was never fully explained and, to this day, there is talk of corrupt practices. The mid-1960s was a sorry era for this scarlet-shirted Glasgow club, named after the Third Lanarkshire Rifle Volunteers. Their odd nickname is derived from their ground's position, looking down on Glasgow from atop a rocky knoll. Forty years after extinction, the site of the ground is now part of a municipal park, but, eerily, some of the terracing still exists.

Kilmarnock showed no sympathy on Boxing Day 1964 and crushed the hapless Thirds 4-0. In the bitterly cold conditions, an icy wind whipped around Cathkin and most of the visiting players wore white gloves. It was tricky underfoot, but Killie danced around their opponents. The conditions assisted the first goal, when young goalkeeper Evan Williams slipped and allowed a McInally miskick to roll into the net. McLean then beat Williams with a ground shot that skidded under him. McIlroy made it three with a header and McLean added another after King's free-kick.

So Kilmarnock were able to say farewell to 1964 from a lofty position in the table. Amid the renditions of *Auld Lang Syne* and the 'first footing' ceremonies, many a supporter must have paused over his drink to wonder if the club was finally on its way to a first League title. The inconsistency of reigning champions Rangers certainly suggested the championship was

Killie get the Jitters (December 1964 – January 1965)

up for grabs this time, and Killie seemed to have as good a chance as anybody. In the *News of the World* the former Rangers and Scotland pivot Willie Woodburn nominated Frank Beattie as his player of 1964 and outlined his hopes that Kilmarnock would lift the title, as no one deserved a medal more than skipper Beattie.

In terms of results, the calendar year of 1964 had been a vintage year for Kilmarnock, with some 35 competitive games won. To put this into historical context, 1964 was the year China acquired the Bomb, Shakespeare appeared on postage stamps, Kruschev was swept from the Kremlin, and Douglas-Home from Downing Street, and a year of four royal babies. It was the year mods and rockers did battle at seaside resorts, *Goldfinger* was the top British film, and *The Fugitive* the top TV show.

Kilmarnock's line-up by now had a good balance to it and was relatively settled. Teenage winger McLean had emerged as a player of huge promise who didn't look like going 'off the rails', thanks to the solid family background he enjoyed. He had two footballing brothers, Jim at Clyde, who had recently gone full-time after years as a part-timer with Hamilton, and the eldest sibling Willie at Raith, and formerly of Alloa, Sheffield Wednesday and Queen of the South. All three sons had their feet kept firmly on the ground by their father, who made sure they took turns on a Sunday to help out at the family bakery business.

On New Year's Day 1965 the Rugby Park groundstaff worked wonders to get the pitch playable for the visit of St Mirren, and the players repaid their efforts with a 4-0 victory. In spring-like sunshine Killie overpowered the opposition from the moment that man-of-the-match Sneddon hooked in the first goal on eight minutes. Hamilton had a fine game, scoring either side of half-time, striking the bar and setting up Eric Murray for the fourth goal. The win was made all the sweeter with the news that Hearts had lost their derby game with Hibs, allowing Killie to open a two-point lead at the top. Mind you, both Killie and the Jambos were looking warily over their shoulders at Dunfermline, who were by now making a determined challenge and had games in hand.

Supporter Alex Milligan, a teenager who would later become a sports reporter on the *Kilmarnock Standard*, recalls the 4-0 win over St Mirren as one of his highlights of the season: 'That game sticks in my memory. It was a New Year's Day derby game and there was a great atmosphere.' He added: 'Rugby Park was pretty basic in those days but had loads of character. I can still smell the Bovril and remember the grease from the piping-hot pies draining on the terracing – and can picture the old Johnnie Walker scoreboard with the guy putting up the half-time scores from other games. On a typical matchday I would travel from nearby Springside village by bus. I mostly went on my own as my mates weren't interested in football, or supported Rangers – same thing really! The terrace banter was good in those days, the food and drink facilities were basic but OK, and the toilets smelled a bit. I remember one boy I used to take along with me to matches is nowadays an Ayr United fan – poor sod! He also became a member of the band Dead End Kids, who had a big hit in 1977 with *Have I The Right?* and appeared on *Top of the Pops*.

'When Celtic or Rangers were in town there were the occasional fights and drinking was predominant back then. We regularly gave them beatings on the park, though, and that helped quieten their fans. One lasting impression I have of those days was standing there at a match watching and listening to men who I knew from my village, who were cursing and swearing and had totally changed character when the whistle blew to start the match. I also remember the sheep mascots that used to wander round the track – a real talking point for the fans.

'I particularly admired Davie Sneddon. He was small in stature but had a great football brain. Chippy, as he was known, provided a great service to wingers McLean and McIlroy – a good old-fashioned inside forward. Killie had a terrific side at that time, and while the fans had their particular favourites, they were all extremely popular. I used to go and watch them training at Rugby Park and they were always kind and courteous to us lads and willing to sign autographs. Later I also used to attend Player of the Year functions and the whole of the first team used to turn up. Supporters of other clubs must have been envious of Killie, I would imagine. We had an amazing record in the early sixties for a provincial team.'

Twenty-four hours after ushering in 1965 with that win over St Mirren, Killie had to tackle struggling Airdrie at Broomfield Park. The home side were second from bottom of the table, but the icy pitch proved to be a great leveller. The conditions might well have been responsible for the accidental handball by Andy King which gave Airdrie a penalty, and saw them take the lead through Jim Rowan on 52 minutes. Sixty seconds later Hamilton converted Sneddon's pass to equalise, but the game's best player, Ian McMillan, engineered a shock victory when he let fly from 25 yards to beat Forsyth. The keeper appeared to misjudge the flight, but probably just lost his footing in the conditions. The goal prompted a pitch invasion and Killie slithered to only their second league defeat of the campaign:

	P	W	D	L	F	A	Pts
KILMARNOCK	20	14	4	2	40	17	32
Hibs	19	14	2	3	46	22	30
Hearts	20	13	4	3	58	27	30
Dunfermline	18	12	2	4	42	20	26
Rangers	18	9	6	3	48	21	24

Killie get the Jitters (December 1964 – January 1965)

Had it just been a temporary blip at Airdrie, or were the leaders losing their touch? A week later St Johnstone visited Rugby Park and Waddell called up Frank Malone for his League debut to replace McFadzean. The lad from Carfin, near Motherwell, had been on Killie's books for more than three years since joining from Fauldhouse United, and his recent goalscoring form in the reserves had caught the eye of Waddell. Davie Sneddon was switched to the wing to provide him with service.

Sneddon didn't look happy out on the flank and, after a lively start, Killie again looked out of sorts. This time there was no icy pitch to blame. Malone did his best and hit a post and had another effort tipped over by Mike McVittie, the Saints' new signing from Brechin. In one late raid McLean looked to have been brought down but St Johnstone survived the appeals and clung on for a goalless draw. Killie fans trudged home, dismayed at how their team always seemed to struggle against lesser opposition. Perhaps it was more a case of opponents raising their game when facing the league leaders? With Rangers hitting form and creeping up the table a Glasgow bookie that week made them 5-2 favourites for the Scottish Cup with Kilmarnock second at 9-2. He quoted Killie as 6-4 favourites for the League with Rangers at 2-1.

Killie's current form meant the last thing they needed was the difficult-looking trip to Dunfermline on Saturday, 16 January, which enticed a good crowd to East End Park. In the first minute Tommy Callaghan clattered into Ronnie Hamilton and the Killie striker needed lengthy treatment. He returned after fifteen minutes but was little more than a passenger. Frank Beattie did sterling work at the back after Waddell reorganised and Killie defended in depth. The big man's tackles and interceptions kept the scores level well into the second half. Bert Paton was the main thorn in Killie's side. After missing an open goal, the former Leeds man tempted Matt Watson into a rash tackle for which the full-back was booked, and then he forced Campbell Forsyth into an excellent double save.

Just when it was looking like Killie had ridden the storm, an unfortunate bounce off Jackie McGrory led to the winning goal. The ball fell kindly for Paton, who looked offside, and he swivelled to crash it home, with the officials ignoring Killie pleas. A feature of the game had been the faultless displays of both keepers, Jim Herriot and Forsyth, who could regard themselves as Scotland's top two on current form. The result put Dunfermline right back in the title race and dropped Killie to second, a point behind Hearts.

The mini-slump of three games without a win prompted a letter to the *Kilmarnock Standard* by an irate fan signing himself as 'No Dossing' of Kilmarnock. He (or she) reckoned the club needed a couple more forwards if they weren't to become eternal bridesmaids and never win anything. If

Dundee United, Morton and Rangers could recruit talented Scandinavian players, why couldn't Killie?

Scandinavian imports were certainly a big talking point in Scotland just now, with five Danes playing at Morton, three at Aberdeen and two at Dundee United; Hearts had a Norwegian and Dundee United a Swede. A point of debate was how long this would be allowed to continue. The press felt the Scottish FA would soon be tempted to exert some sort of control and put a limit on the number of foreign players. SFA President Tom Reid was quoted as saying the players imported so far had been of a high calibre and it was the SFA's duty to encourage all types of football, and not use the rule-book to make it difficult for clubs to provide the best entertainment. He said if things reached a stage where the Scottish-born pros were being 'endangered', that would be a matter for the Players' Union. Morton, who had seen better results and higher gates since their Scandinavians arrived, were certainly not complaining and their manager Hal Stewart joked that if his Danish nursery dried up for any reason, he was planning to head for China next.

So, after the fine victory on New Year's Day, Killie had now dropped five points in three games and allowed this to happen during the very period Waddell had warned would be vital to their title chances. Last season's champions Rangers were creeping back up the table, no doubt taking heart from the way that Killie, Hearts and Hibs had been dropping points. Jock Stein's Hibs were surprisingly beaten 3-4 at Easter Road by Dundee United, but their crunch visit to Rugby Park, scheduled for Saturday, 23 January, was postponed due to a frostbound pitch.

Ronnie Hamilton emerged from the Dunfermline defeat with a knee ligament injury that would keep him out for several weeks. It had the fans debating whether he should be replaced by versatile McFadzean, by thirty-year-old Bertie Black, or by a new signing. Hamilton would be missed, having already bagged sixteen goals. Beattie also took a knock at Dunfermline, but announced himself fit to captain the Scottish League team scheduled to play a full Scotland side in a trial match at Ibrox. Waddell was put in charge of the League XI, but icy weather put paid to the game.

The weather caused havoc with the fixtures. Around this time Waddell appeared on the BBC TV show *Checkpoint*, along with Partick boss Willie Thornton and Motherwell's Bobby Ancell. Waddell spoke about the difficulty in attracting big crowds to Kilmarnock matches: 'There is no doubt in my mind that any change in public interest has resulted from a change in the social habits in this country. Looking at world football the big crowds are in the countries where the standard of living is rather low,' he said. He believed some of the smaller Scottish clubs were facing a mounting crisis, and warned that even though there was still a major public interest in the

Killie get the Jitters (December 1964 – January 1965)

glamour games, the clubs must all take heed of people's changing habits and provide the very best in hospitality and levels of entertainment. He reassured viewers that the standard of play in Scotland was as high, if not higher, than it ever was.

A thaw set in around lunchtime on Saturday, 23 January, but it came too late to save the Hibs fixture at Rugby Park, which became one of five Division One games called off. This meant plans could go ahead for Killie to have a four-day stay at Seamill Hydro – a tranquil spot on the Ayrshire coast – for a mid-season tonic at the seaside. Waddell hoped it would relax the players and boost team spirit after the recent slump. These plans were nearly scuppered when squad player Pat O'Connor was involved in a car crash on his way to collect teammate Frank Malone for the trip to the Hydro. O'Connor's hired car was practically cut in two after a collision with a bus at Baillieston, Lanarkshire, as he headed for Carfin. O'Connor emerged from the vehicle virtually unscathed, but a police spokesman said it was a miracle he'd escaped with his life.

While Killie players relaxed at Seamill, and Hibs and Rangers players also kicked their heels, Hearts beat Partick to extend their lead at the top to three points. Nevertheless it remained the closest and hottest race for the Scottish title in many years.

The recent severe weather must have worried Inter Milan, who were heading for the area for a European Cup-tie with Rangers. The Italian club announced they would be staying in Troon and using Kilmarnock's Rugby Park as a training HQ in advance of their game at Ibrox. The past meetings between Waddell and Inter's coach Helenio Herrera had smoothed the way for these arrangements.

That weekend Sir Winston Churchill died. The great man had strong links with the Kilmarnock area for he'd served with the Ayrshire Regiment many years earlier, commanding the 6th Battalion, the Scots Guards. His last visit to the district had been in 1947 when a crowd of 7,000 gathered at the Ayr ice-rink to hear him speak, with the same number of people locked outside in the car park listening in.

Shortly before Killie's trip to Partick Thistle on Saturday, 30 January, the board of directors announced they had reached agreement for former manager Malcolm 'Malky' MacDonald to return from Brentford to succeed Waddell in July. The news was relayed over the loudspeakers at a reserve game with Airdrie at Rugby Park. Fewer than 500 were present to hear it, but they cheered loudly, for MacDonald had been a popular figure in his previous stint. He'd been at Griffin Park, Brentford, since 1957, winning the Fourth Division championship in 1963 and had recently steered The Bees to a place near the top of the Third. The return of this popular figure was sure to soften the blow of Waddell's impending exit. MacDonald would be signing a five-year contract and earn around £4,000 a year, which he admitted was too good an offer to refuse. It was agreed that Waddell would formally hand over the reins during the summer.

MacDonald admitted he had regrets at having to leave Brentford, as he had made many friends in London. But he viewed the Kilmarnock job as 'returning home' and said he and his wife would be spending the next few months house-hunting in the area. The couple had five offspring, two married, and one living in South Africa. Watson, Beattie, Black and O'Connor were all current Killie players who MacDonald had signed seven or more years earlier. The new manager would find that much else about the club had changed, however, not least the appearance of the ground itself.

The return of MacDonald jostled for front page prominence in the local press with the 'shock' news that Kilmarnock Burns Club had recruited its first ever female member. She was none other than Mrs Lesley Swinton of Sydney, Australia, who was the great-great-great-granddaughter of the poet's sister Isabella Burns.

There was nothing poetic about Killie's display that week at Partick. Tricky conditions again helped them come to grief, with an early Jags goal proving their undoing. Tons of sand were laid on the Firhill pitch to make it playable, but a punchless Killie rarely troubled the home side. Local lad Joe Mason was recalled after a long absence to stand in for Hamilton but he put two chances over the bar and didn't have an afternoon to enjoy. Big Jackie McInally was asked to play wide on the right wing with McFadzean at inside-right, but the ploy didn't work and Killie's disastrous January continued. McInally gamely tried to use his dribbling skills to fashion chances from the flank, but his best run, which saw him beat several defenders in exciting fashion, came to nothing when the ball ran out of play. The winner was created by Dave McParland and Billy Hainey, who worked the ball into the path of Tommy Ewing and he toe-ended it over Forsyth as the keeper advanced. At the other end Jim Gray touched aside a thirty-yarder from Beattie that looked a certain goal. It earned the keeper an ovation that lasted a full minute.

January's results meant there were long faces on the coach trip home from Firhill, but there was some good news when the radio announced that a late goal by seventeen-year-old Archie Gemmill had given St Mirren victory over Hearts. So at least the Edinburgh club wouldn't stretch their lead over Killie. The mid-season 'wobble' was giving great cause for concern at Kilmarnock, but at least the other contenders were having problems too.

CHAPTER 7

UP FOR THE CUP
(February 1965)

There's Death in the cup, so beware!
(Robert Burns, 1795)

For Kilmarnock, February 1965 would be dominated by Scottish Cup matters, but manager Waddell was anxious his players didn't take their eyes off the ball in the League. Following the run of one defeat in their first nineteen league games, January had seen three defeats and a draw in five fixtures. The cracks appearing in the title bid needed quick repair – and cup distractions were probably not what was needed.

As February got under way, Scottish football was buzzing with news that Jock Stein, 42, who in recent years had transformed the fortunes of Dunfermline and Hibs, was to take over as the new boss of Celtic. Managing a football club was still a relatively stable career in the mid-1960s and change at the helm of a big club like Celtic was major news.

The outgoing manager, former Killie boss Jimmy McGrory, had been in charge at Celtic Park for twenty years, latterly cutting an ineffective figure. He had been an old-fashioned, desk-bound manager, and trainer Sean Fallon had more or less been running the Celtic team, which had gone into slow decline since the glory pre-War days. The club had only won the title once in the nineteen seasons since the War (led on that occasion by skipper Jock Stein), gates were down, and change was overdue.

On the day the rumours started about Stein's impending arrival, Celtic's unsettled players were inspired to beat Aberdeen 8-0. The clubs topping the table – Hearts, Kilmarnock, Dunfermline and Hibs – began looking over their shoulders. Surely Celtic were too far adrift, even with a new leader? Stein would formally take over in March, at which point the loyal Fallon would become his assistant and McGrory would move into the new post of Public Relations Manager – something unheard of in Scottish football, not just at Celtic. It looked like a way of easing McGrory aside in a dignified fashion. Stein duly became the first £5,000-a-year manager in the country – and his arrival was greeted with optimism in Glasgow.

Alex Ferguson, then a key member of Dunfermline's attack, recalled this period in his autobiography: 'I played against Celtic in December 1964 and scored the winning goal in a 2-1 win, but the atmosphere at Celtic Park was dreadful, a very small crowd and a typical winter's day in Glasgow ... [by] April 1965 when Dunfermline played Celtic in the Scottish Cup final, things had changed … Jock Stein had overhauled the players' attitude and they had a great belief in themselves.'

It should be remembered that this was a time when the Old Firm clubs were regarded as Kilmarnock's biggest 'local' rivals, even though they were not closest from a geographical point of view. According to David Ross: 'In those days we regarded the Old Firm, and Rangers in particular, as our main rivals. The [true] local rivalry was with St Mirren, however. They had been our 'Ne'erday' [1 January] opponents since the Edwardian era. Ayr weren't registered on the radar at that time. In 1965 they were second bottom of the entire League.'

Another fan of the time, ball-boy Allan Wilson, recalled what it was like when the Old Firm and their boisterous fans descended on Kilmarnock: 'It was like being invaded by some alien culture. Who were these people? They came down, starting about 10 in the morning and [my family] had a bird's eye view as we lived on Munro Avenue, which is a continuation of Western Road in Bonnyton. My mother warned me the previous night not to go outside and not to talk to anybody, as these were "bad people".

'Bad people? These were morons and I don't know who were worse, the Billies or the Tims? As I think back on those days with the benefit of the knowledge I have now gained in the world, and of course speaking as an unbiased Presbyterian Protestant, I think of the Spanish Inquisition when the Catholic Priests gave the soldiers of the Inquisition absolution to rape and pillage! I am convinced that this must have happened in Glasgow in the vicinity of Parkhead on a Friday night before they went off on their noble quest on the Saturday down the A77. I have never seen so many drunken and disorderly priests in my life, sitting in the West Stand, cursing and swearing and calling on every celestial power to crush these "Kilmarnock Bastards". The armada of visiting buses occupied every street in the vicinity of Rugby Park and then by 6 o'clock, they were gone and there were empty Tennents and McEwans cans strewn around the streets as far as the eye could see.'

Killie supporter Anne Marks recalled glumly that the hostile atmosphere surrounding an Old Firm visit meant her parents banned her from attending: 'I was never allowed to go to those games. My dad had a season ticket and I had been banned from joining him there as I had knocked the man in front's hat off in my exuberance when Killie scored a goal.'

David Ross was sometimes kept indoors by his worried parents, too: 'I won't pretend this was some gloriously trouble-free era. It wasn't. I wasn't allowed to go to away games or home ones against the Old Firm at that time. In general though, serious trouble only arrived when the Old Firm entered town, accompanied by their hordes of drunken, sectarian fans, which is why I wasn't allowed to go to those games. Unsegregated fans and copious amounts of alcohol were a recipe for trouble. Usually it started if we had the temerity to take the lead. Killie fans weren't blameless though. There were several occasions when, if visiting teams left Ayrshire with the points, their supporters buses did so minus their windows.'

At this time it was common for youngsters to be allowed in free if an accompanying adult was willing to hoist them over the turnstile, with a nod and a wink towards the turnstile operator in his wooden cubby hole. David Ross recalls that if your father wasn't with you, you had to persuade a passing adult to lift you: 'I used to travel to games by bus from Dundonald, five miles away, with schoolmates. We'd hang around the main entrance with our autograph books at the ready before asking passing adults "gonnae gie's a lift ower, mister?" We would head for the centre of the covered terracing, as that was where the crowd was. There was a TV gantry there and a microphone would be slung down into the crowd to pick up noise, chants and general atmosphere. The programme was pretty basic, twelve pages for threepence, but not much in it by today's standards. Line-ups were still given in a 2-3-5 formation. There were blue rosettes and scarves on sale outside the ground. The Supporters Association ran a hut which sold tea, Bovril and pies. At half-time there were vendors walking around the ground selling chewing gum and macaroon bars. They were readily identifiable by the cry "errachoongumnamakroonbarrrzzz".

'The *Evening Times* and *Evening Citizen* were on sale with the half-time results. These were simply rollered onto the Stop Press section of the paper. We bought one because the scoreboard only gave other Scottish First Division results. It was well-established that the toilets at the Rugby Road end were less disgusting than those at Dundonald Road. The bigger the crowd the worse the conditions. It wasn't at all unusual to use the back walls of houses on Dundonald Road.'

Among his many colourful childhood memories, Ross tells a wonderful anecdote about an Old Firm visit. A record League attendance at Rugby Park witnessed a six-goal thriller: 'Both sides had a man sent off – Rangers' Colin Stein had belted Killie's Tommy McLean and Billy Dickson retaliated by assaulting Stein – and trouble broke out in the crowd. A burly Rangers fan of around eighteen was being marched through the crowd by a policeman when my friend Iain Thomson decided a kick up the backside would help him on his way.

'Unfortunately, Iain's aim was off and he connected with the copper rather than the fan. The policeman turned round to grab whoever had kicked him. Iain ducked and I found myself scooped up by this policeman and ejected from the ground – alongside this terrifying thug who thought I had been trying to kick him! I was twelve years old and wholly terrified at what this guy might do to me.

'There were just the two of us in the street. He eyed me up and down and eventually said: "Is there any other way into this ground?" I stammered out that there was and that if he promised not to kick my head in, I would show him. I walked with him round to the Dundonald Road end where the gates were opened twenty minutes before full-time and with great relief, melted away into the body of the crowd to watch the remainder of the match. I caught up with my friend Iain and we had a furious row about what had happened, although if the roles had been swapped, I would have done exactly the same. This incident has a particular poignancy. My friend grew up to become a pillar of the community – a bank manager. We would later meet up at Killie games as adults and he would mention how he had to reconcile bringing up his children to behave respectably at football matches, alongside this memory of the past.

'The last time we met at a game was in Norway in 2001 for a UEFA Cup-tie against Viking Stavanger and we recalled the incident in detail, laughing at the thought of the two middle-aged men who were once what would have been termed hooligans. I last heard from my friend in an e-mail in March 2003. A day later he suffered a heart attack and never recovered, dying a week later. He was just forty-seven years old.'

Meanwhile, on the same weekend of February 1965 that Scottish bakers launched Fresh Cream Cake Fortnight ('Time to forget about austerity and enjoy yourself'), Killie fans had their appetites whetted by a return to winning form. This new dawn came in the first round of the Scottish Cup and not the League. Cowdenbeath, then mid-table in Division Two, were seen off 5-0 on a slippery pitch at Rugby Park. It had been heavily sanded but still proved hazardous. Sitting in the stand was Malky MacDonald, the man who'd recently been named as Waddell's successor six months hence. He must have been pleased to see Killie attackers in such form, Sneddon and Hamilton setting up McInally to blast home after 32 minutes. McInally then thrashed a strong drive into the roof of the net after clever approach play involving Sneddon. McInally, without a goal since Boxing Day, completed his hat-trick when a McLean effort was deflected goalwards by Jimmy Burns and he nipped in to make sure. The disheartened visitors caved in, and after Bob Wilson handled, McLean tucked home a penalty. The fifth goal was a solo effort by little McLean who forced the ball in after his initial effort had been blocked by the goalkeeper. After the final whistle, reporters attempted to find out what Malky MacDonald thought of the team he would soon inherit, but they were firmly but politely rebuffed with a 'no comment'.

Anxious Killie fans who thought the return to goalscoring ways against Cowdenbeath might spark a return to form in the league were mistaken. On 13 February, Dundee came to Rugby Park and gave Killie a lesson in attacking football, their devastating second half performance sending the home side tumbling to a 1-4 defeat. It was the first home defeat of the season and dumped Killie to fourth. Many felt it could prove a mortal blow to title hopes. Star of the show was 22-year-old Charlie Cooke, signed recently by Dundee from Aberdeen to replace Alan Gilzean. Cooke was one of the shining new stars of Scottish football.

Cooke started the destruction within twenty minutes, side-footing home after Hugh Robertson had beaten keeper Forsyth to a Steve Murray cross. Hamilton levelled with a neat header from McLean's cross, but the relief was merely temporary. Two goals in two minutes on the hour turned the game. First an Alex Hamilton free-kick was deflected to Cooke, who made no mistake, and then Cooke set up Murray to scramble in a third at the near post. By the time of Robertson's late goal Killie were already well-beaten and home fans were heading despondently for the exits.

Dundee's victory had a big impact on young Killie fan William Heron, who remembers it clearly forty years later: 'It was totally out of character for Dundee to come to Rugby Park and completely tear Killie to pieces,' he said. 'Then they went and did exactly the same to Hearts at Tynecastle the same season.' His memory serves him well, for it was only a fortnight later that Dundee scored an amazing 7-1 win in Edinburgh, a result which delighted Killie fans and would later prove highly significant in terms of goal average, too.

Heron, who was then thirteen, was a big fan of winger Brien McIlroy, who would end that season with eighteen goals in all competitions – a fine total for a winger. But Heron admits that most popular of all were Frank Beattie, 'who led the team by example', and the emerging Tommy McLean, who was 'a real treat' to watch. He says: 'Beattie and Jackie McGrory were hard but fair and honest to go with it. They were great servants to the club with their loyalty. I recall that any local lad who managed to make the first team sometimes got a bit of a hard time from the fans – for example Joe Mason, who was a Kilmarnock boy, but eventually went on to score a lot of goals at Greenock Morton.

'On my school holidays I used to go to the local golf club at lunchtimes to see the players and obtain autographs – it was a great thrill to do this. They were very good to meet and speak to. Rugby Park was a fortress in those days and opposition supporters regarded Killie with envy and had to admire the great standard of fitness and teamwork of our side. When the Old Firm clubs came, I went with my dad to the stands or the enclosure below the Main Stand which was usually filled with Kilmarnock fans. It would always be better to be next to your own kind on these occasions. I travelled to games with my father up until my teens and got lifted over the turnstiles. When I was at secondary school I went to games with my pals and like many people who went regularly, we stood at the same place in the ground week in week out.'

To William Heron and the other die-hard fans, the hammering by Dundee at Rugby Park was a depressing blow to Killie's hopes. There was many a long face in the local pubs that night. One disillusioned fan, signing himself 'Aught Six' complained in the *Kilmarnock Standard* that the club's chairman had recently got the extra vocal support he'd called for – and a few extra numbers at the gate too – but now the fans were not getting the improved results they were, by inference, entitled to expect.

Three days later came the re-arranged home game with Hibs – a crunch fixture that had to be won if Killie were to retain serious title ambitions. Before the game Hibs were in second spot behind Hearts, and Killie were down in fourth, their lowest placing of the season thus far. Waddell rang the changes and brought in Bertie Black in place of McIlroy for his first league game of the season. Nineteen-year-old Billy Dickson was given his league debut in place of left-back Matt Watson.

The gamble paid dividends almost instantly, with Black knocking home a McLean cross inside six minutes. Pat Quinn equalised with an eighteen-yarder midway through the first period, but Killie gradually built up a head of steam and after the break took command. Sneddon slipped the ball through for Black to restore their lead and two minutes later Eric Murray hooked home a McLean cross. Within another five minutes the lead had been increased to 4-1 as Andy King blasted a twenty-yard free-kick past Willie Wilson. Big centre-forward Neil Martin pulled two goals back in the dying minutes with headers, but Killie clung on for a first win in six league games, their confidence restored.

Dickson and Black kept their places for the potentially tricky second round Scottish Cup-tie at Second Division outfit East Fife on 20 February. A one-day bus strike didn't have too much impact on the attendance, which was a healthy 9,000-plus. According to one report, the travelling supporters from Kilmarnock, who normally relied on buses, somehow made their way to Bayview 'by devious means and routes ...'

The East Fife part-timers were determined to dish out a shock. They put up a seven-man defensive barrier, hoping to nick a breakaway goal. The plan was half successful. They kept a clean sheet. The tie drifted to a goalless conclusion, but the need for a replay cost at least three Killie players the chance of an Under-23 cap, for it created a clash of dates with the forthcoming Scotland v England fixture at Aberdeen.

A trip to Celtic in the quarter-finals awaited the winner of the replay and Killie got themselves in the driving seat right from the off, McInally firing in a Sneddon cross after ninety seconds. This did not open the floodgates, however, for the Fifers defended stoutly, creating frustration for home fans and players alike. It took another 72 minutes of dour exchanges before McInally picked up a Murray pass to shoot the crucial second goal and settle the tie. In the final minute a Sneddon corner was turned in by Hamilton for a scoreline that flattered Killie.

By one of those quirks of the fixture list, Killie had to face Celtic at Parkhead in the league seven days prior to going back there in the Cup. The Rugby Park faithful couldn't quite decide which game was the most important. The opposition had no such doubts – for their priorities were different. Celtic's modest league position meant the Cup was the last chance of glory. This viewpoint would be reflected in the attendances, with the Cup-tie attracting more than twice as many as the league game.

Things got off to a bad start in the first game, the unfortunate Murray diverting a wayward shot by Steve Chalmers into his own goal. Moments later McIlroy slipped at the vital moment when an equaliser was there for the taking. Killie had more than their share of possession and pressed hard to get back on terms, going close when a Jim McFadzean header was touched on to the post by John Fallon. The killer blow arrived shortly after the interval by way of a controversial John Hughes goal. The big striker clearly handled as he seized on a Chalmers pass and shot home, but to the amazement of all, referee Gordon gave the goal. Protests by Killie players persuaded him to consult a linesman, but the decision stood. The bad feeling cranked up the tension a few notches, and Jackie McGrory and Frank Beattie were both booked as the tackles flew in. Killie had battled bravely, but it was another two vital league points lost.

Although Killie had been beaten by a fluke and a disputed goal, Celtic were, on balance, the better side, with skipper Billy McNeill giving a classy performance as their defensive kingpin. There had been speculation recently that McNeill was disillusioned with life at Parkhead and would be heading to England. But now the impending arrival of Jock Stein as manager seemed to have changed all that.

With Killie introducing McFadzean for the league game in place of wizard McLean, some fans feared Waddell was bringing back the ultra-defensive formation which had yielded some success earlier in the season but wasn't popular on the terraces. They needn't have worried, for the formation had been specifically designed to stifle Celtic, and it wasn't a formation that Waddell would choose for every game. Perhaps more worrying was the fact that Sneddon damaged his wrist at Celtic Park and needed to visit hospital to have it put in plaster. He was expected to be out for a month and this looked to be another serious blow to the club's dwindling title hopes.

Chapter 8

Down and Out in Glasgow

(March 1965)

*Luckless Fortune's northern storms
Laid a' my blossoms low*
(Robert Burns, 1782)

The crucial month of March got under way at Kilmarnock with long-serving left-back Matt Watson being named 1964-65 Player of the Year by the club's Supporters' Association. After counting the votes, they declared the 28-year-old had won by an overwhelming majority of around eight to one, which was a remarkable endorsement of an unsung hero who rarely made headlines at Rugby Park.

Like his full-back partner Andy King, Watson was a great tackler who cleared his lines well and had been a model of consistency. John Livingston says Watson gained extra popularity because of his loyalty and long service. 'I was a full-back myself and loved to watch Watson and King.' Watson's firm tackling also made an impression on supporter Alex Milligan, who pointed out: 'Killie were a good footballing side and didn't have too many hard men; probably Matt Watson and Pat O'Connor were Killie's hardest nuts.'

Watson was born in Paisley but played for Kilmarnock Amateurs and Ayrshire junior club Kilwinning Rangers before signing on at Rugby Park in 1954. Ten years later he could claim to have been a first-team regular for seven uninterrupted seasons. All were agreed it was a well-deserved award, which Watson would receive at the Supporters' Association's annual buffet-dance in the Grand Hall in June.

The forthcoming Scottish Cup quarter-final tie with Celtic at Parkhead was significant in a number of ways, not least because it represented the last game before Jock Stein officially took over the managerial reins of the home side. With Stein watching, the Celtic players would be desperate to impress and anxious to make progress in a competition that represented their last realistic chance of honours this season.

It was the second meeting of the sides in eight days, a fact that revived memories of 27 years earlier, when Celtic hammered Killie in the League only for Killie to pull off a shock victory in the Cup later on. Could history repeat itself? The coincidence stretched further, for, in those 1937-38 games, Killie were managed by Jimmy McGrory, who was now stepping down as Celtic manager to make way for Stein. One newspaperman, with

Down and Out in Glasgow (March 1965) 117

an eye for statistics, pointed out that the two managers had now chalked up eight Cup wins between them (McGrory six and Waddell two) while the 22 players didn't have a single winner's medal between them.

Although Killie had given Celtic the odd hammering at Rugby Park in recent years, their record was not good at Parkhead. A bumper crowd of 47,000 turned out, despite the difficulties posed by another bus strike. Lady Luck didn't smile on the visitors during the early stages, for Celtic opened the scoring with a disputed goal. Goalkeeper Campbell Forsyth insisted he was pushed by John Hughes as he leaped to catch a Bobby Murdoch corner. Play was not halted, however, and the loose ball broke to Bertie Auld, who crossed for Bobby Lennox to head home.

Killie were without Sneddon and McLean, meaning Hugh Brown got a rare run-out on the right flank and it was his accurate cross which set up McInally for the second-half equaliser. Kilmarnock joy lasted just sixty seconds, as Celtic regained the lead with another goal that the visitors felt should have been ruled out. This time Forsyth attempted to gather a backheader by Lennox only to have it bundled out of his hands and into the net by the lively Auld. Referee Phillips came under heavy fire, but the goal stood. Although the legality of his goal was called into question, there was no doubt that Auld was having an influential game. He was a constant thorn in Killie's side and Celtic fans were delighted at how the 26-year-old had pepped their attack since rejoining the club from Birmingham City recently.

Kilmarnock's hopes faded further when Hughes hit Celtic's third, and although they rallied with McInally pulling another one back, it was simply not to be their day. The 3-2 victory meant Stein started his new job in a winning atmosphere, and he was subsequently able to take Celtic through to the final where they beat Dunfermline 3-2 in a Hampden thriller.

Consolation for Killie's Cup defeat came in the shape of a half-share in the bumper £8,507 gate receipts. After the game, the bookies decided that demoralised Kilmarnock were now unlikely to win anything this season. They quoted them as 25-1 to win the League championship, much longer odds than the joint-favourites Rangers and Dunfermline (9-4), with Hearts at 7-2 and Hibs 9-2.

The top of the table after games on Saturday, 6 March read:

	P	W	D	L	F	A	Pts
Hearts	26	16	5	5	67	39	37
Dunfermline	24	16	5	3	57	25	35
Hibs	25	16	6	3	58	34	35
KILMARNOCK	26	15	6	5	45	28	35
Rangers	23	12	4	7	58	23	31

Ayrshire's most famous son, Robert Burns, once wrote about Mary, Queen of Scots, lamenting the arrival of Spring. However her feelings were certainly not shared at Rugby Park 200 years later, for very soon the green shoots of recovery finally started appearing in Killie's results.

Frustrated by the run of just one win in seven league games, the visit of Dundee United on Wednesday, 10 March represented a 'must win' situation for Killie. Home fans weren't optimistic about their chances after news that Sneddon, Beattie and Hamilton would all be missing through injury. It meant Waddell had to field Bertie Black and Frank Malone for only their second league games of the season. Although this situation was forced upon the boss, giving Black the No 9 shirt would subsequently prove a match-winning move.

It was a fast and exciting tussle which deserved more than the sub-6,000 attendance. United looked a much-improved side since the introduction of their four talented foreign internationals – Danes Finn Dossing and Mogens Berg, and Swedes Lennart Wing and Orjan Persson. However it was thirty-year-old Black, by now on Killie's books for more than twelve years, who took the limelight. He netted a brace to take his tally to four goals from two league appearances and was involved in two other goals to hit the Tannadice club's net. Killie got off to a flying start when McIlroy struck a post, with Black snapping up the rebound. Dossing levelled with a spectacular swerving shot, but after the interval McIlroy flicked in a Black cross to restore the lead. Black was then pushed by Doug Smith and McLean slotted in the penalty for the vital third goal.

Although Watson conceded an own-goal to get home fans biting their nails, the outcome was settled when Black rammed home a McIlroy cut-back. The two points left Killie still in fourth place, but in a more positive frame of mind. The title race was still wide open and Killie had seven games remaining, but there was certainly no longer any room for inconsistency. A winning run was essential to stay in the frame.

The results of Saturday, 13 March underlined the growing feeling that this year's title race was moving towards its tightest finish for many years. A fighting 2-0 win at Motherwell meant Killie's bid for glory was very much back on track. The contest at Fir Park was a colourful game with the thrills of a cup-tie but the standard of marksmanship on display would have made a bunch of disorganised juniors blush – that was the verdict of one reporter, anyway. Certainly a host of chances went begging, but it was Kilmarnock who struck twice in the final half-hour to atone for their wayward finishing earlier. The two points saw them rise to second in the table, two points behind Hearts, both sides with six games left. Killie's situation was aided by the fact that Dunfermline had only drawn and the Old Firm teams both lost.

Down and Out in Glasgow (March 1965) 119

The win was achieved with a somewhat makeshift side, with Forsyth dropped and Watson, Beattie and Sneddon all nursing injuries and watching from the stands. It was Brien McIlroy, with his eighth goal of the season, who broke the deadlock, racing in from the left to net a McLean cross with a neat flick. Former Killie favourite Joe McBride went close to an equaliser as Motherwell battled hard. The two young deputies – Bobby Ferguson, in his second league game in goal, and full-back Billy Dickson – had fine games, while the experience of King, McGrory and McFadzean steadied the ship under a Motherwell barrage. Killie's win was assured five minutes from time when McInally set up Joe Mason, who joyfully netted in only his second outing of the season.

Manager Waddell was highly encouraged by the efforts at Fir Park and kept faith with the young keeper Ferguson, who had just celebrated his twentieth birthday. He felt Ferguson would cope with the following Saturday's game, even though it was a nerve-jangling trip to Ibrox, where an intimidating crowd of around 30,000 could be expected. Mason and Black also kept their places for a game Killie couldn't really afford to lose. Rangers had recently gone out of the European Cup to Inter Milan, out of the Scottish Cup to Hibs, and had been surprisingly beaten in a league game at Aberdeen. There seemed a distinct danger that Kilmarnock might feel the backlash.

Waddell's decision to stick with Ferguson in goal was partly influenced by the fact that Campbell Forsyth had that week taken a stack of criticism for a midweek performance for the Scottish League against the English League at Hampden. The game ended 2-2 and Forsyth was blamed for the English goals by Jack Charlton and Barry Bridges. Waddell said that some of the criticism was unfair, but told Forsyth it would do him a favour to get out of the limelight for a while and play for the reserves. The big man took his 'punishment' well and duly put in a starring performance in a 2-0 win over Rangers' second string. His display included a fine penalty save from Roger Hynd. Forsyth put a brave face on being dropped and didn't sulk in public – he agreed he would just have to fight for his place again: 'I have done it before and I'm sure I can do it again,' he said.

To avoid defeat at Ibrox on Saturday, 20 March, Killie would surely need to summon up all their resourcefulness and energy and hope that Lady Luck would smile on them. Alas – for the second successive visit to Glasgow – they didn't get the rub of the green. As against Celtic, a puzzling refereeing decision favoured the host club and turned the match completely. To Kilmarnock eyes, a 75th-minute penalty award to Rangers was a clear case of the referee panicking in the heat of the moment, making a knee-jerk reaction to the loud appeals of home players and an intimidating big crowd.

Mason had given Killie the lead just before half-time when McLean fed Beattie from a free-kick and the skipper's drive cannoned off the defensive wall into Mason's path. As they tried to build on this lead, Killie were hampered when McInally suffered bad bruising to his ribs and became little more than a passenger up front. Rangers' controversial penalty equaliser came at the point when Killie had begun to look capable of holding out for a famous victory. The incident came with fifteen minutes left, when a through-ball was fed into the Killie box and in the chase to deal with it, McFadzean was tripped by Scottish international Ralph Brand. McFadzean seemed to retaliate and the two men clashed a second or two after the initial foul. Referee Mr Hamilton presumably missed the first offence, for he sparked anger in the Killie ranks as he pointed to the spot. Brand slotted the kick past Ferguson and it needed a brave rearguard action by Killie to keep the scores level in the hectic closing minutes.

On paper, a draw at Ibrox looked a good result, but Killie came away from the game feeling justice had not been done. Indeed the loss of that extra point saw them slip to fifth in the table. It remained very tight, however, with only a couple of points separating all the challengers and it seemed certain the title race would go to the last day.

These were exciting times at Rugby Park, and fans welcomed the splash of colour in their lives brought about by supporting a winning football team. The only cloud on the horizon was the continuing low gates at Rugby Park. With one or two exceptions, many home games now failed to bring in more than 6,000 people, a disappointing level of support which upset chairman Willie McIvor. He simply couldn't understand why Killie's continuing search for honours didn't bring in higher numbers.

There was no lack of atmosphere on the terraces, though. According to David Ross, if you went into the covered terrace area known as The Middle, you could have a 'good old sing-song' and shelter from the rain while yelling lusty songs of praise for the heroes: 'Football fans show great ingenuity in adapting songs to suit their needs,' Ross said recently. 'None more so than when a piece of outdated, imperialistic claptrap was turned into a paean of praise to Jackie McGrory. Just because it rhymed!'

'Land of hope and glory
                Home of Kilmarnock FC
We shall never be beaten
                On to victory
Men like Jackie McGrory
                Boys like Tommy McLean
Here in the west of Scotland
                We'll bring Ayrshire fame'

Down and Out in Glasgow (March 1965)

Jackie McInally's bruised ribs kept him out for the visit of Aberdeen on the final Saturday in March, but the Dons' recent indifferent form meant Killie still started the game as hot favourites. The visitors, managed by former Hibs and Scotland star Eddie Turnbull, had recently signed two Danish forwards – Leif Mortensen and Jorgen Ravn – who had been among the goals and would need watching.

All looked well by half-time, for by then Killie had surged into a two-goal lead through an Eric Murray header and a typical McIlroy strike. The second half was a different story, however. McLean and Hamilton both picked up bad injuries and Killie's effectiveness as an attacking unit disappeared. McLean had been badly fouled by full-back Ally Shewan and would need X-rays later on his ankle. Don Kerrigan pulled a goal back for the Dons and from then onwards it was backs-to-the-wall stuff for the home side. Beattie and McFadzean had superb games, fighting off wave after wave of late Aberdeen raids. McFadzean was wearing the No 3 shirt and his versatility was proving invaluable, for here was a man who could not only cover for virtually anyone, he could be relied upon to play a big part in the team effort. Killie clung on for the two points in front of a disappointingly low crowd of under 5,200. The high number of walking wounded meant that Walter McCrae and Jock Murdoch would have a busy few days in the treatment room as a result.

A board meeting took place in the final week of March and it was announced afterwards that Waddell would end his stint as manager in June – a month before his contract was due to expire, thus allowing Malky MacDonald to take charge for the summer trip to America.

As well as Killie's championship challenge, the talk of the town around now was the forthcoming Scotland game against England at Wembley. Killie's away game at Falkirk had been brought forward by three days to avoid a clash and Killie supporters were offered a return rail trip to the big game for 85 shillings. The special excursion would leave Kilmarnock station on the evening of Friday, 9 April, arriving at London Euston early the following morning. The train would return around midnight after the game, allowing time for Scotland fans to celebrate or commiserate, whichever was appropriate. There was no shortage of takers to join the huge army which ultimately made the trip south of the border, to see Scotland bid for a fourth successive win over the 'Auld Enemy'. Having lost his place in the Kilmarnock side, it was no surprise when Scotland overlooked keeper Forsyth for this game, instead calling on veteran Tottenham custodian Bill Brown.

CHAPTER 9

'COME BACK WITH YOUR SHIELDS – OR ON THEM'

(April-June 1965)

I'll sit me down upon this turf,
And wipe the rising tear
(Robert Burns, 1787)

On the first day of April 1965, the only clubs feeling like April fools were the big two – Rangers and Celtic – both of whom were in the unfamiliar position of being out of the reckoning as the Scottish championship race began its final lap.

On Saturday, 3 April, Kilmarnock kept the pressure on leaders Hearts by scrambling their way to a 2-1 home win over Clyde. Although languishing in mid-table, the 'Bully Wee' surprisingly proved to be one of the most skilful sides to visit Rugby Park this year, and Killie were made to toil for their two points. By coincidence this game followed an almost identical pattern to the previous week's 2-1 home win over Aberdeen. As then, the two Killie goals came in the tenth and fortieth minutes, the visitors struck back after the break, and the match ended with Killie hanging on grimly.

Jackie McInally had made the breakthrough, outstripping the defence to convert Bertie Black's through pass. Ronnie Hamilton's second was even better, a dipping shot from thirty yards, again set up by Black. After the interval, Matt Watson handled a goalbound header from Jim McLean, elder brother of Killie's Tommy, to allow Clyde to pull a goal back from the spot. Killie were a shade lucky to stay in front, but it was a result which brought them back into the reckoning. Hearts and Dunfermline both won, but Hibs slipped up with defeat at Dundee.

	P	W	D	L	F	A	Pts
Hearts	31	21	5	5	86	46	47
Hibs	31	20	4	7	68	38	44
KILMARNOCK	31	19	6	6	56	33	44
Dunfermline	30	19	4	7	72	32	42

Killie's trip to Falkirk's Brockville Park, scheduled for Saturday, 10 April was brought forward into midweek, to avoid a clash with the England-Scotland international at Wembley. It gave them the chance to pick up points while two of their rivals – Hearts and Dunfermline – were not in action. At No 8 was Jim McFadzean, one of eight different shirts he'd so far worn this season. The part-timer had played in both full-back roles, at right and left-half, centre-half, inside-left, outside-left and now inside-right.

For the third successive match, Killie got their noses in front and then had to survive a pounding from the opposition. Andy King's free-kick after 35 minutes found Black, who pulled the ball back for McIlroy to pounce from close range. The small but enthusiastic home crowd roared their favourites on, but to no avail. It left Killie in second place with two games remaining, and a nine-day rest period before their next game.

Fans who'd recently enjoyed seeing most Scotland games screened in full on TV the following day were disappointed to find that the game at Wembley would only feature in highlights. The *Kilmarnock Standard* called this 'a poor show' for those local folk who could not afford to travel to London. With Killie's recently-capped Forsyth and McGrory both currently out of favour, Scotland forced a 2-2 draw at Wembley, maintaining the unbeaten run against the English in the aftermath of 1961's 3-9 thrashing. There was some Kilmarnock involvement, however, for Walter McCrae was making his 'debut' as Scotland trainer.

While Killie kicked their heels, Dundee United held leaders Hearts to a 1-1 draw at Tannadice, and Dunfermline won 2-1 at doomed Third Lanark to go third. These results left Killie two points behind Hearts with both sides having two games to play. It was building up to a dramatic finish, for these two sides would have to face each other at Tynecastle on the final day. If both chalked up wins in their penultimate games, it would mean the title hinged on that last game. It meant more drama than twelve months earlier, when Rangers had finished streets ahead of the rest.

On Wednesday, 14 April Dunfermline played their game in hand, at home to Rangers, and won 3-1 to draw level with Kilmarnock on points (but with a better goal-average) which made things even tighter at the top. Celtic, with Jock Stein now settled behind the manager's desk, were shocked the same night at lowly Falkirk, going down 2-6. Considering the season now had less than a fortnight to run, this night must go down as an all-time nadir in the fortunes of the Old Firm clubs. Both of them were outside the top four and unlikely to finish inside. After the 14 April games the top of the table read:

	P	W	D	L	F	A	Pts
Hearts	32	21	6	5	87	47	48
Dunfermline	32	21	4	7	77	34	46
KILMARNOCK	32	20	6	6	57	33	46
Hibs	32	20	4	8	68	42	44

The penultimate Saturday of the season dawned bright and chilly with three clubs in serious contention – Hearts, Dunfermline and Kilmarnock. The bottom line was that all three contenders needed to win that day to stay in contention and take the race into the final day. But if Killie and Dunfermline were to slip up, the whole issue could be decided in Hearts' favour. It was white-knuckle time.

Killie's opponents on Saturday, 17 April were mid-table Morton, the side who'd ended their unbeaten start to the season with that 1-5 hammering back in December. Dunfermline had the easier-looking task – at home to lowly St Johnstone – while title favourites Hearts had a tricky-looking encounter at mid-table Aberdeen.

Morton might normally have expected to entice around 5,000 to Rugby Park, but more than twice that amount turned up to see the fun in what would be Willie Waddell's final competitive home match. A tense first period ended goalless, but after the break Killie imposed themselves. Black chested down a high ball from Beattie and shot home off a post. Most of the tension evaporated and two goals inside a minute soon had the home crowd in party mood. Man-of-the-match Black slotted home after Morton keeper Erik Sorensen punched the ball straight at McIlroy. Within seconds McInally's cross was converted by McIlroy.

Sorensen had made a number of fine saves, but Killie's cause was helped by injury to the visitors' key striker Allan McGraw. The four-goal hero at Cappielow last December was carried off with a suspected broken leg. The game had its lighter moments – notably when referee Paterson gave up trying to understand the broken English of Morton full-back Kaj Johansen. Unable to make sense of the Dane's spelling, the ref handed his notebook to the full-back and instructed him to book himself!

There was delight at Rugby Park with the news that Dunfermline had been held to a 1-1 draw by St Johnstone, a result that ended The Pars' challenge. But leaders Hearts had won 3-0 at Pittodrie, which meant they remained two points clear of Killie at the top, with just the one game left, and a fractionally better goal-average. The situation was soon clear: Killie had to go to Tynecastle the following Saturday and win by two clear goals. Anything less would see Hearts crowned champions. Hearts' goal-average stood at 1.915 and Killie's 1.818 (inferior by 0.097 of a goal). If Killie won by, say, 2-0, they would have the better goal average by 0.042 of a goal. If, however, Killie were to win by only 1-0, then Hearts would have the superior goal average by 0.027 of a goal. It doesn't get much closer than that.

	P	W	D	L	F	A	Pts
Hearts	33	22	6	5	90	47	50
KILMARNOCK	33	21	6	6	60	33	48

The form book, and common sense, suggested that Hearts were still firm favourites. Nevertheless, it was in Killie's own hands. Thousands of Ayrshire folk made their plans to invade Edinburgh with Waddell's Army. Pictures of the team were pinned up in local shop windows as the days leading up to the game took on an atmosphere normally reserved for the build-up to a cup final.

The leader writer of the *Kilmarnock Standard* got caught up in the general fervour and urged the players into battle by echoing the rallying cry of Spartan women of yesteryear: 'Come back with your shields – or on them!'

'For years now, those of us who support Kilmarnock FC have been prophesying or expecting that the team would bring home one of the major trophies in the game. And for years we have had to be content with the runners-up position – in the Scottish Cup, American Tournament, League Cup and Scottish League. This afternoon we follow the team to Tynecastle, Edinburgh, in the hopeful mood we have been in for so long. Once more Kilmarnock are on the verge of landing a major honour, for today's game with Hearts will decide the League championship. All we need to land is a two-goal victory. Dare we anticipate success with any degree of confidence? I think we can, if only for the obvious reason that the oftener we reach the final stages of competitions, the likelier we are to win.'

The game was built up as the biggest in the club's history and in both Ayrshire and Edinburgh the little matter of the Scottish FA Cup final, between Celtic and Dunfermline on the same day, was relegated to an item of minor interest. Hearts had won the title twice since the War, but Killie had never been champions. What a way to say farewell to popular manager Waddell if they could do it. There were two good omens, for Killie had a good recent record at Tynecastle, and, secondly, goalkeeper Bobby Ferguson had yet to play on a losing Killie side.

Despite the huge anticipated influx from Kilmarnock, Hearts announced the game would not be all-ticket. It would be a case of first come, first served, to all parts of the ground, including seating in the main stand. A minor distraction during the build-up was a story in the Glasgow press that Manchester City had offered their manager's job to Waddell, but the 44-year-old publicly confirmed his intention to quit football after the end of the season. The City job would subsequently go to Joe Mercer.

Waddell made no special arrangements or changes to routine in that final week. Davie Sneddon recalled: 'The week prior to the big decider … was similar to any other, for the Boss and Walter [McCrae] made sure it was that way. On the Saturday morning the bus picked up the locally-based players at Rugby Park, the rest we met in Glasgow. We had something to eat at BAE in St Enoch Square and then went on to Edinburgh to Tynecastle.'

An estimated 10,000 Killie fans trekked to Tynecastle, some by train, but many tackling the seventy-mile journey along the A71 by bus or car. They certainly made themselves heard inside Tynecastle and both teams received a hearty welcome as they took the field.

Killie's top priority had to be to keep Hearts out in the early stages. To go a goal behind would make their task monumental. In view of this, it was comforting to see young Bobby Ferguson – making only the eighth senior appearance of his life – looking as cool as a cucumber. John Malkin of the *Kilmarnock Standard* echoed what many thought when he wrote later how reassuring it was for Killie players and fans to see the young man keeping calm under early pressure, taking his time with goal-kicks. Ferguson's discipline and maturity in such a cauldron of tension was inspiring.

There was one big scare in the early minutes, however, as winger Roald Jensen struck a post. Killie refused to panic and turned in great displays right from the first whistle. Sneddon, celebrating his 29th birthday, fetched and carried all game long, Murray and Beattie 'romped and charged wherever the ball was to be found', McGrory shackled Hearts centre-forward Willie Wallace, and full-backs Watson and King looked like they had the measure of wingers Jensen and Johnny Hamilton.

After a scrappy 26 minutes, Killie's target suddenly looked more attainable. The golden goal came from an unlikely source. Out on the right, Jackie McInally took a short pass from Brien McIlroy, juggled with the ball and left his marker Willie Polland standing before knocking it to McLean, 'the wee fellow in the baggy breeks', according to one reporter. Sneddon takes up the story: 'Tommy saw me at the far post and put the cross over perfectly on to my head. To be honest, I thought I'd miss – I never scored many with my head. Big Jim Cruickshank came right back across the goal and threw himself at the ball. By the time it hit the net, he had dived beyond the post, so that shows how close he came to stopping it.'

The Killie fans went crazy. This was the early goal they'd craved, and, of all people, it had come from the head of wee Sneddon. They were still dancing when, two minutes later, their heroes unbelievably made it 2-0: Bertie Black seized a clearance from Watson on the left and stabbed the ball past Alan Anderson to McIlroy. The Rangers reject wearing the No 11 shirt ignored appeals for offside and cracked the ball low into the far corner of the net. It was a stunning strike and like a blow in the guts for the home side. According to the *Kilmarnock Standard*, Hearts now found themselves 'walking upstairs with a bag of coal on their backs'.

Even in their wildest dreams, Killie fans hadn't expected to achieve the two-goal lead they needed so early on. It was thrilling and frightening at the same time – for now they had to spend the remaining 61 minutes making sure Hearts didn't pull a goal back.

Finger-nails might have needed less chewing had a fine run by McIlroy not ended with McLean hesitating in front of goal to allow Cruickshank to come barreling out and thwart the danger. Hearts ended the first half with the expected siege on Ferguson's goal, and after the break the action resumed in the same hectic fashion. Central defenders Barry and Beattie both fell heavily after a nasty clash of heads and, after being helped to his feet, Barry went bravely upfield to head over the bar.

Killie had the odd half-chance to make it 3-0, but as the final whistle loomed Hearts once again began to throw everything at them. The tension was unbearable on the terraces and on the sidelines too – a fine photo of Waddell and McCrae chain smoking in the dug-out can be seen to this day hanging at Rugby Park. By now almost every Hearts man was in the last third of the field with all eleven visiting players behind the ball. McInally recalled: 'I was so tired the last ten minutes felt like a week.' McLean was in agreement and collapsed three times with cramp near the end.

Hearts were annoyed when the game was stopped by referee Wilson who lectured McGrory and then Ferguson about time-wasting. With the fans roaring 'Killie, Killie' and screaming for the final whistle, play went past 93 minutes when the contest then reached its defining moment. Weary Barry, his socks round his ankles, lobbed forward. The ball eluded Beattie and fell to Hearts' twenty-year-old local boy Alan Gordon. It was a clear chance to win the title. Just ten yards out, Gordon fired goalwards. It looked a goal all the way and the roars of delight had left the Hearts throats by the time Ferguson sprang acrobatically across his line to turn it round for a corner. It was a save that in this setting almost defied belief.

Gordon's 'miss' would be debated in Edinburgh for years afterwards. But the Jambos' No 10 should not be blamed, according to Sneddon: 'Gordon has taken some stick for that, but the truth is Ferguson made a great save. I thought [Gordon] did ever so well, he took the ball on the up really skilfully and was able to keep his shot down. He smashed it into the ground and it was going high into the net, but Bobby got to it.' Forty years on, the whole breathtaking sequence, and more, can be seen on a special DVD produced for sale in the Kilmarnock club shop.

Seconds after Ferguson's save, the final whistle sounded and all hell was let loose. In one wild, forty-yard sprint on to the pitch, the normally calm Waddell shed his image as an unflappable and dour manager. Attempting to button his overcoat as he ran, Waddell showed exactly why he used to be one of Rangers' finest wingmen, racing across to his skipper Beattie to administer the mother of all bear-hugs. McGrory, too, could be seen bouncing up and down like a hyperactive schoolboy.

Not far behind Waddell's glory run came chairman McIvor, cutting a more portly figure as he wove his way around the Hearts players, several of whom had collapsed to their knees. McGrory jumped into McIvor's arms and nearly knocked his chairman over. Fans swarmed on to mob the Killie heroes and the players needed the help of the police to escape to the dressing room. Soon afterwards, with the almighty din unabated, they returned to the pitch to take the cheers, emerging from the tunnel behind the dancing figure of Waddell, who was skipping along with a huge smile. This moment was captured for posterity by a photographer and prints can be seen around Kilmarnock's stadium forty years on.

Stunned Hearts simply couldn't believe it. Years later Alan Gordon would tell *The Scotsman*: 'I still have people mentioning it to me, and it makes the hairs on the back of my neck prick up. It was hard to believe that it actually happened, and I don't suppose that for a minute the Kilmarnock players thought they would end up being league champions. We had played good football all the way. Kilmarnock were much more defensive-minded. If it had been goal difference in 1965 [instead of goal-average], we would have won the league by a couple of miles.'

Once the dust had settled, on the game and on the wild scenes in Kilmarnock town centre that night, the big talking point in Scottish football was how Killie had lifted the crown with so little resistance from the Old Firm. The *Kilmarnock Standard* was outraged by 'hysterical trumpetings' in the popular press which suggested Scottish football would never regain its former glory until the Glasgow giants went out and bought new players. Such talk was an insult to Kilmarnock, reckoned the *Standard*.

'We are told that these particular clubs owe it to the game in Scotland, and their fans, of course, to get back to their rightful place at the top of the honours list. This sort of mush does the game infinite harm. It emanates from an erroneous belief that certain clubs alone have some almost divine right to win everything the game has to offer. The role of all others is seen as permanently inferior, always to be accepted tacitly as such. Thus it is that we get this insistent demand in the press for certain clubs to import as much skilled football talent as their bank balances will allow. It's all for the good of Scotland, we are told. Well, here in Kilmarnock we now have a team which is decisively giving the lie to this lackey talk. The team which has just won the championship is predominantly an Ayrshire one. The only player to be bought on the transfer market is Davie Sneddon and he hails from Kilwinning. Kilmarnock have shown that football talent is not necessarily confined to players with expensive price tags on their heads. Success in football does not depend on the importation of so-called stars and we'll soon have a flag at Rugby Park to prove it. I hope Kilmarnock's success will inspire other town clubs to go all out to emulate Saturday's achievement at Tynecastle. We want new names in the honours list of Scottish football.'

Skipper Beattie recalled two of his clearest memories of that weekend – firstly, having to leave his heavily pregnant wife at home as he headed for Edinburgh, and secondly 'the mad figure' of Waddell running on the pitch to hug him. Beattie modestly brushed off suggestions from far and wide that it was he who should have been Scotland's Player of the Year that season, an award which went to Celtic's Billy McNeill. 'It was just one of those things, but an Old Firm player winning the honour would obviously sell more newspapers,' he said with a wink.

In *Charles Buchan's Football Monthly*, writer W G Gallagher, also known as 'Waverley' of the *Daily Record*, eulogised about Beattie's contribution to the title win: 'There is a no more wholehearted player in British football than Frank Beattie. He is essentially a team man and as such has been a constant inspiration. He has never been looked upon as one of the glamour boys of football, and has seen less skilful men transferred from Rugby Park to wealthy English clubs without once seeking a move for himself. Maybe it is because of his contentment that he has been such an important factor in his club winning their first ever league championship. He has been most unfortunate in not achieving international rating. Were I Scotland's team manager I would be happy, ever so happy, to have Frank Beattie at my call.'

Sneddon attempted to explain Kilmarnock's success in an interview: 'Waddell wasn't a great tactician but his man management was just right. He made the players think for themselves. That's what makes a good side, there's only so much a manager can do. We weren't a great side but we were very solid. And we had players like Bertie Black, Jackie McInally and Brien McIlroy who could win a game by themselves.' Skipper Beattie backed up Sneddon's view on Waddell: 'He could motivate players and he got the best out of Kilmarnock players.'

Waddell himself explained that giving the players three-year contracts had helped to maintain continuity: 'That is a good thing and it gave the players a sense of security they would otherwise not have had. It is hard at times to convince youngsters nowadays that they should not become grasshoppers. And by that I mean wanting to jump about from club to club. Promising youngsters can get every chance to make a name for themselves with Kilmarnock and that applies to second team men as well as first, as is instanced by the breaking through this season of Ferguson and McLean. There is definitely a future for good young players at Rugby Park. We felt that local boys will take a keen interest and pride in their local club. Often in the past local lads were prophets never honoured by their own folk and when things went wrong with them they had to take a buffeting from their own supporters. That is part of the set up: local players must face this sort of criticism; it is part of asking them to turn pro. Happily there's not been much of that with our local lads in recent times because they have all been good lads to work with and have shown the skill and the urge needed to get on in football.'

The trophy was paraded for the first time at Rugby Park on the Monday night after the Hearts game, prior to the Ayrshire Cup final between Killie and Ayr United. Even a thunderstorm failed to dampen spirits as the champions were applauded onto the pitch by the Ayr team and officials. Even referee Wilson got a cheer, for it was he who had officiated at Tynecastle. The game that night was of secondary importance to the party atmosphere, and Second Division strugglers Ayr won 1-0. John Livingston recalls that Ayr skipper Sam McMillan was so surprised to have won the cup that he managed to drop it when it was presented to him.

The season was not over, for there were six Summer Cup fixtures to come in May, followed by the New York international tournament, then a special match with Hearts, sanctioned by FIFA, in which the offside law was to be scrapped as an experiment. In the meantime, on Friday, 30 April, Kilmarnock Supporters' Association paid tribute to the departing Waddell at a special function laid on at David Lauder's restaurant in Kilmarnock.

Waddell's wife had to miss the event as she was soon to give birth to their third child, but the manager enjoyed the chance to explain his reasons for quitting, which had still not been made entirely clear. The Association chairman Jim Heaney presented him with a parting gift of a projector for showing still transparencies. In his response, Waddell continued to frustrate the press by refusing to reveal much about his future plans.

He said: 'I am leaving Kilmarnock FC, but I am not leaving the town. I will still be here and I only hope I can go to Rugby Park and see the team week after week. I am going out of football and I am not sorry I am leaving. I have had my fill of it. It is a hard, hard job. But any little I have done to help Kilmarnock FC gave me a great thrill and a lot of pleasure. In spite of brusqueness, brashness and sometimes intolerable rudeness, deep down I am a sentimental fellow. I have spoken seven or eight times to this association in the past seven years and the same record could probably have been played, for each time I said "We didn't win anything this year but we will next year" – and now at long last we have.

'I have been a long time in this game, for nearly thirty years as a professional footballer and manager and last Saturday's result and display in Edinburgh provided the biggest thrill I have had in all that time.'

Chairman McIvor added: 'Mr Waddell made his own decisions, his own defeats and his own victories. He had a complete free hand during his time with us and we on the board are proud that he has had this great achievement before demiting office. We admired his attitude and his reasons for taking this step [retirement] and I want to tell you that we made every endeavour to get him to change his mind and continue as manager but he'd made his mind up and we were forced to accept the position. However, before leaving he has achieved a personal ambition – to do something for the club, the team and the board as well as for himself. Something history will put down in the record books, something that cannot be taken away from Mr Waddell or anyone else who helped to achieve it.'

After the toasts, the group adjourned to an upstairs hall to be entertained by a concert party and after a hearty rendition of 'For he's a jolly good fellow' there was clearly a tear or two in Waddell's eyes.

Financially, winning the League with 50 points earned Kilmarnock £4,000 from the Pools company payouts (£80 per point). The total handout to all clubs was £103,680 and every club except Third Lanark received sums of at least £1,000. As the Thirds came bottom of the table with just seven points, their payout was a modest £560. The financial year ending 31 July 1965 yielded a Kilmarnock club profit of £21,401, which was largely due to the money-spinning Fairs Cup-ties with Eintracht and Everton, plus a small surplus on the transfer market. The club's accounts this year would be the first to be subject to a new Corporation Tax announced by the Chancellor of the Exchequer in his recent budget.

Fans were informed that although Kilmarnock's newly renovated Main Stand was without a flagpole, this would be remedied before the start of the new season, to enable the club's first championship flag to fly. There had once been a flagpole at the back of the Rugby Road terrace, but it was temporarily in storage during building work. The club confirmed receipt of a cheque from the Scottish FA to buy themselves a championship flag.

Despite the title, the public voted with its feet over the ill-fated Summer Cup and gates were disappointingly low for Killie's six ties. For example, only 667 turned out at Third Lanark to see Killie's 3-0 win. Other matches involving the Thirds proved even less popular. Only the group winners would go through and Killie finished second, despite winning four games. This second staging of the competition would be the last.

With Waddell remaining vague on his plans, speculation mounted that he might become the next Scotland manager. Sports writers tipped him as a front runner now that Ian McColl had departed. Jock Stein had agreed to take temporary charge for the imminent World Cup 1966 qualifiers against Poland and Finland, but this was only a stop-gap. By now, Killie's trainer Walter McCrae was part of the Scotland set-up and was making himself 'popular' with his tough regime. Rangers' Davie Wilson told one reporter: 'Trainer McCrae really puts us through the hoop. He gave us every conceivable thing to do. I've never had such a rigorous routine.' But the reporter noted with admiration that McCrae never asked players to do anything he couldn't do himself – and this approach seemed to have inspired the players under his charge, at both Kilmarnock and Scotland.

Waddell said little about the Scotland job, but admitted in June that he'd been approached by relegated Wolves, who were looking for a manager to replace Andy Beattie. Waddell took his time before turning this job down, which suggested he was still open to persuasion despite his pledge to quit the game. The Wolves job carried a high £7,000 salary. By now Waddell's name had been linked with many jobs, including positions at a whisky firm, a car manufacturer, a carpet firm, and his former club Rangers. According to the *Evening Citizen*: 'To all such stories Waddell says now't. Yet as one recalls the scenes at Tynecastle, and the obvious delight football provides for him, it is hard to believe that all the Waddell know-how and experience and influence is going to be lost to football.'

Waddell's final game in charge of Killie came on Saturday, 19 June, when Hearts won 8-2 in a FIFA experimental game in which offside was abandoned altogether in the first half and then restricted to within eighteen yards of the goals in the second. Soccer VIPs from all over the globe came to Tynecastle to see the effect of these rule changes. FIFA had chosen Scotland to stage this game, and, as they were now the top two clubs in the country, the privilege fell to Killie and Hearts. Three of the eight Hearts goals were a direct result of the offside rule being scrapped. According to John Livingston, Killie were heavily beaten because they tried all sorts of intricate tactics to cope with the changes, but only managed to bamboozle themselves. The FIFA observers were clearly not impressed by what they saw, for the offside rule remained unchanged.

A few days later Waddell officially handed over to Malky MacDonald. On his last day, Frank Beattie presented him, on behalf of the players, with a silver tray, crystal decanter and six crystal glasses. The tray bore the inscription 'To the boss, William Waddell, manager, Kilmarnock FC, 1957-65, with pride and appreciation'.

It had taken eight years, but Waddell had turned a moderately successful club into a major force in Scotland. His eight seasons in charge saw Killie finish champions once, runners-up four times, fifth twice and eighth once – not to mention a series of cup runs. It had been a wonderful period for the club and the man himself was immensely proud to be leaving with that championship flag flying high above Rugby Park (metaphorically speaking, at least!).

POSTSCRIPT: Hearts followers have always bemoaned the fact that had the 'goal-difference' rule operated in 1965, instead of 'goal-average', they would have won the League and not Kilmarnock. This rule was later changed, but – amazingly – Hearts suffered again in 1986, for they lost the title to Celtic on goal-difference, but would have won it had goal-average still been in operation!

CHAPTER 10

THE PAIN IN SPAIN
(1965-66)

Yet they, even they, with all their strength,
Began to faint and fail:
Even as two howling, ravenous wolves
To dogs do turn their tail.
(Robert Burns, 1789)

Today, a glance down the list of Scottish champions finds Kilmarnock's name standing isolated, shining out like a beacon. A true 'blip' on the pattern of history. In the six decades since the 1939-45 War, the title has been won 48 times by either Rangers or Celtic. The remaining champions all come from the cities of Edinburgh, Dundee or Aberdeen – except, that is, little Kilmarnock, the only town with a population of under 100,000 to have hoisted the championship flag.

However, Killie's ground-breaking triumph wasn't the signal for other 'small' clubs to come marching into prominence. In fact, it marked the end of an era of opportunity for the less privileged. Immediately afterwards, the Old Firm not only regained their grip on Scottish football, they carried their dominance to a new level. After the arrival of Jock Stein in 1965, Celtic were able to forget twenty years of post-War mediocrity and went on a spree that featured nine successive championships, six Scottish FA Cups, six League Cups, seven losing cup finals, and European glory.

It is clear now that in the late 1950s and early '60s Celtic had stagnated, a situation blamed by many on chairman Bob Kelly. In 1998, authors Tom Campbell and David Potter wrote of Kelly: 'His arrogance in determining every aspect of Celtic's policy bordered on the pathological.' They went on: 'The maladministration of the club amounted to dereliction of duty by the board of directors ... at Celtic Park the important matches during this time were fated to end in disaster, often self-inflicted through bizarre team selections.' Other observers pointed the finger of blame at manager Jimmy McGrory, the former Kilmarnock boss, who'd been appointed at Celtic Park in 1945 but proved to be an office-bound figure who made little impact in his twenty years at the helm.

During Celtic's post-War hiatus, neighbours Rangers blew hot and cold, but were still by far the top dogs in Scottish football. They won the 'treble' twice during this period, ten of the nineteen championships on offer, plus eight Scottish Cups. But instead of sharing the limelight with Celtic,

Rangers intermittently conceded the title to the likes of Hibs, Aberdeen, Dundee, Hearts and then Kilmarnock. It meant a level of healthy competition that has been rarely evident before or since.

Once Celtic got their act together under Stein in 1965, the 'smaller' clubs were put in their place in resounding fashion. The season that followed Kilmarnock's success, 1965-66, proved to be arguably the Old Firm's most successful ever. The pair finished winners and runners-up in all three major competitions — for the first time.

Post-War Scottish football suffered from so much talent going south of the border, even though the maximum wage system operated in England (until 1961) and not in Scotland. In the mid-to-late 1950s, for example, more than 100 Scottish players played in the English First Division. The maximum wage of £20-per-week meant there wasn't untold riches to be had, but nevertheless the English game was a big pull for those with ambition and itchy feet. The majority of players in Scotland were part-time in the 1950s and '60s, including many of those in the First Division. Kilmarnock only went 'full-time' in 1959 but abandoned this policy in 1971 and it wasn't until 1989 that full-time contracts were issued again.

Most Scottish clubs couldn't afford generous wages and there were few attempts to exploit the maximum wage system by offering English stars big money to come north — a rare example was Syd Puddefoot joining Falkirk. Even wealthy Rangers didn't splash out — by the time they sold Jim Baxter for a club record £70,000 to Sunderland in 1965 their own record purchase was still less than £30,000. Rangers liked to raid clubs like Queen's Park in the 1950s for players who didn't cost a fee.

Strangely, the Celtic 'revival' began on the same day that Kilmarnock clinched the title. While Killie were celebrating in Edinburgh, Celtic were simultaneously doing a lap of honour at Hampden, after a 3-2 Scottish FA Cup final win over Dunfermline. It was their first silverware in seven seasons and there would be no looking back.

Meanwhile, Willie Waddell's departure from Rugby Park was, perhaps inevitably, followed by the steady break-up of the title-winning squad. Only three players — Beattie, Black and Forsyth — had passed their thirtieth birthdays, so this was not an ageing side, but with a new manager in place and new challenges ahead, changes were inevitable.

During the busy summer Forsyth was tipped to move to England, having lost his place in the Killie team to young Bobby Ferguson. First Division newcomers Northampton were keen on Forsyth, but their interest waned and subsequently he joined Southampton, helping The Saints win promotion to the English top flight for the first time. A week or two after Forsyth bade farewell, Ronnie Hamilton moved to St Mirren in a swap deal involving Gerry Queen.

The Pain in Spain (1965-66)

Jackie McGrory refused the new terms offered and was not the only one unhappy over how the players had been rewarded for winning the title. Interviewed by the fanzine 'Killie Ken' years later, McInally didn't pull his punches: 'The directors wouldn't reward the players the way they should have. It was very short-sighted. I know [Kilmarnock] weren't one of the most fashionable clubs and didn't get the crowds they deserved, but I don't accept the argument that they paid us what they could afford.'

McInally said the players had speculated among themselves over how much they might get in bonuses if they finished top. Figures of £800 to £1,000 were bandied about, but these would prove wide of the mark. According to McInally, the sum on offer was £180 (before tax) for those who played in every game (only Eric Murray did so) and proportionately less for the others. It equates to around £4,000 per man in today's terms for the regulars. In another interview, Davie Sneddon recalled receiving £169 for winning the title. The offer caused uproar and led to various meetings and formal complaints from the players. The sum was eventually raised to around £360 per man, according to McInally.

'Big Jake' reckoned the pay row, which continued into the following season, signalled the start of a decline in Kilmarnock's fortunes that would ultimately result in relegation eight years later. 'I saw a lot of the players become uneasy and unhappy at the club and if you have a situation like that then you won't have a successful team. There were a few players who were moved on, and a few who had contract problems. I think that was the biggest factor in the start of the decline.'

As a result of his intransigence over pay, McGrory was omitted from the party that departed for the USA on 2 July, under the command of Malky MacDonald for the first time. Having played 56 games in the previous eleven months, it was a weary squad which flew out from Renfrew. The American tournament was not a success. In six group games Killie suffered four defeats and enjoyed just one victory (2-0 over West Brom), the competition ultimately won by Polish side Polonia Bytom. Due to an odd ruling by the Scottish FA, Killie were the only participating side forbidden to use substitutes. The American organisers asked Killie's opponents to refrain from using them, as a goodwill gesture, but Ferencvaros apparently ignored this and sneaked two new faces into their team at half-time.

And so the post-Waddell era began with player unrest and disappointing results. True, few cared much about the USA tournament, but the new manager would have preferred a more positive start to his incumbency, particularly in view of the bad feeling in the squad about pay.

On returning from New York in early August, McGrory was absent from pre-season training. The situation between him and the club became deadlocked. McGrory said he did not intend to approach the club again about his future, and MacDonald said the club's attitude was unchanged. McGrory wanted a transfer and said he wouldn't play for Killie again. He took a job as a barman in a Renfrew pub.

The atmosphere of unease at the club wasn't ideal, but things looked jovial enough when well-known broadcaster Bill Tennent joined the players on the training field for a feature to be screened on Scottish TV. A few days later, at the end of August, McGrory ended his dispute and put pen to paper. Unfortunately, this came too late to comply with a UEFA deadline and he found himself ineligible for Killie's forthcoming campaign in the European Champions Cup.

The club's baptism in this elite competition saw them paired against fellow novices – the strangely named '17 Nendori' club from the Albanian capital, Tirana. (They are variously referred to as Nandori, Nendori, Nantori, and Nentori in football record books, but '17 Nendori' is the version given in the club's own literature). Formerly known as SK Tirana, they had changed their name in mysterious circumstances soon after the 1939-45 War, reportedly following instructions from Albania's ruling Communist authorities. With little or no notice, the men in charge decreed that 'Partizani' would be the new Defence Ministry team and 'Dinamo' the Internal Affairs Ministry team. The plan was to make these two new 'clubs' as strong as possible. SK Tirana, or 17 Nendori as it would now be known, lost many of its 'stars' to one or other. Afterwards, 17 Nendori finished third in the Albanian league several times before finally winning the title in 1965 (just like Kilmarnock).

Albania seemed a grim, mysterious Communist outpost and Killie hadn't a clue what would greet them. The country's recent history was complex, both before and after communists had seized control in 1944. Enver Hoxha, a college instructor who had earlier led the communist resistance against fascist invaders, had become leader of the People's Republic of Albania. His pre-War predecessor had been the dictator King Zog.

While the Albanian champions made plans to face Kilmarnock, their national leader was planning and launching a violent campaign to extinguish religious life in the country, an episode which would lead in 1967 to the creation of the self-styled 'world's first atheist country'.

Against this background it was not surprising that diplomatic problems arose when Killie officials attempted to make travel arrangements for the first leg. Britain had no direct diplomatic contact with Albania and the club was told it would have to fly via London and Rome, changing planes to get to Tirana, making the trip awkward and expensive. Attempts by Scottish pressmen to obtain visas were blocked, with Killie also unsuccessful with their block application for a party that included players, officials and reporters. John Wilson, the Rangers vice-chairman whose day job was at a travel agency, assisted as best he could, but found that Hoxha's henchmen would only grant visas to fifteen players, the manager, trainer, club doctor, chairman and one director. The rule was strictly no reporters.

The *Kilmarnock Standard* reckoned few other British clubs engaging in European competition could have faced a more awkward baptism. The reduced allocation of visas arrived shortly before departure. Asked about the arrangements, MacDonald commented: 'I'm not so worried about getting into the country, as getting out of it!' It seems likely this rather undiplomatic comment had been intended to be 'off the record'.

The party set out from Renfrew on Monday, 6 September, given sprigs of white heather as they boarded. Local MP William Ross, Secretary of State for Scotland, was present to wish them well. The final stage of the journey was scary as the chartered plane from Rome ran into a violent storm and, according to an account by correspondent Hugh Taylor, its wings were struck by lightning. The welcome in Tirana was reassuringly warm, however, and the players were given bouquets and ushered into a luxury hotel for a pre-match banquet. Facilities and hospitality were far better than MacDonald and his men had dared to expect.

As the Tirana stadium had no floodlights, the game took place on the Wednesday afternoon and the noisy 35,000 crowd was presumably a Scot-free zone. In gruelling, stamina-sapping conditions under a hot sun, Killie did well to hold out for a 0-0 draw, giving a disciplined defensive performance, despite McGrory's absence. Trainer Walter McCrae was a regular visitor on the pitch, particularly to care for Jackie McInally, who was singled out for robust treatment.

One of the heroes of the 0-0 draw was Bobby Ferguson, twenty, who was by now widely tipped as a future international goalkeeper. He told reporters he planned to go full-time after finishing his apprenticeship as an engineer at the ICI factory at Ardeer.

For the second leg, manager MacDonald warned that the attendance at Rugby Park would need to be at least 20,000 to meet commitments and expenses over the two legs. The Albanian opponents would be playing under floodlights for the first time and would also be playing with a heavier ball than they were used to. MacDonald reckoned they were a talented bunch and at least as good as most Scottish First Division clubs. The visitors were due to be met at London Airport by chairman Willie McIvor and director David McCulloch, who must have accepted that Kilmarnock would struggle to match the hospitality they'd been shown in Tirana. Asked what was on offer, MacDonald said 'nothing special, we will wait to see what they would like to do'.

Rooms were booked for the visiting delegation at the Marine Hotel in Troon and Killie negotiated with a language college in London for the use of an interpreter. For their first cup-tie outside their own country, the visitors arrived at Troon exhausted after a 48-hour journey, which included a long spell stranded in Budapest due to a visa mix-up. Kilmarnock had been told of the delay via a telegram in French from Budapest. With no one in the office able to translate, the message was passed to the Scottish FA, who in turn turned to the Home Office. After a good sleep on the Sunday night the Albanians trained the following morning and evening at Rugby Park, the latter specifically to get used to floodlights. They had a look around the town and on the Tuesday went shopping in Glasgow before attending a friendly between Rangers and Benfica. An overworked representative of the London School of Oriental Languages came to Scotland to help, but seemed to struggle with the Albanian dialects.

Scenes of jubilation and relief greeted the narrow win that Kilmarnock recorded on Wednesday evening. Weakened by the absence of McGrory, Murray and Sneddon, Killie could thank a half-fit Bertie Black for their late winner. Stand in right-half Pat O'Connor exchanged passes with McLean before placing a fine pass into the box, where Black raced in to shoot past the heroic Janku. Black later took a clearance from Menna full in the face. The resulting concussion left him unaware that he'd scored the winner until much later in the dressing room.

The Albanians left for home deflated but grateful for their treatment, and clutching gifts of tartan travelling rugs and Stewarton 'bunnets'.

Kilmarnock hearts soared when the draw for the second round was made in Brussels in mid-October and paired Killie with the mighty Real Madrid. Said MacDonald: 'We couldn't have had a better draw. It's fantastic.' Chairman McIvor added: 'This is a wonderful tie for Kilmarnock; it's even beyond the realm of Eintracht owing to the worldwide reputation of this great club [Real Madrid]. This is a game the like of which our supporters have never seen before.'

Five-times winners of the still-young European Cup, Madrid were well known in Scotland for having knocked Rangers out two years earlier. Killie appealed to the authorities for permission to play McGrory in the tie, but the earlier ban was re-affirmed. Strangely enough Madrid were no strangers to humble Rugby Park, for on at least two occasions they'd visited Scotland, stayed at Troon and trained on Killie's pitch.

The date for the home leg was fixed for 17 November, and the press were quick to see the coincidence – for the previous opponents' name, when translated, meant '17 November'. The *Kilmarnock Standard* urged local fans not to get too carried away about their heroes' chances: 'It would be futile to underestimate what must be the greatest club team in soccer history. Real are the supreme masters of the sport. When aroused they can be ruthless, and when they strike form they can be positively devastating. We saw that when they played Eintracht in the European Cup final at Hampden a few years ago.'

MacDonald flew to Spain to spy on Real and tickets went on sale in various Kilmarnock town-centre shops as well as the Supporters Club, prices ranging from five shillings for boys to £1 for the best adult seats. Killie's build-up was not helped when they suffered a shock home defeat by lowly Clyde, defensive blunders giving the visitors a 2-1 win. Andy King's error for the first goal – a wayward back-pass – may have contributed to his being dropped that week from the Scotland World Cup 1966 pool of 22. The pool was pruned to seventeen prior to a qualifying tie with Italy and King was in good company, for another man axed was Denis Law.

The Clyde defeat was followed by one at Aberdeen, watched by Real coach Miguel Munoz and the Spanish side's London agent George Stirrup. Munoz said he was optimistic of beating Killie, but had been impressed by their defence, and in particular the half-back line. 'We will not treat Kilmarnock lightly because of this display, they were not at their best. We could see that, despite the defeat, they have first-class players.'

After their earlier words of warning, the local paper now tried to rally support: 'So let it rip lads and lasses. Chant and cheer, sing and shout as much as you like, but let Killie know that you are with them and for them all the way.'

Real were at the time second in the Spanish League and many felt they were not quite the force they once were, with star man Ferenc Puskas now 39 years old, albeit still leading scorer and a formidable opponent. To Killie's dismay they had to go into the game without key man Frank Beattie who was out with a thigh injury.

Rugby Park was blue and white bedlam on the night, large numbers of special constables with their walkie-talkies shepherding the huge crowd of nearly 25,000 into the ground. Pre-match entertainment was provided by the Band of the Royal Marines and the City of Glasgow Pipe Band, who started up ninety minutes before kick-off. The home crowd provided superb support throughout, apart from the spate of bottle-throwing which greeted an ugly foul on McLean by Gento. Puskas also received the sort of cat-calls usually reserved for famous opponents. It proved a busy night for Kilmarnock photographer J Stewart McLauchlan, who in conjunction with an international press agency, set up a photograph wire machine in his nearby studio to cope with the demand for pictures of the game from foreign sources. Twenty minutes after kick-off the first photos were on their way to London, Paris and Madrid and more followed at twenty-minute intervals. Kilmarnock folk marvelled later on when told that pictures of the game had been plastered across the newsstands in Madrid just two hours after the game.

The match was a thriller. Killie turned on their Eintracht form in an absorbing first half, but bad luck and over-anxious finishing – plus a questionable offside call – combined to keep the score 1-1 by half-time. After just eight minutes Ronnie Hamilton had lofted the ball into the path of Brien McIlroy and the winger fired a splendid shot into the far corner – but the roars turned to groans as a German linesman flagged for offside. Later, the same linesman flagged Hamilton offside when Santamaria was clearly two yards nearer the goal. It earned the poor linesman a massive ear-bashing for the remainder of the game.

Real were quiet early on, apart from a snapshot by Gento which Ferguson was alert to. After twenty minutes Killie had taken the lead. Driven forward by the irrepressible O'Connor, they won a penalty when McInally was dragged down. McLean slotted the ball home – his 27th successful spot-kick in all competitions, with none missed. Real were level within four minutes, when the otherwise quiet Puskas shook off several defenders and supplied Martinez, who waltzed round Matt Watson to drive high into the net. Killie remained in command, however, and rained more efforts on goal without success.

After half-time McInally was floored inside the box by Zoco, but the referee was not impressed. King snuffed out the ageing Gento on the wing, Watson held his own against the most agile and menacing forward – Amancio – and Murray and McFadzean performed superbly at the heart of the defence. McLean had a fine game and linked up well with McInally to create a constant threat down the right, but Sneddon and McIlroy struggled to make headway in their private battles.

The overweight Puskas helped set up Real's second goal, against the run of play. Gento's cross was met by Amancio, who flicked past Ferguson. Within two minutes a high cross by Hamilton found McInally who nodded in the equaliser. Gento hacked down McLean late in the game and was booked, but the scores remained level at 2-2. It had been a cold night in Ayrshire, but an absorbing game had warmed the enthusiastic crowd.

Kilmarnock's brave display left them with a crop of injures and their patched up side were hammered 0-5 at Rangers in the league three days later. Real, too, felt the effects, for they went down 1-2 to lowly Seville on the Sunday. Young Ferguson barely had time to catch his breath around now, for three days after the Rangers hammering, he made his full debut in goal for Scotland in a 4-1 win over Wales.

Killie's European adventure came to an emphatic end in the vast Bernabeu Stadium in the second leg, even though the Scots made a wonderful start. Defensive blunders then let Real back into the game and, despite fighting to the end, Killie were humbled 1-5 on the night, 3-7 on aggregate. The scoreline flattered Real and Killie were not disgraced.

The Pain in Spain (1965-66)

With kingpin Beattie missing again, Killie had started brightly. After eighteen minutes McLean got through and rounded the keeper, squaring the ball to McIlroy, who hooked high over the bar when it seemed easier to score. He made amends nine minutes later when O'Connor sent away McInally, who rounded a defender and slipped the ball to McLean. His cross was met by McIlroy who dived to head a picture goal. The frustrated home fans put their men under pressure and got a response just minutes later. Grosso equalised after Watson was slow to clear. Ruiz then raced though to fire past Ferguson.

A great chance to level things came when McInally beat the keeper but missed an open goal. It looked a costly miss on 35 minutes when Ferguson misjudged a high cross and in the ensuing scramble Grosso forced home. The 3-1 half-time lead was not a fair reflection on the balance of play. Killie looked apprehensive and disorganised after the break, however, and Gento shot the fourth goal on 58 minutes. Then McIlroy was shoved as he jumped for a header, whereupon McLean missed a spot-kick for the first time in his career, his low shot being so soft it was comfortably saved. In the final minute Grosso tucked in a fifth.

With the European Cup out of the way, Killie could now concentrate on the more prosaic matter of attempting to defend their league title. The post-Cup blues saw them struggling in eighth place for several weeks, but a New Year revival led to a finishing position of third in 1965-66, which was pretty much what realists on the Rugby Park terraces had expected.

Chapter 11

How the Mighty are Fallen
(1966 and beyond)

Should auld acquaintance be forgot,
And never brought to mind?
Should auld acquaintance be forgot,
And auld lang syne?
(Robert Burns, 1788)

Malky MacDonald's second stint at Rugby Park would last three seasons. He was, perhaps, unlucky that his return to Kilmarnock coincided with the resurgence of Celtic under Jock Stein. Celtic would succeed Killie as champions in 1966 and subsequently win the league nine seasons in a row.

MacDonald guided Killie to third, seventh and seventh again, and oversaw two big cup runs – to the last four of the League Cup in 1965-66, and to the semi-finals of the Inter-Cities Fairs Cup in 1966-67. His reign included some magical nights in Europe, including the enthralling meetings with Real Madrid and 17 Nandori in the European Cup, and, one year later, a 2-4 aggregate defeat by Leeds in the Fairs Cup.

The second coming of MacDonald was not without excitement, but the consistency of the Waddell era had gone. The parting of the ways came after a 0-6 home rout by Celtic in March 1968, whereupon MacDonald was replaced by trainer Walter McCrae. MacDonald became a scout for Spurs and later Celtic, but this courteous man was only really happy when working with players day-to-day. Overall, his managerial record at Killie was fairly good, but stepping into Waddell's shoes had been a thankless task.

Curiously, MacDonald's 1960s stint at Killie included a spell when he was also in charge of the Scottish national team. Ian McColl had taken the Scotland job in November 1960 – the first man not to combine the job with managing a club. But when McColl was sacked in May 1965, the SFA used a series of men on a seemingly part-time/caretaker basis. Jock Stein was followed by John Prentice. Then, in October 1966, MacDonald spent five months in the hot seat before Bobby Brown took over. Kilmarnock had finished in Scotland's top three for four years, but Malky's time as part-time Scotland boss coincided with the club slipping to seventh. The post-championship decline was by now clearly well under way.

Several decades on, MacDonald looked back with fondness on his time at Rugby Park: 'I was very lucky with the people who were at the club when I was there. To many of the players, I wasn't the manager, I was still

Malcolm MacDonald the player. I was fortunate that I made some great friends. I did things that would be frowned upon today, for example socialising with the players. I always remember them saying, 'You cannae dae this Malky or you cannae dae that!' I did try to promote the club. If a foreign team was coming over to this country to play, we would try to fix up a game with them. If I was proud of anything, it was that I encouraged a lot of foreign teams to come to Rugby Park, opening the club up to new methods and ideas. I had my ups and downs as a player and a manager, but I suppose that you have that in any walk of life.'

As for Waddell, he did indeed leave football, returning to journalism and a job on the *Scottish Daily Express*. David Ross recalled: 'He was a qualified journalist who wrote all his own material with no ghostwriters. He'd had a year in journalism before joining Killie. As far as I can recall he only wrote about football – big match reports and opinion pieces mainly.'

Waddell worked for the *Express* – a major paper whose sales were in steady decline – for four years before the lure of the manager's job at Rangers tempted him back into football in 1969. Just after his appointment at Ibrox, a *Sunday Post* reporter phoned Waddell, expecting co-operation from a former fellow journalist. He was taken aback by the response: 'I am no longer a colleague [of yours]. I am the manager of Rangers and things are different. Our jobs are no longer the same, and neither will our relationship be as it was.' Waddell had instantly reverted to the mindset of a manager, and was again treating the media as an occupational hazard.

Waddell, 'the old growler', as sections of the press called him, was inspired by the challenge at Ibrox. In 1966 he'd been offered the national job but turned it down. 'The pity of it all is that we were not able to synchronise our ideas,' he said, referring to the men of the SFA. 'It would be disloyal of me to go into any detail further than that.' His decision not to manage Scotland came shortly after he'd also finally refused the offer of a directorship at Kilmarnock – an issue unresolved for months.

Killie fans watched their team slip slowly into decline, while Waddell was rebuilding Rangers. He provided strong leadership in the aftermath of the 1971 Ibrox disaster, and led the club to the 1970-71 League Cup and 1972 European Cup-Winners' Cup. He would hand over the reins to assistant Jock Wallace in 1972, becoming general manager, managing director and then vice-chairman before his death in 1992 aged 71.

And so Walter McCrae, trainer for twelve years, and also the national team's sponge-man, took up the challenge of the manager's job at Rugby Park in 1968. His first full season saw a finishing position of fourth, with many of the goals coming from new local hero Eddie Morrison. In April 1969 Eintracht Frankfurt were invited back to Rugby Park to celebrate the Killie centenary and the game ended 1-1. Around the same time, the 1964-

65 championship flag mysteriously went missing, only to be found days later in a locker at Glasgow's Queen Street Station.

The disappearance of the flag in 1968 was portentous, for it seemed to signal the end of the Kilmarnock's stint as one of Scotland's top club sides. It would be a long time before they challenged seriously again.

1969-70 was another mediocre season, lit only by runs to the Scottish Cup semi-final and Fairs Cup third round. Full-back Billy Dickson won his third full cap for Scotland when he faced England. He would be the last Killie outfield player to win senior honours for 28 years (until Ally McCoist in September 1998). The following season was even worse, as Killie won just ten of their 34 games and finished thirteenth. The low point was a home defeat in the Fairs Cup by Northern Irish part-timers Coleraine.

The decline was inevitably mirrored by financial woes. Tommy McLean, probably the most gifted player ever produced by the club, was sold to Rangers in 1971 for a modest fee of £65,000 and a few months later the club went part-time. Current full-time contracts were allowed to expire. The future looked bleak. Although the side battled to the 1971-72 Scottish Cup semi-final, they were beaten 1-3 by Celtic, and could only manage eleventh in the league. Many fans feared that relegation was on the horizon.

Their fears became reality in 1972-73. Failure to beat Falkirk on the season's final day, despite being 2-0 up at half-time, saw Kilmarnock slip out of the top flight after nineteen years – eight years after winning the League title. They'd finished second from bottom and lost nineteen of their 34 league games. The only bright spot was ever-present Eddie Morrison banging in 22 goals in all competitions. Shortly after the start of the following season, manager McCrae was fired and the last real link with the championship side was broken.

Football fans often deal with misery in a humorous way and the gloom of Kilmarnock's relegation was reflected by the adoption of an unlikely song as the new Rugby Park anthem. To the bewilderment of many, the tacky chart hit *Paper Roses* by Marie Osmond started echoing incongruously from the terraces. Why were big beefy Scotsmen singing about 'tender looks mistaken for love' as they munched their pies under slate grey skies? It seems the fans had become so fed up with 'empty promises' by Killie's board of directors that they adopted this song as a form of protest. It stuck, and remains an anthem to this day.

But although *Paper Roses* can still be heard at Kilmarnock, songs about the heroic 'Boys of 1965' no longer echo around Rugby Park. Forty years later, the men who gave Kilmarnock its first and only championship success are spread far and wide. Furthest afield is Bobby Ferguson, who decided to settle in Australia following a fine career in which he won seven full caps. He left Kilmarnock in 1967 when West Ham parted with a world record fee for a goalkeeper of £65,000. He spent twelve years at Upton Park, mostly in the English top flight. Two other players ultimately settled abroad: wing-half Pat O'Connor, who headed for the USA and joined Chicago Spurs in 1967, and inside-left Frank Malone, who never made the Killie team again after the title win, later making South Africa his home.

Among those remaining closer to home is trainer and manager Walter McCrae, who still lives close to Rugby Park. His managerial stint ended in 1973 but he returned in 1980 as club secretary, before retiring in November 1991. A fine servant to Scottish football, he was awarded an OBE in 1992. Another man still often seen locally is former midfield ace Davie Sneddon, who had three seasons at Raith after leaving Killie in 1968. He returned to Rugby Park as manager in 1977, took the club into the Premier League and also led Killie to an unlikely victory in the Tennent's Caledonian Cup preseason tournament at Ibrox. He left Rugby Park for a second time in early 1981, and was later manager of Stranraer for several years. Recently he has worked for Killie in PR and marketing.

In 2004 fans and former colleagues were saddened to hear of the death of centre-half Jackie McGrory, who played 476 senior matches in more than a dozen years at Rugby Park. He only ever scored one goal, sparked several contractual disputes, but was always a big favourite of the fans. For a player who remained largely injury-free over ten years it was a bitter pill to swallow when injury caused his retirement in 1972.

Two other members of the title-winning side have passed away – both of them goalscorers. Bertie Black, scorer of 129 goals between 1952 and 1967, died in 1984. In 2005 he was still the fifth-highest Killie goalscorer of all time. Even higher, at number three, is Brien McIlroy, who banged in 152 goals in a ten-year period, including the goal that won the league championship in 1965. McIlroy died in the late 1990s, after which his widow revealed that for his entire career his name had been misspelt. Everyone regarded him as 'Brian', but she said his first name was James, although he'd always preferred 'Brien' which was his Irish middle name. It was misspelt so often that he never bothered to correct it.

Nestling at No 4 in Killie's goalscoring chart, between McIlroy and Black, is Jackie McInally, who continued in Killie's attack for two years after the title win, before joining Motherwell and later Hamilton. Now based in Ayr, McInally's son Alan had a short spell at Killie before finding fame as a striker at Celtic, Aston Villa and Bayern Munich.

Skipper Frank Beattie, nowadays living in the Bonnybridge area, went on to make 602 first-class appearances, a club record until overtaken by Alan Robertson in 1989. Beattie was granted a testimonial in 1971 against Celtic, during which Jock Stein fielded a prodigy called Kenny Dalglish, who startled everyone by scoring six times. Beattie had broken his leg in a collision with Celtic's Jimmy Johnstone in December 1969 and, despite a brief comeback, had to call it a day. Many thought him the best uncapped wing-half in the game. After leaving Killie, he managed Albion Rovers and Stirling Albion for a season each before becoming a newsagent.

Along with goalkeeping colleague Ferguson, Campbell Forsyth was the only title-winning man who ended up going south, playing 48 league games for Southampton over a three-year period. Some Saints fans remember him mainly as the keeper beaten by Peter Shilton's 100-yard drop kick in 1967. Forsyth retired through injury in June 1968. Twinkle-toed winger Tommy McLean amassed 313 first-class appearances and 73 goals for Killie. He would earn six full caps and enjoyed ten trophy-winning years on Rangers' books after his transfer in 1971. He went on to manage Morton, Raith, Hearts and Motherwell, with whom he won the Scottish Cup.

Full-backs Matt Watson and Andy King are among the unsung heroes of the title-winning team, appearing 821 times between them. Now based in Paisley, Watson chalked up 474 appearances in fourteen years before moving to St Mirren and Queen of the South. King was a regular for ten years at his only league club and still lives locally. Eric Murray also rarely grabbed the headlines, but was the only ever-present in the title-winning season. He left Killie to play for St Mirren and is nowadays based at Symington, where he established a book-keeping business.

Although Sneddon would manage the club, Ronnie Hamilton went one better by having a spell as club chairman in the 1990s. Despite missing much of the final three months of the 1964-65 season, Hamilton still topped the goal chart for league games that year with fifteen. He later scored goals for Queen of the South, before quitting in 1975. He still lives locally, as does Jim McFadzean, a remarkably versatile performer, who combined his football with duties as a school PE instructor.

The surviving members of the title-winning squad were formally reunited for the first time at Towans Hotel, Prestwick, for a 25th anniversary dinner-dance in 1990. Ten years later they gathered again and were invited onto the pitch at half-time during a Killie game, to make the lucky draw and help promote the reprinting of John Livingston's souvenir publication 'We Were the Champions'. The old pals have assembled several times since, and today's visitors to Rugby Park can see reminders of the glory season. There are photos of Waddell dancing out of the tunnel at Tynecastle, for example, and Davie Sneddon's name is engraved on the Moffat Stand as part of the club's Brick in the Wall initiative.

Killie and its stadium have changed beyond recognition since 1964-65, but as former commercial manager Jim McSherry said: 'The title-winning team will always be remembered. They are our version of Celtic's Lisbon Lions. It was a tremendous achievement that might never be repeated.'

Guide to Seasonal Summaries

Col 1: Match number (for league fixtures); Round (for cup-ties).
e.g. 4R means 'Fourth round replay.'

Col 2: Date of the fixture and whether Home (H), Away (A), or Neutral (N).

Col 3: Opposition.

Col 4: Attendances. Home gates appear in roman; Away gates in *italics*.
Figures in **bold** indicate the largest and smallest gates, at home and away.
Average home and away attendances appear after the final league match.

Col 5: Respective league positions of Killie and opponents after the game.
Killie's position appears on the top line in roman.
Their opponents' position appears on the second line in *italics*.
For cup-ties, the division and position of opponents is provided.
e.g. 2:12 means the opposition are twelfth in Division 2.

Col 6: The top line shows the result: W(in), D(raw), or L(ose).
The second line shows Killie's cumulative points total.

Col 7: The match score, Killie's given first.
Scores in **bold** show Killie's biggest league win and heaviest defeat.

Col 8: The half-time score, Killie's given first.

Col 9: The top line shows Killie's scorers and times of goals in roman.
The second line shows opponents' scorers and times of goals in *italics*.
A 'p' after the time of a goal denotes a penalty; 'og' an own-goal.
The third line gives the name of the match referee.

Team line-ups: Killie line-ups appear on top line, irrespective of whether
they are home or away. Opposition teams are on the second line in *italics*.
Players of either side who are sent off are marked !
Killie players making their league debuts are displayed in **bold**.

SCOTTISH DIVISION 1

Manager: Willie Waddell

SEASON 1964-65

148

No	Date	Att	Pos	Pt	F-A	H-T	Scorers, Times, and Referees	1	2	3	4	5	6	7	8	9	10	11
1	H THIRD LANARK	5,197	1	2	W 3-1	0-0	Watson 68, O'Connor 75, Hamilton 85 Todd 49 Ref: W Syme	Forsyth Mitchell	King McGillivray	Watson Davis	O'Connor Little	McGrory McCormack	Beattie Geddes	Murray Todd	McInally Jackson	Hamilton Murray	Sneddon Evans	McIlroy Kerr

Killie look a little disjointed and struggle for the first hour. Bobby Evans' men go ahead via Todd's drive. After McInally hits the bar, Watson fires in a long-range equaliser. This lifts the home side and O'Connor fires a third from close range.

| 2 | A ST MIRREN | 4,636 | 1
16 | 4 | W 2-0 | 0-0 | McIlroy 51, Hamilton 63
Ref: A Kidd | Forsyth
Liney | King
Murray | Watson
Wilson | Murray
Clark | McGrory
Clunie | Beattie
Gray | McIlroy
McIntyre | McInally
Beck | Hamilton
Queen | Sneddon
Allan | McIlroy
Robertson |

Well beaten in Germany in midweek, Waddell changes the line-up again. McInally miskicks a great chance early on. The breakthrough arrives when Hamilton tries his luck from distance and the ball rebounds off the bar for McIlroy to net. A Sneddon corner is headed in by Hamilton.

| 3 | H AIRDRIEONIANS | 5,299 | 1
18 | 6 | W 2-0 | 1-0 | Hamilton 25, McInally 78
Ref: W Brittle | Forsyth
Samson | King
Jonquin | Watson
Keenan | Murray
Stewart | McGrory
Hannah | Beattie
Wishart | McIlroy
Ferguson | McInally
Reid | Hamilton
Hastings | McFadzean
Murray | Sneddon
Newlands |

A dour game is enlivened when Hamilton slots in at the end of a slick move. The two points are finally made safe when McInally converts a hopeful lob forward by Sneddon. Keenan is booked after clashing with Beattie. Forsyth keeps a fifth successive clean sheet in domestic games.

| 4 | A ST JOHNSTONE | 4,829 | 1
10 | 8 | W 1-0 | 0-0 | McInally 55
Ref: R Wilson | Forsyth
Fallon | King
McFadyen | Watson
Coburn | Murray
Richmond | McGrory
McCarry | Beattie
Renton | McIlroy
Hawkshaw | McInally
Harrower | Hamilton
Kerray | McFadzean
McLindon | Sneddon
Kemp |

Waddell is delighted as his controversial 4-2-4 formation helps achieve another clean sheet. Saints have an early goal unluckily disallowed. After the interval McInally slots the winner past Fallon after combining with McIlroy. Renton is booked for two hefty challenges on McInally.

| 5 | H DUNFERMLINE | 10,755 | 1
6 | 10 | W 1-0 | 0-0 | Hamilton 53
Ref: H Phillips | Forsyth
Herriot | King
Thomson | McFadzean
Callaghan W | Murray
Callaghan T | McGrory
McLean | Beattie
Miller | McLean
Edwards | McInally
Ferguson | Hamilton
McLaughlin | Sneddon
Sinclair | McIlroy
Melrose |

Buoyed by midweek heroics against Eintracht, Killie give a league debut to teenager McLean. After a hat-trick last week, Alex Ferguson has to be tightly marked. The Pars battle hard, but Killie get the vital goal when a corner finds McInally, whose fierce shot is prodded in by Hamilton.

| 6 | A HIBERNIAN | 15,471 | 1
5 | 12 | W 2-1 | 1-0 | Hamilton 44, 71
Martin 79
Ref: W Syme | Ferguson
Wilson | King
Fraser | Watson
Peake | Murray
Stanton | McGrory
McNamee | Beattie
Baxter | McIlroy
Cormack | McInally
Hamilton | Hamilton
Scott | McFadzean
Martin | Sneddon
Stevenson |

Ferguson has a fine debut with Forsyth away on Scotland duty. Hamilton opens the scoring against the run of play, netting at the end of a swift raid led by Sneddon. Hamilton heads a second from McInally's cross. The run of clean sheets ends as a Stanton lob is diverted in by Martin.

| 7 | H PARTICK THISTLE | 8,379 | 1
12 | 13 | D 0-0 | 0-0 | Ref: J McConville | Forsyth
Niven | McFadzean
Hogan | Watson
Timney | Murray
Davis | McGrory
McKinnon | Beattie
Cunningham | McLean
Fleming | McInally
Ferguson | Hamilton
Hainey | Sneddon
Duffy | McIlroy
McParland |

Killie's front-runners have an off day and the 100 per cent league record is ended. Thistle's defence are in defiant mood. Martin Ferguson is booked for a foul on Sneddon. Keeper George Niven is the day's star man, making fine saves. Hearts are now one point behind leaders Killie.

| 8 | A DUNDEE | 13,171 | 1
11 | 15 | W 3-1 | 0-1 | Murray 62, Sneddon 64, McInally 68
Murray 23
Ref: J Hamilton | Forsyth
Donaldson | King
Hamilton | Watson
Totten | Murray
Seith | McGrory
Ryden | Beattie
Stuart | McLean
Penman | McInally
Murray | Hamilton
Waddell | McFadzean
Cousin | Sneddon
Robertson |

Stevie Murray wins a race with Forsyth to reach a loose ball and scramble Dundee ahead. Killie are on a roll and within minutes McInally heads a third after a mix-up. Sneddon fires home after a King free-kick is not properly cleared. Killie level up after a corner. Two minutes later Eric Murray levels after a corner.

| 9 | H CELTIC | 19,122 | 1
6 | 17 | W 5-2 | 3-0 | McInally 7, 38, Ham' 26, McFa' 53, 55
Gemmell 62, Gallagher 79
Ref: J Paterson | Forsyth
Fallon | King
Young | Watson
Gemmell | Murray
Brogan | McGrory
Cushley | Beattie
Kennedy | McIlroy
Johnstone | McInally
Murdoch | Hamilton
Chalmers | McFadzean
Gallagher | Sneddon
Lennox |

Waddell has announced he'll quit in eight months, but this is a great night under the lights. McInally nets Hamilton's cross and Hamilton leaps to make it two. Sneddon's corner is cracked in by McInally for a big interval lead. Versatile McFadzean heads two before a mini Celtic revival.

| 10 | A DUNDEE UNITED | 8,567 | 1
16 | 19 | W 1-0 | 0-0 | McInally 69
Ref: T Wharton | Forsyth
Mackay | King
Millar | Watson
Briggs | Murray
Munro | McGrory
Smith D | Beattie
Fraser | McIlroy
McManus | McInally
Graham | Hamilton
Howieson | McFadzean
Gillespie | Sneddon
Smith R |

Tannadice fans are furious when the referee misses Watson's handball in the area. A Fraser cannonball shot lays out poor Beattie. Hamilton sends McInally away with a through ball and he beats four defenders before curling in a wonderful solo goal, good enough to win any game.

| 11 | H MOTHERWELL | 9,698 | 1
7 | 20 | D 1-1 | 1-0 | Hamilton 40
Lindsay 47
Ref: W Syme | Forsyth
Wylie | King
Thomson | Watson
McCallum R | Murray
McCann | McGrory
Delaney | Beattie
McCallum W | McIlroy
Hunter | McInally
Murray | Hamilton
McBride | McFadzean
Weir | Sneddon
Lindsay |

Killie are down to ten men for a long spell when Murray is hurt, but they bombard the visiting defence in the first half. McIlroy feeds Hamilton for the breakthrough goal, but after this the home side goes off the boil. Forsyth pushes a Lindsay shot against a post but it rolls over the line.

#	H/A	Date	Opponent	Attendance	Res	W/D/L	P	Pos	Score	Scorers	Forsyth	King	Watson	Murray	McGrory	Beattie	McLean	McInally	Hamilton	McFadzean	Sneddon
12	H	14/11	RANGERS	32,021	1 D 7 21				1-1 0-0	Beattie 74 / Baxter 63 Ref: W Brittle	Forsyth Ritchie	King Provan	Watson Caldow	Murray Greig	McGrory McKinnon	Beattie Wood	McLean Brand	McInally Millar	Hamilton Forrest	McFadzean Baxter	Sneddon Johnston

Forsyth bounces back from his Everton midweek nightmare to see the reigning champs put under huge pressure. The majestic Jim Baxter nets a low drive, but Beattie bullets in a fine equaliser with his head after a Hamilton shot is parried to him.

| 13 | H | 21/11 | ABERDEEN | 9,101 | 1 D 13 22 | | | | 1-1 0-1 | McInally 89 / Morrison 35 Ref: J Callaghan | Forsyth Ogston | King Shewan | Watson Hogg | Murray Burns | McGrory McCormack | Beattie Smith | McLean Lister | McInally Cooke | Hamilton Morrison | McFadzean Kerrigan | Sneddon Kerr |

Ex-Killie favourite Kerr sets up Morrison for the opening goal. A battling second-half performance in the fog is rewarded seconds from the end when a grounded McInally hooks a wayward shot by Hamilton in off the post. A valuable point won, but the 100 per cent away record is gone.

| 14 | A | 28/11 | CLYDE | 4,863 | 2 W 8 24 | | | | 2-1 2-0 | McFadzean 6, McInally 37 / Knox 63 Ref: A Webster | Forsyth McCulloch | King Glasgow | Watson Mulherron | Murray McHugh | McGrory Fraser | Beattie White | McLean Bryce | McInally Gilroy | Hamilton Knox | McFadzean McLean | Sneddon Hastings |

McFadzean heads home a Sneddon corner and the lead is doubled as McIlroy's cross is nodded by McInally. The Bully Wee the most of complacency and dominate the second half. Debutant Kenny Knox pulls one back. Killie drop to second place, level on points with Hearts.

| 15 | H | 5/12 | FALKIRK | 5,535 | 1 W 13 26 | | | | 2-0 2-0 | McInally 35, Sneddon 41 / Ref: A Kidd | Forsyth Whigham | King Lambie | Watson Hunter | Murray Fulton | McGrory Markie | Beattie Scott | McLean Stewart | McInally Allan | Hamilton Casgrove | McFadzean Moran | Sneddon Gourlay |

A routine win, but Killie's display generally matches the gloomy weather. Sneddon, returning to inside-left, is man of the match against a poor Bairns outfit. Sneddon crosses for McInally to head the first goal and shortly afterwards scores himself with a fierce shot from outside the box.

| 16 | A | 12/12 | MORTON | 10,306 | 2 L 8 26 | | | | 1-5 0-2 | Hamilton 66p / Caven 7, McGraw 41, 48, 71, 83 Ref: J McConville | Forsyth Sorensen E | King Boyd | Watson Johansen | Murray Smith | McGrory Anderson | Beattie Higgins | McLean Strachan | McInally Sorensen J | Hamilton Caven | McFadzean McGraw | Sneddon Wilson |

Caven sprints clear to slip the first past Forsyth. Killie slowly crumble to their first league defeat with Alan McGraw in devastating form. Boyd fouls McInally for a consolation penalty. McGraw's foursome leads to jubilant home fans calling for a lap of honour, but he modestly refuses.

| 17 | H | 19/12 | HEARTS | 18,285 | 2 W 1 28 | | | | 3-1 2-1 | McIlroy 20, Sneddon 44, McIlroy 84 / Gordon 18 Ref: R Davidson | Forsyth Cruikshank | King Sheviane | Watson Holt | Murray Polland | McGrory Anderson | Beattie Higgins | McLean Wallace | McInally Traynor | Hamilton White | McFadzean Gordon | Sneddon Hamilton |

A tense top-of-the-table clash sees Wallace's cross converted by Gordon's spectacular overhead kick. McIlroy drives in a quick response and Killie go ahead as Sneddon cashes in on a Shevlane error. Hamilton knocks in a McIlroy centre and the Rugby Park faithful roar Killie home.

| 18 | A | 26/12 | THIRD LANARK | 2,549 | 2 W 17 30 | | | | 4-0 2-0 | Forsyth / McInally 14, McLean 34, 87, McIlroy 84 Ref: J Stewart | Forsyth Williams | King McKay | Watson Baillie C | Murray Little | McGrory Baillie D | Beattie Geddes | McLean McDonald | McInally Kilgallon | Hamilton Murray | McFadzean Jackson | Sneddon Kirk |

Thirds are torn apart at Cathkin. With most players wearing gloves in the bitter cold, McInally miskicks, but keeper Evan Williams slips and allows it past. McLean's shot then slips under the unhappy keeper. A picture goal by McIlroy is followed by a McLean effort to sew things up.

| 19 | H | 1/1 | ST MIRREN | 12,039 | 1 W 11 32 | | | | 4-0 2-0 | Sneddon 8, Hamilton 33, 61, Murray 81 / Ref: R Wilson | Forsyth Liney | King Murray | Watson Riddell | Murray Gray | McGrory Clunie | Beattie Wilson | McLean Robertson | McInally Quinn | Hamilton Carroll | McFadzean Ross | Sneddon Queen |

The frosty pitch is passed playable in spring-like sunshine. Man-of-the-match Sneddon hooks the first goal. Hamilton grabs a pair as Killie attack relentlessly. Hamilton sets up Murray for the fourth and with Hearts losing to their neighbours Hibs, Killie are back on top of the table.

| 20 | A | 2/1 | AIRDRIEONIANS | 7,808 | 1 L 17 32 | | | | 1-2 0-0 | Hamilton 53 / Rowan 52p, McMillan 72 Ref: D Weir | Forsyth Samson | King Jonquin | Watson Keenan | Murray Reid | McGrory Hannah | Beattie Marshall | McLean Ferguson | McInally McMillan | Hamilton Rowan | McFadzean Moonie | Sneddon Murray |

On another icy pitch, lowly Airdrie battle hard and another of their regular 'Houdini' acts looks underway. Jim Rowan's penalty is cancelled out by Hamilton, who converts a pass by Sneddon. Ian McMillan lashes a 25-yarder past Forsyth to signal a pitch invasion and a shock result.

| 21 | H | 9/1 | ST JOHNSTONE | 6,694 | 1 D 15 33 | | | | 0-0 0-0 | Ref: J Callaghan | Forsyth McVittie | King McFadyen | Watson Coburn | Murray McCarry | McGrory McKinven | Beattie Renton | McLean Flanagan | McInally Harrower | Hamilton Whitelaw | McFadzean Kemp | Sneddon Moonie |

After the miserable Broomfield defeat, in-form reserve striker Frank Malone gets a call up. He fails to pep the attack, however, and Saints are spared by poor finishing. Killie are rarely troubled in defence but the Rugby Park fans go home disappointed by this lack-lustre performance.

| 22 | A | 16/1 | DUNFERMLINE | 9,766 | 2 L 5 33 | | | | 0-1 0-1 | Paton 80 Ref: R Crockett | Forsyth Herriot | King Callaghan W | Watson Lunn | Murray Thomson | McGrory McLean | Beattie Callaghan T | McLean Edwards | McInally Paton | Hamilton McLaughlin | Malone Duffy | Sneddon Sinclair |

Hamilton is injured early on and is a virtual passenger for most of the game. A tight and tense affair is decided ten minutes from time when a loose ball spins to Bert Paton, who crashes it past Forsyth. The Fifers are back in the title hunt, but Killie are off the top again.

| 23 | A | 30/1 | PARTICK THISTLE | 6,560 | 2 L 12 33 | | | | 0-1 0-1 | Ewing 15 Ref: H Phillips | Gray Campbell | King Muir | Watson Davis | Murray Harvey | McGrory McParland | Beattie McLindon | McLean Cunningham | McInally Hainey | Hamilton Ewing | Mason Kilpatrick | McFadzean |

On a tricky pitch, Killie again lack punch. Muir lobs a free-kick forward and after a crucial intervention by Hainey, Ewing beats the advancing Forsyth to poke the ball into the net. Joe Mason gets a rare appearance in place of the injured Hamilton, but cannot lift the out-of-sorts visitors.

SCOTTISH DIVISION 1   Manager: Willie Waddell   SEASON 1964-65

150

No	Date			Att	Pos	Pt	F-A	H-T	Scorers, Times, and Referees	1	2	3	4	5	6	7	8	9	10	11
24	13/2	H	DUNDEE	7,158	4	L	1-4	1-1	Hamilton 22 Cooke 19, 57, Murray 59, Robertson 86 Ref: W Elliott *Charlie Cooke, a new signing from Aberdeen, sidefoots Dundee ahead but Hamilton's header cancels it out. Two in two minutes from the boots of Cooke and Stevie Murray condemn Killie to another defeat. Hugh Robertson bangs in the final goal and Killie slip down the table.*	Forsyth Donaldson	King Hamilton	Watson Cox	Murray Cousin	McGrory Easton	Beattie Stuart	McLean Penman	McNally Murray	Hamilton Cameron	Sneddon Cooke	McIlroy Robertson
25	16/2	H	HIBERNIAN	10,535	4 2	W	4-3 35	1-1	Black 6, 53, Murray 55, King 60 Quinn 20, Martin 87, 89 Ref: T Wharton *Billy Dickson debuts and Black returns to pep off-form Killie. Black taps in the opener. Pat Quinn fires Hibs level, but Killie roar back with three quick goals, the best being Murray's spectacular hooked shot from the edge of the area. Late headers by Neil Martin add to the tension.*	Forsyth Wilson	King Fraser	Dickson Davis	Murray Stanton	McGrory McNamee	Beattie Baxter	McLean Quinn	McNally Hamilton	Hamilton Cormack	Sneddon Martin	Black Stevenson
26	27/2	A	CELTIC	21,875	4 7	L	0-2 35	0-1	Murray 15 (og), Hughes 49 Ref: J Gordon *Steve Chalmers' shot is unluckily deflected past Forsyth by Murray to hand Celtic the lead. Killie apply pressure and a fine diving header by McFadzean is touched on to a post. Moments later John Hughes appears to handle before shooting home but, to Killie dismay, the goal stands.*	Forsyth Fallon	King Young	Watson Gemmell	Murray Clark	McGrory McNeill	Beattie Brogan	McIlroy Chalmers	McNally Murdoch	Hamilton Hughes	McFadzean Lennox	Sneddon Auld
27	10/3	H	DUNDEE UNITED	5,756	4 10	W	4-2 37	1-1	Black 4, 87, McIlroy 54, McLean 64p Dossing 25, Watson 85 (og) Ref: A Crawley *Black nets after McIlroy hits a post but Finn Dossing levels. McIlroy flicks Killie's second, then McLean nets a penalty after Black is pushed. Watson beats his own keeper before lively Black settles Killie nerves from close range. A spirited response to the cup exit four days earlier.*	Forsyth Mackay	King Millar	Watson Briggs	Murray Gordon	McGrory Smith D	McFadzean Wing	McLean Berg	McNally Munro	Black Dossing	Malone Gillespie	McIlroy Persson
28	13/3	A	MOTHERWELL	4,098	2 14	W	2-0 39	0-0	McIlroy 62, Mason 85 Ref: W Mullan *The outside hopes of the title are boosted by this fighting display. McIlroy flicks in McLean's cross on a swift counter-attack. Led by ex-Killie star Joe McBride, The 'Well pile on the pressure but Killie hold out superbly. Mason ensures two points from close range, set up by McNally.*	Forsyth Wylie	King Moore	Dickson McCallum R	Murray McCann	McGrory Delaney	McFadzean Murray	McLean Lindsay	McNally Hunter	Black McBride	Mason Weir	McIlroy Thomson
29	20/3	A	RANGERS	30,574	3 5	D	1-1 40	0-0	Mason 49 Brand 75p Ref: J Hamilton *Killie acquit themselves well in the Ibrox cauldron, with Mason firing them ahead after Beattie's shot is blocked. Near the end, the visitors are stunned to have a penalty appeal turned down, and then at the other end have one controversially awarded against McFadzean. Brand raps it in.*	Forsyth Ritchie	King Provan	McFadzean Caldow	Murray Greig	McGrory McKinnon	Beattie Wood	McLean Brand	McNally Millar	Black Forrest	Mason Beck	McIlroy Wilson
30	27/3	H	ABERDEEN	5,193	3 11	W	2-1 42	2-0	Murray 10, McIlroy 40 Kerrigan 49 Ref: W Syme *McIlroy's cross is headed in by Murray and the lead is extended when Hamilton's through-ball sets up McIlroy. After the break the Dons force the issue and, after Kerrigan's goal, it needs a monumental effort by the home defence to keep them at bay. McLean and Hamilton are injured.*	Ferguson Ogston	King Bennett	McFadzean Shewan	Murray Stewart	McGrory McCormack	Beattie Smith	McLean Little	Mason Winchester	Black Ravn	Hamilton Kerrigan	McIlroy Mortensen
31	3/4	H	CLYDE	5,816	3 8	W	2-1 44	2-0	McInally 10, Hamilton 40 McLean 65p Ref: A Kidd *Coincidentally, Killie go two-up with goals after 10 and 40 minutes, as per last week. McInally outpaces the defence to ram home the first and Hamilton's 30-yard dipper makes it two. McLean's elder brother Jim pulls Clyde back into it and the visitors make life uncomfortable late on.*	Ferguson McCulloch	King Glasgow	Watson Mulheron	Murray White	McGrory McHugh	Beattie Soutar	McLean Bryce	McFadzean Gilroy	Black Knox	Hamilton McLean	McIlroy Hastings
32	7/4	A	FALKIRK	2,569	2 16	W	1-0 46	1-0	McIlroy 35 Ref: R Henderson *Brought forward into midweek to avoid a clash with England v Scotland, this was another grim battle, with Killie repelling pressure. King's free-kick is turned back by Black and McIlroy nets a typical opportunist goal. The win puts Killie back to second, and things are hotting up.*	Ferguson Whigham	King Lambie	Watson Hunter	Murray Pierson	McGrory Baillie	Beattie Scott	McNally Graham	McFadzean Fulton	Black Wilson	Hamilton Moran	McIlroy Halliday
33	17/4	H	MORTON	10,605	2 11	W	3-0 48	0-0	Black 52, 80, McIlroy 81 Ref: J Paterson *If Dunfermline and Hearts slip up today, Killie could be on the verge of the title. Black shoots in off a post and doubles the lead from close range. McIlroy nets a McInally cross to crown a great afternoon. Hearts win 3-0 at Pittodrie, but Dunfermline are out of it, having only drawn.*	Ferguson Sorensen E	King Johansen	Watson Mallon	Murray Smith	McGrory Strachan	Beattie Neilsen	McLean Wilson	McNally Stevenson	Black McGraw	Sneddon Sorensen J	McIlroy Adamson
34	24/4	A	HEARTS	36,346	1 2	W	2-0 50	2-0	Sneddon 26, McIlroy 29 Ref: R Wilson *The decider! Killie have to win by two goals to take the title on goal-average from their hosts. Amid unbearable tension, Sneddon heads in a McLean cross and then McIlroy nets a fine drive from Black's pass. Killie are in dreamland. 61 nail-biting minutes later they are champions.*	Ferguson Cruikshank	King Ferguson	Watson Holt	Murray Polland	McGrory Anderson	Beattie Higgins	McLean Jensen	McNally Barry	Black Wallace	Sneddon Gordon	McIlroy Hamilton

Average   Home 10,507   Away 11,358

League Cup – Section 3

			F-A	H-T	Scorers, Times, and Referees	1	2	3	4	5	6	7	8	9	10	11
S3	H	HEARTS	D 1-1	0-0	McIlroy 53	Forsyth	King	Watson	O'Connor	McGrory	Beattie	McLean	McInally	Hamilton	Sneddon	McIlroy
	8/8	8,832			Higgins 69	*Cruikshank*	*Shevlane*	*Holt*	*Polland*	*Barry*	*Higgins*	*Hamilton*	*Cumming*	*Murphy*	*Sandeman*	*Traynor*
					Ref: R Davidson	Waddell's new 4-2-4 formation, said to be modelled on Inter Milan, is criticised for being negative after this lifeless display. A rainstorm delays the second half. McIlroy hooks in a fine shot to put Killie ahead, but Higgins levels by heading Traynor's left-wing cross past Forsyth.
S3	A	PARTICK THISTLE	D 0-0	0-0		Forsyth	King	Watson	O'Connor	McGrory	Beattie	Murray	Brown	McInally	Sneddon	McIlroy
	12/8	7,767				*Niven*	*Hogan*	*Tinney*	*McParland*	*Harvey*	*Staite*	*Cowan*	*Ewing*	*Hainey*	*Duffy*	*Fleming*
					Ref: J Stewart	The defence certainly looks at home in the new formation, shutting out Thistle with some ease, but fans and opposition remain a little baffled over shirt numbering and who is playing where. Closest thing to a goal is when King tries a 20-yard screamer that beats Niven but goes wide.
S3	A	CELTIC	L 1-4	0-1	Watson 62	Forsyth	King	Watson	O'Connor	McGrory	Beattie	Murray	Brown	McInally	Sneddon	McIlroy
	15/8	22,017			Gallagher 42, 65, Chal' 77, J'stone 79	*Fallon*	*Young*	*Gemmell*	*Clark*	*McNeill*	*Brogan*	*Johnstone*	*Murdoch*	*Chalmers*	*Gallagher*	*Lennox*
					Ref: A Crossman	With Killie one down, the new system falls apart after Watson is injured on 57 minutes and becomes a passenger on the wing. His presence is missed at the back and the home side win with ease. Killie's only goal comes from the limping Watson, who fires home a pass from McInally.
S3	A	HEARTS	W 1-0	0-0	McInally 50	Forsyth	King	Watson	O'Connor	McGrory	Beattie	Murray	McInally	Hamilton	Sneddon	McIlroy
	22/8	10,391				*Cruikshank*	*Shevlane*	*Holt*	*Polland*	*Barry*	*Higgins*	*Wallace*	*Ferguson*	*White*	*Gordon*	*Traynor*
					Ref: W Syme	The players seem to be adapting to Waddell's new ideas and at Tynecastle things go like clockwork, the talented home side looking subdued. Sneddon and McIlroy cause confusion by swapping roles. A Hamilton cross is fired in via the underside of the bar by McInally to win the tie.
S3	H	PARTICK THISTLE	W 4-0	2-0	Hamil' 42, 52, Murray 43, McInally 55	Forsyth	King	Watson	O'Connor	McGrory	Beattie	Murray	McInally	Hamilton	Sneddon	McIlroy
	26/8	6,344				*Niven*	*Hogan*	*Tinney*	*McParland*	*Harvey*	*Staite*	*Cowan*	*Ewing*	*Hainey*	*Duffy*	*Fleming*
					Ref: R Rodger	Hamilton's swirling shot and Murray's fine header put the home side in command. However, by half-time Celtic are 3-0 up against Hearts, effectively ending Killie's interest in this competition. Hamilton nets the third goal from close range and McInally streaks clear for the last.
S3	H	CELTIC	W 2-0	0-0	Hamilton 50p, McIlroy 89	Forsyth	King	Watson	O'Connor	McGrory	Beattie	Murray	McInally	Hamilton	Sneddon	McIlroy
	29/8	10,834				*Fallon*	*Young*	*Gemmell*	*Clark*	*McNeill*	*Kennedy*	*Johnstone*	*Murdoch*	*Chalmers*	*Gallagher*	*Hughes*
					Ref: A McKenzie	Although nothing is at stake, this turns into a stormy affair. Billy McNeill and Bobby Murdoch end up in hospital with leg injuries. Amid the free-kicks and crashing tackles, McIlroy and Hamilton snatch a goal apiece. Missiles are thrown and Celtic fans invade the pitch at the end.

Qual							
	Celtic	6	4	1	1	18	5	9
	KILMARNOCK	6	3	2	1	9	5	8
	Partick Thistle	6	1	2	3	6	14	4
	Hearts	6	1	1	4	7	16	3

SCOTTISH DIVISION 1 (Scottish Cup)   Manager: Willie Waddell   SEASON 1964-65

Scottish Cup

1   H   COWDENBEATH   2   W   5-0   1-0
6/2   6,276   2:17

Scorers, Times, and Referees: McNally 32, 57, 75, McLean 81p, 89
Ref: D Weir

1	2	3	4	5	6	7	8	9	10	11
Forsyth	King	Watson	Murray	McGrory	Beattie	McLean	McNally	Hamilton	Sneddon	McIlroy
Ritchie	*Wilson*	*Jack*	*Burns*	*Clinton*	*Rolland*	*Menzies*	*Dawson*	*Lamont*	*Clark*	*Matthew*

Killie dominate matters on a heavily sanded and slippery pitch. McNally breaks through and goes on to notch the first Killie hat-trick of the season. Second Division Cowdenbeath crumble after the interval and McLean adds two late goals. It's relief after the recent poor league form.

2   A   EAST FIFE   3   D   0-0   0-0
20/2   9,003   2:9

Ref: A Webster

1	2	3	4	5	6	7	8	9	10	11
Forsyth	King	Dickson	Murray	McGrory	Beattie	McLean	McNally	Hamilton	Sneddon	Black
Hamilton	*Stirrat*	*Smith*	*Aitken*	*Walker*	*Donnelly*	*Rodger*	*Dewar*	*Young*	*Stewart*	*Waddell*

At Bayview Park, the Second Division battlers have already knocked Aberdeen out of the Cup and they give Killie much to worry about today. They work hard in defence and employ lightning raids forward. Murray and Hamilton go close but are foiled by superb saves by Ian Hamilton.

2R   H   EAST FIFE   3   W   3-0   1-0
24/2   10,201   2:9

Scorers: McNally 2, 75, Hamilton 88
Ref: A Webster

1	2	3	4	5	6	7	8	9	10	11
Forsyth	King	Dickson	Murray	McGrory	Beattie	McLean	McNally	Hamilton	Sneddon	McIlroy
Hamilton	*Stirrat*	*Smith*	*Aitken*	*Walker*	*Donnelly*	*Cunningham*	*Dewar*	*Young*	*Stewart*	*Waddell*

An opportunist strike early on by McNally puts the Methil side behind, but they bravely keep Killie at bay for the next 73 minutes, much to the home fans' immense frustration. Then McNally nets again to book a quarter-final trip to Celtic Park. Hamilton's late goal is merely academic.

QF   A   CELTIC   4   L   2-3   0-1
6/3   10,834   8

Scorers: McNally 59, 73
Lennox 15, Auld 60, Hughes 67
Ref: H Phillips

1	2	3	4	5	6	7	8	9	10	11
Forsyth	King	Watson	Murray	McGrory	Beattie	Brown	McNally	Hamilton	Sneddon	McIlroy
Fallon	*Young*	*Gemmell*	*Clark*	*McNeill*	*Brogan*	*Chalmers*	*Murdoch*	*Hughes*	*Lennox*	*Auld*

Bobby Lennox nets a disputed goal after a blatant push on Forsyth. Brown's cross finds McNally, who nets an equaliser. Poor Forsyth is again heavily buffeted before Bertie Auld regains the lead. John Hughes makes it three, but McNally ensures a nail-biting finish by pulling one back.

Inter Cities Fairs Cup

1   A   EINTRACHT FRANK'   L   0-3   0-0
2/9   (W Germany) 35,000

Scorers: Stein 55, Trimbold 57, Stinka 75
Ref: A Hauben (Belgium)

1	2	3	4	5	6	7	8	9	10	11
Forsyth	King	Watson	McFadzean	McGrory	Beattie	Murray	McNally	Hamilton	Sneddon	McIlroy
Loy	*Weber*	*Hofer*	*Lindner*	*Landerer*	*Stinka*	*Stein*	*Trimbold*	*Huberts*	*Solz*	*Schamer*

After a goalless first half, Stein seizes on Huberts' miskick to crash the ball in. Trimbold scores at the second attempt to increase the lead. Stinka, who played superbly despite his name, fires in a loose ball for the third. The German crowd sportingly applauds Killie off the park.

1   H   EINTRACHT FRANK'   1   W   5-1   2-1
22/9   14,930

Scorers: Hamil' 12, 88, McIlroy 15, McFad' 52, Huberts 2   [McNally 80]
Ref: J Adair (N Ireland)
(Killie win 5-4 on aggregate)

1	2	3	4	5	6	7	8	9	10	11
Forsyth	King	McFadzean	Murray	McGrory	Beattie	McLean	McNally	Hamilton	Sneddon	McIlroy
Loy	*Blusch*	*Herbert*	*Lindner*	*Weber*	*Stinka*	*Kraus*	*Trimbold*	*Stein*	*Huberts*	*Schamer*

Huberts cracks in a beauty after 90 seconds for 0-4 on aggregate. What follows defies belief. Hamilton hooks in a cross, then McIlroy steers one through Loy's legs. McFadzean heads a third and McNally stoops to level it. Hamilton's deflected shot climaxes an unforgettable night.

2   H   EVERTON   1   L   0-2   0-0
11/11   (England)   23,561   E:8

Scorers: Temple 54, Morrissey 59
Ref: A Albrecht (Holland)

1	2	3	4	5	6	7	8	9	10	11
Forsyth	King	Watson	Murray	McGrory	Beattie	McIlroy	Black	Hamilton	McFadzean	Sneddon
Rankin	*Stevens*	*Brown*	*Gabriel*	*Labone*	*Harris*	*Temple*	*Young*	*Pickering*	*Vernon*	*Morrissey*

After the Eintracht excitement, this become an anti-climax. Derek Temple nets a soft goal after Forsyth is beaten in a race for a loose ball. Then a drive by John Morrissey is helped into the net by the big keeper. He pulls off a great save from Jimmy Gabriel, but the damage is done.

2   A   EVERTON   1   L   1-4   1-2
23/11   30,730   E:5

Scorers: McIlroy 6
Harvey 24, Pickering 34, 70, Young 64
Ref: K Tschenscher (W Germ)
(Killie lose 1-6 on aggregate)

1	2	3	4	5	6	7	8	9	10	11
Forsyth	King	Watson	Murray	McGrory	Beattie	O'Connor	McNally	Hamilton	McFadzean	Sneddon
Rankin	*Harris*	*Brown*	*Gabriel*	*Labone*	*Stevens*	*Temple*	*Young*	*Pickering*	*Harvey*	*Morrissey*

McIlroy shoots home early and Killie force five corners in the opening minutes. The optimism evaporates as Colin Harvey and Fred Pickering crack home smart goals. Classy Alex Young seals Killie's fate. Forsyth handles outside his area and Pickering nets directly from the free-kick.

League Table

	P	W	D	L	F	A	W	D	L	F	A	Pts
			Home						Away			
1 KILMARNOCK	34	12	4	1	38	17	10	2	5	24	16	50
2 Hearts	34	11	3	3	46	24	11	3	3	44	25	50
3 Dunfermline	34	14	2	1	55	14	8	3	6	28	22	49
4 Hibernian	34	11	2	4	44	26	10	2	5	31	21	46
5 Rangers	34	9	5	3	42	16	9	3	5	36	19	44
6 Dundee	34	9	4	4	47	32	6	6	5	39	31	40
7 Clyde	34	10	3	4	35	22	6	5	6	19	36	40
8 Celtic	34	9	2	6	33	18	7	3	7	43	39	37
9 Dundee U	34	10	1	6	38	24	5	5	7	21	27	36
10 Morton	34	9	4	4	38	21	4	3	10	16	33	33
11 Partick T	34	5	5	7	28	30	6	5	6	39	28	32
12 Aberdeen	34	8	5	4	33	27	4	3	10	26	48	32
13 St Johnstone	34	6	6	5	31	24	3	6	8	26	38	29
14 Motherwell	34	4	4	9	24	31	6	4	7	21	23	28
15 St Mirren	34	8	2	7	27	32	4	2	11	11	38	24
16 Falkirk	34	6	5	6	27	26	1	2	14	16	59	21
17 Airdrieonians	34	3	3	11	26	48	2	1	14	22	62	14
18 Third Lanark	34	2	0	15	11	41	1	1	15	11	58	7
	612	146	59	101	623	473	101	59	146	473	623	612

Odds & ends

Double wins: (8) St Mirren, Hibs, Hearts, Dundee U, Clyde, Third Lanark, Motherwell, Falkirk.
Double losses: (0).
Won from behind: (4) Third Lanark (h), Dundee (a), Hearts (h), Eintracht Frankfurt (h) (FC).
Lost from in front: (1) Everton (a) (FC).
High spots: Clinching the club's first title in dramatic fashion. A sensational win over Eintracht Frankfurt after being four down. The 5-2 hammering of Celtic on a great night in October. Jackie McInally's solo goal, which beat Dundee United in October.
Low spots: Willie Waddell quitting after eight years as manager. The poor run in Jan-Feb which nearly scuppered title hopes. The double penalty 'injustice' at Ibrox Park in March.
Distasteful scenes at the August League Cup-tie at home to Celtic.
Hat-tricks for: (1) Jackie McInally (H, v Cowdenbeath, SC).
Hat-tricks against: (1) Alan McGraw (A, v Morton).
Ever-presents: (1) Eric Murray.
Leading scorers: (21) Jackie McInally, Ronnie Hamilton.

Appearances & Goals

	Lge	LC	SC	FC	Lge	LC	SC	FC	Tot
Beattie, Frank	31	6	4	3	1				1
Black, Bertie	9		1	2	6				6
Brown, Hugh	1	2	1						
Dickson, Billy	2		2						
Ferguson, Bobby	8								
Forsyth, Campbell	26	6	4	4					
Hamilton, Ronnie	28	4	4	3	15	3	1	2	21
King, Andy	33	6	4	4	1				1
Malone, Frank	2								
Mason, Joe	4			4	2				2
McFadzean, Jim	26		1	4	3			1	4
McGrory, Jackie	32	6	4	4					
McIlroy, Brien	29	6	3	4	9	2		2	13
McInally, Jackie	32	6	4	3	11	2	7	1	21
McLean, Tommy	19		3	1	3		2		5
Murray, Eric	34	6	4	4	4	1			5
O'Connor, Pat	1	6		1	1				1
Sneddon, Davie	28	6	3	4	5				5
Watson, Matt	29	6	2	3	1	1			2
19 players used	374	66	44	44	62	9	10	6	87

SCOTTISH DIVISION 1 — Manager: Malky MacDonald — SEASON 1965-66

No	Date		Att	Pos	Pt	F-A	H-T	Scorers, Times, and Referees	1	2	3	4	5	6	7	8	9	10	11
1	H 25/8	PARTICK THISTLE	7,806		W 2	2-1	0-0	McIlroy 71, 74; Roxburgh 89; Ref: A Fleming	Ferguson Niven	King Campbell	Watson Muir	Murray McKinnon	Beattie	McFadzean McParland	McLean Gibb	Hamilton Hainey	Black Rae	Sneddon Closs	McIlroy Roxburgh
								Ferguson makes key saves and Thistle hit the woodwork. A nicely-flighted McLean cross is headed in by McIlroy, racing in at speed. Three minutes later he fires in Black's pass. Late on, Andy Roxburgh's hopeful shot ends up in the net. McGrory settles his long-running wages row.											
2	A 11/9	HIBERNIAN	13,385	5 4	D 3	3-3	2-0	McIlroy 32, 33, 71; Martin 51, Cormack 54, Scott 69; Ref: W Syme	Ferguson Wilson	King Simpson	Watson Davis	Murray Stainton	Beattie McNamee	McFadzean Baxter	McLean Cormack	McInally Quinn	Black Scott	Sneddon Martin	McIlroy Stevenson
								McIlroy heads in after a Sneddon free-kick. Wilson fails to hold McInally's shot and McIlroy nets again. Martin pulls one back, then Cormack stabs an equaliser. Scott fires in from 22 yards before McIlroy heads his third. Murray impedes Martin but Cormack's penalty strikes the post.											
3	H 18/9	ST MIRREN	6,536	2 15	W 5	3-1	2-0	McFad' 25, McLean 35p, Ham' 64; Faulds 88; Ref: R Rodger	Ferguson Liney	King McLardy	Watson Riddell	Murray Murray	McGrory Young	McFadzean Kiernan	McLean Robertson	Hamilton Mitchell	Hamilton Queen	McFadzean Faulds	McIlroy Adamson
								In a reshuffled line-up, McFadzean shoots home McLean's through ball. Young hauls down McIlroy and McLean nets from the spot. Ferguson drops a couple of crosses but gets away with it. Killie make it three, set up by McFadzean's throw to Hamilton. Faulds nods a late consolation.											
4	A 25/9	DUNFERMLINE	7,104	6 3	L 5	0-1	0-0	Robertson 90p; Ref: J Hamilton	Ferguson Martin	King Callaghan W	Watson! Lumn	O'Connor Thomson	McGrory McLean	Beattie Callaghan T	McLean Edwards!	McInally Smith	Hamilton Maxwell	Sneddon Ferguson	McIlroy Robertson
								Killie are a shadow of the side which played here earlier in the League Cup. Ferguson keeps them in the match with superb saves. In a stormy finish, King handles Ferguson's header and Robertson converts the winner. Watson and Edwards then tangle on the touchline and are sent off.											
5	H 2/10	HAMILTON	5,155	5 18	W 7	3-1	2-1	McIlroy 27, McLean 45p, King 63; Alexander 22; Ref: J Stewart	Ferguson Lamont	King Forest	Watson Holton	O'Connor Bowman	McGrory Small	Beattie McCann	McLean Horne	McInally Anderson	Black Alexander	Hamilton Gilmour	McIlroy McClare
								Anderson and Alexander combine to give Ferguson no chance. McIlroy nets a fine cross by Black to level it. In first-half injury-time Lamont pulls down Hamilton and McLean scores from the spot. Lowly Accies are spared more punishment until King cracks home a deflected drive.											
6	A 9/10	STIRLING	3,985	4 11	W 9	3-2	1-1	McIlroy 17, Hamilton 52, 68; Murray 27, Westwater 48; Ref: J MacConville	Ferguson Taylor	King McGuinness	Dickson Murray	Murray Reid	McGrory Robb	Beattie Sutherland	McLean Westwater	McInally Fyfe	Hamilton Fleming	Hamilton Duncan	McIlroy Hall
								MacDonald fails in a bold bid to sign Everton's Alex Young and switches his focus to Ipswich's Gerry Baker. McIlroy touches in Hamilton's pass, then a cross by Murray swirls past Ferguson. Killie defend badly to let in Westwater, but Hamilton bags two, the second in a breakaway.											
7	H 16/10	DUNDEE	7,829	3 8	W 11	5-3	2-2	Ham' 4, 79, McFad' 6, 65, McLean 55p; McLean 14, Penman 16, Cameron 87; Ref: T Wharton	Ferguson Donaldson	King Hamilton	Dickson Cox	Murray Cooke	McGrory Easton	Beattie Stuart	McLean Murray	McInally Penman	Hamilton Cameron	McFadzean McLean	McIlroy Harvey
								Hamilton swoops as Donaldson drops the ball and then McFadzean fires home a beauty. Rugby Park is silenced as the lead is quickly wiped out. Easton upends Hamilton for a McLean penalty. McFadzean's header and a Hamilton drive make it safe, before Cameron pulls one back.											
8	A 23/10	MORTON	8,458	2 7	W 13	4-1	2-0	McIlroy 30, 48, 82, Hamilton 43; Watson 67; Ref: N Watson	Ferguson Sorensen	King Loughan	Dickson Gray	Murray Neilsen	McGrory Madsen	Beattie Strachan	McLean Watson	McInally Graham	Hamilton Stevenson	Hamilton McGraw	McIlroy McIntyre
								McFadzean dummies Beattie's cross for the first, then Hamilton fires a fine goal. McIlroy completes his hat-trick after the break with Watson hooking a consolation for the Cappielow men, who have penalty claims turned down. Two are booked and home fans hurl on bottles and cans.											
9	H 30/10	CLYDE	6,362	5 12	L 13	1-2	0-0	Hamilton 52; McFarlane 48, Hastings 75; Ref: D Small	Ferguson McCulloch	King Glasgow	Dickson Mulheron	Murray McHugh	McGrory Fraser	Beattie White	McLean McFarlane	McInally Gilroy	Hamilton Knox	McFadzean Bryce	McIlroy Hastings
								Ferguson and King in Scotland's 1966 World Cup pool and need to give a good display. King concedes an unnecessary corner, from which McFarlane nets a fierce drive. Hamilton quickly whips in an equaliser. MacDonald announces plans to spy on cup opponents Real Madrid.											
10	A 6/11	ABERDEEN	8,907	6 7	L 13	0-1	0-0	Melrose 67; Ref: E Thomson	Ferguson Clark	King Whyte	Watson Shewan	Murray Petersen	McGrory McMillan	Beattie Smith	McLean Little	Black Melrose	Hamilton White	Sneddon Winchester	McIlroy Wilson
								Clark saves well and Hamilton goes close in the first half. The Dons miss chances before pressure pays off: a Melrose shot beats Ferguson as he goes down late. Killie enjoy a good spell but cannot find an equaliser.											
11	H 13/11	MOTHERWELL	6,689	5 14	W 15	5-0	1-0	McInally 23, McIlroy 66, 69, Ham' 75, [Murray 86]; Ref: A Webster	Ferguson McCloy	King Thomson M	Watson McCallum	Murray Aitken	McGrory Martis	McFadzean Murray	McLean Moffat	McInally Hunter	Hamilton McLaughlin	Sneddon Thomson I	McIlroy Campbell
								McInally heads in after Hamilton hits a post. McCloy is injured in a clash with McInally and McIlroy swoops to score with the keeper prone. He is replaced by McCallum who is beaten three times, including by Hamilton, who is clearly yards offside. Killie also hit the crossbar twice.											

154

#	H/A	Date	Opponent	Att	W/L/D	Pos	Score	Scorers / Ref	Team	Match Report
12	A	20/11	RANGERS	33,225	L	15	0-5	McLean 19, 23p, 50, Johnston 42, 79 Ref: J Barclay	Ferguson, King, Dickson, Murray, McGrory, O'Connor, McLean, McInally, Hamilton, Sneddon, McIlroy / Ritchie, Johansen, Provan, Watson, McKinnon, Greig, Henderson, Willoughby, Forest, McLean, Johnston	Rangers are rampant and this is one-sided. George McLean shows fine control to net the first from Henderson's cross. McLean scores from the spot after Henderson is fouled. A wayward Killie pass sets up Johnston for the killer third and the winger completes the job with a solo effort.
13	A	27/11	CELTIC	21,131	L	15	0-3	McIlroy 57 Hughes 67p, McBride 83 Ref: A McKenzie	Ferguson, King, Dickson, Murray, McGrory, O'Connor, McLean, McInally, Hamilton, Sneddon, McIlroy / Simpson, Craig, Gemmell, Murdoch, Cushley, Clark, Johnstone, McBride, Chalmers, Lennox, Hughes	Killie put up a valiant fight against the other half of the 'old firm'. On a tricky pitch, Killie surge into the lead, McIlroy tucking the ball home with Celtic screaming in vain for offside. Ferguson and Chalmers tangle and a penalty provides the equaliser. McBride slams in a late winner.
14	A	11/12	FALKIRK	2,617	L	15	1-1	McLean 44p, McFadzean 89 Graham 23, 61, Lambie 51 Ref: J Kelly	Ferguson, King, Dickson, Murray, McGrory, O'Connor, McLean, McInally, Hamilton, Sneddon, McIlroy / Whigham, Markie, Hunter, Rowan, Baillie, Fulton, Haddock, Lambie, Moran, Graham, McKinney	Graham shoots the Brockville men ahead but Killie level after the ball strikes Hunter's arm for a spot-kick. Lambie finishes off good work by McFadzean, who adds the third himself. McFadzean raises brief hopes. Beattie has now won just once in seven games.
15	A	18/12	DUNDEE UNITED	7,170	D	16	0-0	Ref: H Phillips	Ferguson, King, Dickson, Murray, McGrory, Beattie, Brown, McInally, Hamilton, McFadzean, McIlroy / Mackay, Millar, Briggs, Neilson, Smith, Wing, Seeman, Munro, Dossing, Gillespie, Persson	Lady Luck at last smiles on Killie and the Tannadice men can't believe they fail to win this one. Ferguson performs heroically while under constant siege. Beattie gives Dickson a torrid afternoon. Killie nearly snatch a late winner but Mackay saves.
16	H	25/12	ST JOHNSTONE	4,493	W	18	3-1	McLean 25p, McIlroy 35, Hamilton 57 Cowan 80 Ref: W Syme	Ferguson, King, Dickson, McFadzean, McGrory, Beattie, McLean, McInally, Hamilton, McFadzean, McIlroy / McVittie, Michie, Coburn, McCarry, McKinven, Renton, Cowan, McPhie, Kerray, Duffy, Kemp	A Christmas Day return to winning ways. Coburn's tackle on McInally is deemed a penalty despite fierce protests. McIlroy makes it two with a diving header from McFadzean's cross. A half-hit Hamilton shot finds its way in for a third goal. Kemp's cross is converted by Cowan late on.
17	A	1/1	ST MIRREN	3,906	W	20	7-4	McIlroy 9, 64, Mason 14, McLean 29, Robertson 23, 53p, Adamson 47, 75 [McInally 35, 43, Murray 87] Ref: R Wilson	Ferguson, King, Dickson, Murray, McGrory, Beattie, McLean, McInally, Mason, McFadzean, McIlroy / Thorburn, Murray, Clark, Mitchell, Kiernan, Pinkerton, Aird, Queen, Adamson, Gemmell, Robertson	Lowly St Mirren battle hard and play their part in this goal feast. McIlroy's low drive and McFadzean's glancing header get things moving. McLean hits a fierce third and McInally nets a pair, including a typical solo effort. McIlroy grabs the sixth and Murray gets in on the act with a header.
18	H	3/1	HIBERNIAN	11,298	W	22	1-0	Mason 45 Ref: H Phillips	Ferguson, King, Dickson, Murray, McGrory, Beattie, McLean, McInally, Mason, Sneddon, McIlroy / Simpson, Davis, Stainton, McNamee, Baxter, Hogg, Cousin, Hainey, Scott, O'Rourke, Cormack	Sneddon strikes wood and Killie miss chances, finding man-of-the-match Willie Wilson in splendid form in the Hibs goal. Ten seconds before the interval Murray floats a high ball into the box and Mason outjumps Wilson to head Killie in front. A deserved win and the revival goes on.
19	A	8/1	PARTICK THISTLE	6,310	L	22	0-1	Hainey 44 Ref: A McKenzie	Ferguson, King, Dickson, Murray, McGrory, Beattie, McLean, McInally, Mason, McFadzean, McIlroy / Niven, Campbell, Muir, Cunningham, McKinnon, Gibb, McLindon, Hainey, Rae, McParland, Duncan	Firhill has become a bogey ground for Killie. Today they find The Jags full of fight and McParland, returning from injury, plays a key role. Hainey picks up a pass a long way out and moves forward, poking his shot through a crowd of defenders and in at Ferguson's left-hand post.
20	H	15/1	DUNFERMLINE	8,526	W	24	1-0	McInally 86	Ferguson, King, Dickson, Murray, McGrory, Beattie, McLean, McInally, Mason, Sneddon, McIlroy / Martin, Callaghan W, Lumm, Smith, McLean, Thomson, Edwards, Fleming, Hunter, Ferguson, Robertson	On a frozen pitch, Killie only get to grips with the game in the later stages, storming to an exciting victory. With the Fifers wilting, Sneddon's corner is headed home by the diving figure of McInally. MacDonald brings in Gerry Queen, signed from St Mirren in exchange for Hamilton.
21	A	22/1	HAMILTON	2,573	W	26	4-1	Mason 5, Queen 44, 52, McInally 78 Anderson 56 Ref: W Mullan	Ferguson, King, Dickson, Murray, McGrory, Beattie, McLean, McInally, Mason, Queen, McIlroy / Brown, Forrest, Halpin, Hinshelwood, Gaughan, King, Currie, Anderson, Alexander, Gilmour, Holton	Mason flicks the first goal past Brown. Debutant Queen goes close twice before a low, angular shot flies in and then after the break he buries another. Anderson has a shot deflected away from Ferguson by the unlucky Murray. McInally runs on to Queen's pass to crash home a fourth.
22	H	29/1	STIRLING ALBION	5,651	W	28	2-1	McGuinness 35 (og), Queen 67 Hall 88 Ref: D Weir	Ferguson, King, Dickson, Murray, McGrory, Beattie, McLean, McInally, Mason, Queen, McIlroy / Taylor, McGuinness, Dickson, Reid, Robb, Thomson, Grant, McKinnon, Fleming, Gardiner, Hall	In a drab game, Killie get lucky as Taylor misses a high ball and it rebounds off McGuinness into the net. Mason and McLean combine on the right to feed home debutant Queen, who shoots his third goal for the club. Albion rarely look threatening, but late on a Hall shot swerves in.
23	A	12/2	DUNDEE	8,782	W	30	2-0	Black 29, 40 Ref: W Anderson	Ferguson, King, Dickson, Murray, McGrory, Beattie, McLean, McInally, Mason, Black, McIlroy / Donaldson, Hamilton, Cox, Beattie, Easton, Stuart, Murray, Scott, Penman, McLean, Cameron	Alec Hamilton's header back to Ally Donaldson is fumbled badly and McIlroy swoops to set up Black from 12 yards. Black and Queen swap passes before Black fires home a firm, low drive. Dundee heads drop and their only real chance sees King clear a Penman effort off the line.

SCOTTISH DIVISION 1 — SEASON 1965-66

Manager: Malky MacDonald

156

No	Date		Att	Pos	Pt	F-A	H-T	Scorers, Times, and Referees	1	2	3	4	5	6	7	8	9	10	11
24	A 26/2	CLYDE	5,137	4 10	W 32	4-1	1-1	Queen 20, Murray 49, Black 85, Hastings 42p [McLean 87p] Ref: R Crockett	Ferguson *McCulloch*	King *Glasgow*	Watson *Mulheron*	Murray *McHugh*	McGrory *Fraser*	Beattie *White*	McLean *McFarlane*	McInally *Stewart*	Black *Knox*	Queen *Bryce*	McIlroy *Hastings*
								Queen fires in a neat back-heeled pass by Black. Bryce is pulled down by Murray for Hastings' penalty. Murray's fierce shot regains the lead. Black makes the points safe after McLean sends a perfect pass through the mud to him. Black is impeded and McLean fires in the penalty kick.											
25	H 28/2	MORTON	7,148	3 11	W 34	4-0	2-0	McInally 13, 63, Queen 41, Murray 70 Ref: T Wharton	Ferguson *Sorensen*	King *Boyd*	Dickson *Kennedy*	Murray *Strachan*	McGrory *Madsen*	Beattie *Gray*	McLean *Stevenson*	McInally *Smith*	Black *McIntyre*	Queen *Arentoft*	McIlroy *Watson*
								An unwell McIlroy is replaced by Sneddon. After Kennedy's lob is pushed onto the bar, McInally beats two men before crashing in a beauty. A McLean drive hits the bar. Black is the provider for Queen and then McInally, who sweeps in his second. Murray prods in a Sneddon cross.											
26	H 9/3	ABERDEEN	5,592	3 8	L 34	1-3	0-0	McLean 60p Beattie 50 (og), Melrose 55, Smith 58 Ref: I Foote	Ferguson *Clark*	King *Whyte*	McFadzean *Shewan*	Murray *Petersen*	McGrory *McMillan*	Beattie *Smith*	McLean *Little*	McInally *Melrose*	Bertelsen *White*	Queen *Winchester*	McIlroy *Wilson*
								Dane Carl Bertelsen signs from Dundee for £6,000 and has a reasonable debut. The Dons stun Killie with three in eight minutes. Beattie's back pass deceives Ferguson, Melrose nets a fine drive and Smith scores after a mix-up. Queen is tripped and McLean pulls one back from the spot.											
27	A 12/3	MOTHERWELL	4,383	3 15	W 36	3-0	2-0	McInally 1, 62, McIlroy 14 Ref: J Stewart	Ferguson *Wylie*	King *Delaney*	McFadzean *McCallum R*	Murray *McCallum W*	McGrory *Campbell*	Beattie *Murray*	McLean *Deans*	McInally *Hunter*	Bertelsen *Cairney*	Queen *Thomson*	McIlroy *Donnachie*
								McInally scores a typical goal in under 30 seconds, dribbling past two men, evading another and lashing in a cracking shot. It's easy for Killie and McIlroy has plenty of time to nonchalantly tuck in a second with Wylie all at sea. McInally is hurt, colliding with Wylie in netting a third.											
28	H 19/3	RANGERS	25,372	3 2	D 37	1-1	0-0	McLean 89 Forrest 81 Ref: R Wilson	Ferguson *Ritchie*	King *Johansen*	McFadzean *Provan*	Murray *Mathieson*	McGrory *McKinnon*	Beattie *Greig*	McLean *Henderson*	McInally *Miller*	Bertelsen *Forrest*	Queen *McLean*	McIlroy *Johnston*
								Defences dominate and there is stalemate until near the end. Title-chasing Rangers take the lead as Forrest heads in a fierce cross by Johnstone. O'Connor feeds McLean, whose hopeful shot is left by Greig and Ritchie for each other, and drifts into the net off a post for a lucky equaliser.											
29	H 29/3	CELTIC	25,035	3 1	L 37	0-2	0-2	Lennox 10, 35 Ref: A Webster	Ferguson *Simpson*	King *Young*	McFadzean *Gemmell*	Murray *Murdoch*	Beattie *McNeill*	O'Connor *Clark*	McLean *Johnstone*	McInally *McBride*	Black *Chalmers*	Queen *Lennox*	McIlroy *Auld*
								Jock Stein's men are close to clinching the title after crushing Killie in the first half. Murdoch's long ball finds Lennox who carefully arrows his shot past Ferguson. Johnstone's low cross into the area beats Ferguson, is blocked on the line by King, but falls nicely for Lennox to net.											
30	H 4/4	HEARTS	5,026	3 7	D 38	2-2	0-2	McInally 55, Bertelsen 80 Wallace 2, 37 Ref: W Syme	Ferguson *Cruickshank*	King *Shevlane*	McFadzean *Holt*	Murray *Anderson*	McGrory *Barry*	Beattie *Higgins*	McLean *Hamilton*	McInally *Murphy*	Bertelsen *Wallace*	Queen *Gordon*	McIlroy *Traynor*
								Wallace races into the area from Hamilton's cross. He sweeps home another from Hamilton's cross. McInally launches the fight for a point by crashing in a McLean cross. McFadzean's free-kick is met by Bertelsen who heads a fine equliser with his first league goal for Killie.											
31	A 9/4	HEARTS	6,209	3 7	W 40	3-2	1-2	Bertelsen 39, McIlroy 51, 84 Hamilton 10, Traynor 42 Ref: A Crawley	Ferguson *Cruickshank*	King *Shevlane*	Watson *Holt*	Murray *Anderson*	McGrory *Barry*	Beattie *Higgins*	McLean *Hamilton*	McInally *Murphy*	Bertelsen *Wallace*	Queen *Gordon*	McIlroy *Traynor*
								Goalmouth scambles produce a goal for each side, before Traynor lashes in a tremendous solo effort. Hearts are unhappy over five refused penalty appeals and a disallowed goal. After Bertelsen miskicks. McIlroy nets a winner from a tight angle. Hearts have a fine game, but both defences hold firm in a fast and furious finish.											
32	H 16/4	FALKIRK	3,773	3 10	W 42	1-0	1-0	McIlroy 39 Ref: R Davidson	Ferguson *McDonald*	King *Markie*	Watson *Hunter*	Murray *Rowan*	McGrory *Rae*	Beattie *Smith*	McLean *Brown*	McInally *Fulton*	Bertelsen *Moran*	Queen *Graham*	McIlroy *McKinney*
								In search of a Fairs Cup place, Killie do little to warm up the low crowd in the bitterly cold conditions. Ferguson's long punt upfield is headed on by Bertelsen and McIlroy, in superb form just now, glides in a shot, despite Rae's attempts to block. There's little else to entertain the fans.											
33	H 23/4	DUNDEE UNITED	5,711	3 5	W 44	1-0	0-0	Queen 65 Ref: W Anderson	Ferguson *Davie*	King *Millar*	Watson *Briggs*	Murray *Neilson*	McGrory *Smith*	Beattie *Wing*	McLean *Hainey*	McInally *Munro*	Bertelsen *Dossing*	Queen *Gillespie*	McIlroy *Mitchell*
								Billed as a Fairs Cup place 'decider', both sides go hell for leather for the win. The stalemate is broken when a long clearance by Ferguson is pushed on by Bertelsen for Queen to convert from close range. Wing has a fine game, but both defences hold firm in a fast and furious finish.											
34	A 30/4	ST JOHNSTONE	2,441	3 15	D 45	1-1	0-0	Bertelsen 75 McDonald 74 Ref: D Weir	Ferguson *Donaldson*	King *Richmond*	Watson *Coburn*	Murray *Walker*	McGrory *McKinven*	Beattie *Renton*	McLean *Cowan*	McInally *Whitelaw*	Bertelsen *McDonald*	Queen *Clark*	McIlroy *Kemp*
								Cowan's pass is netted by McDonald, with a well-placed shot. Seconds later Bertelsen heads in Watson's cross. Frustratingly, Killie are below par and pass up the chance to make absolutely certain of Fairs Cup qualification. Dunfermline lose at Celtic later on, so all is well eventually.											

Home 8,706 Away 8,573 Average 8,573

League Cup – Section 3

				F-A	H-T	Scorers, Times, and Referees
S3	A	ST JOHNSTONE	W	1-0	1-0	McIlroy 10
	14/8	5,810				Ref: R Wilson
S3	H	PARTICK THISTLE	W	2-0	1-0	Black 29, McIlroy 88
	18/8	9,758				
S3	A	DUNFERMLINE	W	3-1	0-1	McLean 68, Sneddon 76, McIlroy 90, Robertson 44
	21/8	9,073				Ref: R Henderson
S3	H	ST JOHNSTONE	W	3-0	0-0	Black 78, 88, Sneddon 83
	28/8	7,309				Ref: J Paterson
S3	A	PARTICK THISTLE	W	2-1	1-1	McIlroy 38, McInally 82, Roxburgh 44
	1/9	3,926				Ref: A Webster
S3	H	DUNFERMLINE	L	0-1	0-0	Paton 89
	4/9	6,858				Ref: D Weir

Qual					
KILMARNOCK	6	5	0	1	11	3	10
Dunfermline	6	3	1	2	14	9	7
St Johnstone	6	3	0	3	7	10	6
Partick Thistle	6	0	1	5	3	13	1

QF	H	AYR	W	2-0	0-0	McIlroy 64, Black 77
1	15/9	10,728 2:13				Ref: T Wharton
QF	A	AYR	D	2-2	1-2	Murray 7, McIlroy 79, Murphy 19, McMillan 28
2	22/9	8,495 2:16				Ref: J Stewart
						(Killie win 4-2 on aggregate)
SF	N	RANGERS	L	4-6	1-3	McInally 36, McLean 70, 77p, 85, McLean 12, 44p, 50, Willoughby 32,
	6/10	54,702 1				Ref: J Paterson
	(At Hampden)					[Forrest 64, Henderson 66]

Line-ups

Date	1	2	3	4	5	6	7	8	9	10	11
14/8	Ferguson / McVittie	King / McFadyen	Watson / Coburn	Murray / McCarrie	Beattie / McKinven	McFadzean / Renton	McLean / McGrogan	McInally / Whitelaw	Black / Kerray	Sneddon / Maxwell	McIlroy / Kemp
18/8	Ferguson / Niven	King / Campbell	Watson / Muir	Murray / Hogan	Beattie / McKinnon	McFadzean / Gibb	McLean / Hainey	McInally / McParland	Black / Rae	Sneddon / Roxburgh	McIlroy / Closs
21/8	Ferguson / Martin	King / Callaghan W	Watson / Lunn	Murray / Thomson	Beattie / McLean	McFadzean / Callaghan T	McLean / Edwards	McInally / Smith	Black / Hunter	Sneddon / Ferguson	McIlroy / Robertson
28/8	Ferguson / McVittie	King / McFadyen	Watson / Coburn	Murray / Richmond	Beattie / McKinven	McFadzean / Renton	McLean / Kerray	McInally / Duffy	Black / Whitelaw	Sneddon / Maxwell	McIlroy / McGrogan
1/9	Ferguson / Gray	King / Campbell	Watson / Muir	Murray / Hogan	Beattie / McKinnon	McFadzean / Gibb	Brown / Cowan	McInally / McParland	Black / Rae	Sneddon / Roxburgh	McIlroy / Kilpatrick
4/9	Ferguson / Martin	King / Callaghan W	Watson / Lunn	Murray / Smith	Beattie / Thomson	McFadzean / Callaghan T	Brown / Edwards	McInally / Paton	Black / Hunter	Sneddon / Ferguson	McIlroy / Robertson
15/9	Ferguson / Paton	King / Malone	Watson / Murphy	Murray / Thomson	McGrory / Monan	Beattie / McAnespie	McLean / Grant	McFadzean / McMillan	Black / Moore	Sneddon / Hawkshaw	McIlroy / Paterson
22/9	Ferguson / Paton	King / Malone	Watson / Murphy	Murray / Oliphant	McGrory / Monan	Beattie / McAnespie	McLean / Grant	McFadzean / McMillan	Hamilton / Moore	Sneddon / Hawkshaw	McIlroy / Paterson
6/10	Ferguson / Ritchie	King / Johansen	Watson / Provan	Murray / Wood	McGrory / McKinnon	Beattie / Greig	McLean / Henderson	McInally / Willoughby	Black / Forrest	Hamilton / McLean	McIlroy / Johnston

Match reports

14/8: McLean tricks Coburn and hammers in a shot which McFadyen blocks on the line, but McIlroy steams in to pounce and score. Killie miss chances to make it safe, with Black the main culprit. McGrory is missed in defence and is mainly due to Ferguson's sterling work.

18/8: The championship flag is officially unfurled for the first time over Rugby Park before kick-off, but a scrappy game follows. Black's low drive puts Killie ahead from McLean's assist. The second goal finally arrives near the end as McIlroy beats Niven to the ball to bury a neat header.

21/8: The East End Park side attack furiously in the first period and go ahead through Robertson from close range. Killie take command after the break and McLean's long-range shot is deflected in. Sneddon's first time shot gives Martin no chance and McIlroy nets just before the close.

28/8: Killie only look like champs in the final stages. Black breaks the deadlock with 12 minutes left, looking offside. McLean's through-ball finds Sneddon who smashes home a fierce drive. Kilmarnock have to make two goalline clearances before Black's ate header ensures the victory.

1/9: Sneddon sends McIlroy away and he races down the left, cuts in and fires a low shot home. Roxburgh brings the game level from close range. The Jags press hard for a winner but find Martin in fine form. Chances go begging and in the second half tempers fray. Paton and T Callaghan are booked. With frustration growing, Smith suddenly darts past Watson and squares for Paton to flick a surprise last ditch-winner past Ferguson.

4/9: Killie start at a cracking pace but find Martin in fine form. Chances go begging and in the second half tempers fray. McInally decides the match late on and this goal also clinches section victory.

15/9: In this first-leg local derby, the young underdogs from Ayr look lively and keep the score-line goalless until past the hour mark. McIlroy bursts clear from Sneddon's pass and his shot squeezes in after being only half-saved. Sneddon's cross is nodded on by Murray for Black to score.

22/9: Murray hits a left-foot drive high into the net and the contest appears to be over. Ayr have other ideas and press forward continually. Murphy fires an equaliser with the aid of a deflection and McMillan flicks in the second. McIlroy stabs home a late face-saver for the nervous visitors.

6/10: Rangers turn on the style early, but McInally's brilliant goal stems the flow. The walkover then resumes and with 20 minutes left Rangers are cruising at 6-1. Little McLean then nets an astonishing quick-fire hat-trick to save Killie blushes, including a penalty after McInally is floored.

SCOTTISH DIVISION 1 (Scottish Cup)   Manager: Malky MacDonald   SEASON 1965-66

Scottish Cup

			F-A	H-T	Scorers, Times, and Referees	1	2	3	4	5	6	7	8	9	10	11
1	A MORTON	4 D 1-1	0-1	Queen 78	Ferguson	King	Watson	Murray	McGrory	Beattie	McLean	McInally	Mason	Queen	McIlroy
	5/2	9,735 15			McGraw 44	Sorensen	Boyd	Loughan	Strachan	Madsen	Kennedy	Harper	Smith	McGraw	Stevenson	Watson
					Ref: T Wharton	An end-to-end first half culminates with Ferguson failing to gather a Boyd shot and local hero McGraw pounces to crash the ball in from close range. Huge relief for the travelling fans when McLean's corner bobbles around and falls for Queen, who cracks in the deserved equaliser.
1R	H MORTON	4 W 3-0	2-0	Beattie 8, Black 29, Queen 46	Ferguson	King	Watson	Murray	McGrory	Beattie	McLean	McInally	Black	Queen	McIlroy
	9/2	11,109 15				Sorensen	Boyd	Loughan	Strachan	Madsen	Kennedy	Harper	Smith	McGraw	Stevenson	Watson
					Ref: T Wharton	After a McLean corner, Beattie finds the net from close range. Black takes a pass from Queen, swivels and sends a rocket into the Morton net for one of the goals of the season. A minute after the restart the contest is over as Queen's pot-shot from 25 yards sneaks its way past Sorensen.
2	H MOTHERWELL	4 W 5-0	2-0	Queen 4, McIlroy 11, McInally 67,	Ferguson	King	Watson	Murray	McGrory	Beattie	McLean	McInally	Black	Queen	McIlroy
	21/2	13,209 15			(McCallum W 82 (og), Black 84]	McCloy	Delaney	McCallum R	McCallum W	Martis	Murray	Cairney	Lindsay	McLaughlin	Thomson	Campbell
					Ref: A Webster	This tie is put back two days due to a blizzard. Black feeds Queen for a clinical finish. McIlroy then makes the most of Delaney's hesitation. McInally nets a third after a long run. McIlroy's free-kick flies in off McCallum's head. Black bursts through the middle to add a superb fifth.
3	A DUNFERMLINE	4 L 1-2	1-0	McInally 39	Ferguson	King	McFadzean	Murray	McGrory	Beattie	McLean	McInally	Black	Queen	Sneddon
	5/3	19,363 3			Paton 67, Edwards 88	Martin	Callaghan W	Lumb	Thomson	McLean	Callaghan T	Edwards	Smith	Maxwell	Ferguson	Robertson
					Ref: T Wharton	McInally races clear and prods in after going round Martin. Killie's splendid defence is finally pierced as Paton brushes Beattie aside and rifles high into the net. An absorbing and tense contest is settled near the end as Edwards picks up a neat pass, draws Ferguson out and shoots home.

European Cup

			F-A	H-T	Scorers, Times, and Referees	1	2	3	4	5	6	7	8	9	10	11
1:1	A 17 NANDORI TIRANA	D 0-0	0-0		Ferguson	King	Watson	Murray	Beattie	McFadzean	McLean	McInally	Black	Sneddon	McIlroy
	8/9 (Albania)	35,000			Ref: R Meyer (Austria)	Janku	Frasheri	Halilli	Kasmi	Menna	Byluku	Xhacha	Bakoviku	Cjoka	Ishka	Hyka
						Reports that the Albanians (whose name means 'November 17th') would be easy meat prove incorrect. They have pace and flair, although lack class in front of goal. In scorching heat, McInally is singled out for rough treatment, but off the field this trip has seen Killie treated like kings.
1:2	H 17 NANDORI TIRANA	6 W 1-0	0-0	Black 77	Ferguson	King	Watson	O'Connor	Beattie	McFadzean	McLean	McInally	Black	Black	McIlroy
	29/9	15,717				Janku	Frasheri	Halilli	Kasmi	Menna	Byluku	Xhacha	Bakoviku	Hyka	Bykici	Ishka
					Ref: B Nilson (Norway)	Killie struggle to break down a resolute side, well marshalled by Menna. McInally hits the woodwork and a scrambled goal is disallowed, but Killie keep plugging away. Late on, O'Connor's fine pass is diverted into the net by Black. The scorer is knocked out and suffers concussion.
		(Killie win 1-0 on aggregate)														
2:1	H REAL MADRID	5 D 2-2	1-1	McLean 20p, McInally 60	Ferguson	King	Watson	O'Connor	Murray	McFadzean	McLean	McInally	Hamilton	Sneddon	McIlroy
	17/11 (Spain)	24,325			Martinez 24, Amancio 55	Betancourt	Miera	Sanchiz	Ruiz	Santamaria	Zoco	Amancio	Martinez	Grosso	Puskas	Gento
					Ref: G Shulenberg (W Germany)	The maestros are given a tough time and Killie have a goal disallowed before McInally is pulled down and McLean nets the penalty. Puskas then sets up Martinez for a classy goal. Amancio flicks Real ahead, but Killie hit back with McInally nodding in. A fine game on a cold night.
2:2	A REAL MADRID	8 L 1-5	1-3	McIlroy 27	Ferguson	King	Watson	O'Connor	Murray	McFadzean	McLean	McInally	Hamilton	Sneddon	McIlroy
	1/12	35,000			Grosso 30, 35, 89, Ruiz 31, Gento 58	Betancourt	Miera	Sanchiz	Tejada	De Felipe	Zoco	Amancio	Ruiz	Pirri	Grosso	Gento
					Ref: S Campanati (Italy)	Without Beattie and McGrory, Killie stun the Bernabeu as McIlroy dives to head home. Grosso then punishes ponderous defending and Ruiz streaks clear to score. Grosso nets after a scramble and Gento hits a fourth. McLean has a penalty saved before Real are flattered by a fifth.
		(Killie lose 3-7 on aggregate)														

158

League Table

		P	W	D	L	F	A	W	D	L	F	A	Pts
					Home						Away		
1	Celtic	34	16	1	0	66	12	11	2	4	40	18	57
2	Rangers	34	15	1	1	49	10	10	4	3	42	19	55
3	KILMARNOCK	34	12	2	3	36	18	8	3	6	37	28	45
4	Dunfermline	34	11	2	4	52	29	8	4	5	42	26	44
5	Dundee U	34	10	3	4	45	27	9	2	6	34	24	43
6	Hibernian	34	8	6	3	45	22	8	0	9	36	33	38
7	Hearts	34	7	5	5	28	21	6	7	4	28	27	38
8	Aberdeen	34	8	3	6	35	26	7	3	7	26	28	36
9	Dundee	34	9	2	6	35	29	5	4	8	26	32	34
10	Falkirk	34	10	1	6	32	26	5	0	12	16	46	31
11	Clyde	34	7	2	8	33	29	6	2	9	29	35	30
12	Partick	34	9	5	3	34	25	1	5	11	21	39	30
13	Motherwell	34	9	0	8	31	26	3	4	10	21	43	28
14	St Johnstone	34	6	6	5	34	36	3	2	12	24	45	26
15	Stirling	34	7	2	8	25	29	2	6	9	15	39	26
16	St Mirren	34	6	3	8	27	34	3	1	13	17	48	22
17	Morton	34	4	5	8	18	31	4	0	13	24	53	21
18	Hamilton	34	3	1	13	19	56	0	1	16	8	61	8
		612	157	50	99	644	486	99	50	157	486	644	612

Odds & ends

Double wins: (6) Dundee, Hamilton, Morton, Motherwell, St Mirren, Stirling.
Double losses: (2) Aberdeen, Celtic.
Won from behind: (4) Dunfermline (a) (LC), Hamilton (h), Hearts (a), Stirling (a).
Lost from in front: (3) Celtic (a), Dunfermline (a) (SC), Real Madrid (a) (EC).
High spots: The astonishing 7-4 away win at St Mirren. Taking the lead in the Bernabeu Stadium, Madrid. The capture of forwards Queen and Bertelsen in early 1966.
Low spots: Facing Real Madrid without kingpins Beattie and McGrory. Conceding six and then five in autumn games against Rangers. Failing to beat the 'old firm' clubs in five attempts.
Hat-tricks for: (3) Brien McIlroy v Hibs (a) & v Morton (a); Tommy McLean v Rangers (n) (LC).
Hat-tricks against: (3) George McLean v Rangers (a) & Rangers (n) (LC), Grosso v Real Madrid (a).
Ever presents: (1) Bobby Ferguson.
Leading scorer: (28) Brien McIlroy.

Appearances and Goals

	Appearances				Goals				
	Lge	LC	SC	EC	Lge	LC	SC	EC	Tot
Beattie, Frank	30	9	4	2			1		1
Bertelsen, Carl	8		3	2	3				3
Black, Bertie	9	9	3	2	3	4	2	1	10
Brown, Hugh	1	2							
Dickson, Billy	10			4					
Ferguson, Bobby	34	9	4	3					
Hamilton, Ronnie	13	2		4	9				9
King, Andy	33	9	4		1				1
Layburn, Stuart	1								
Malone, Frank	1								
Mason, Joe	9		1		3				3
McFadzean, Jim	19	8	1	4	4				4
McGrory, Jackie	30	3	4	4	20	6	1	1	28
McIlroy, Brien	32	9	3	4	10	2	2	1	15
McInally, Jackie	31	7	4	4	9	4		1	14
McLean, Tommy	33	7	4	4	4	1			5
Murray, Eric	31	9	4	3					
O'Connor, Pat	7			3					
Queen, Gerry	14		4		6		3		9
Sneddon, Davie	9	8	1	3		2			2
Watson, Matt	19	9	3	4	1		1		2
(own-goals)									
21 players used	374	99	44	44	73	19	10	4	106

160   *Kilmarnock: Champions of Scotland 1964-65*

Two Kilmarnock championship stalwarts: Eric Murray and Matt Watson

LIST OF SUBSCRIBERS AND VOTES FOR THE MOST IMPORTANT KILLIE PLAYER 1964-65

Gordon Allison	Frank Beattie	John McGhee	Jackie McGrory
Gordon Andrews	Tommy McLean	Mark & Kyle	
Allan Auld	Frank Beattie	MacKenzie	Frank Beattie
Ian Barr	Frank Beattie	James McSherry	
Alan Brown	Tommy McLean	David Mawson	Eric Murray
Eric Brown		Alan Muir	Brien McIlroy
Alistair Campbell	Brien McIlroy	James & Alison Rankin	Jackie McInally
Bob Coburn	Jackie McGrory	Barry (Baz) Richmond	Davie Sneddon
G Coulburn		Walker Roberts	
Raymond Devlin		David Ross (Snr)	Davie Sneddon
Alastair Dow	Davie Sneddon	Paul Skilling	Davie Sneddon
John G Farmer	Brien McIlroy	Graeme Stevenson	
Stuart Ferguson	Tommy McLean	J Gary Torbett	Ronnie Hamilton
James H Findlay	Frank Beattie	Sandy Tyrie	Frank Beattie
Fraser John Gall		Charlie Walker	Tommy McLean
Peter Gemmell	Eric Murray	David Woodison	Bertie Black
John Gilmour	Bobby Ferguson		
David Graham	Davie Sneddon	FAVOURITE PLAYERS	
Jamie Hewitson	Bobby Ferguson	1ST =	FRANK BEATTIE
Neil Laird	Davie Sneddon	1ST =	DAVIE SNEDDON
Stuart W Little	Eric Murray	3RD	TOMMY MCLEAN
John Livingston	The Whole Team	4TH =	BRIEN MCILROY
Andy & Matthew		4TH =	JACKIE MCGRORY
McCutcheon	Ronnie Hamilton	4TH =	ERIC MURRAY